D1649208

First edition February 2013

Published by Design Community College Inc,

Design Community College Inc.
PO Box 1153
Topanga CA 90290 USA

info@curedale.com
Designed and illustrated by Robert Curedale

ISBN-10:0988236249
ISBN-13: 978-0-9882362-4-0

Structured Workshops
The author presents workshops online and
in person in global locations for executives,
engineers, designers, technology professionals
and anyone interested in learning and applying
these proven innovation methods. For
information contact: info@curedale.com

Design Thinking

process and methods manual

Robert Curedale

Dedication

Dedicated to aidan and liam

introduction

Design Thinking is an approach to designing products, services, architecture, spaces and experiences that is being quickly adopted by designers, architects and some of the world's leading brands such as GE, Target, SAP, Procter and Gamble, IDEO and Intuit. It is being taught at leading universities including Stanford and Harvard. Design Thinking creates practical and innovative solutions to problems. It drives repeatable innovation and business value. Design Thinking can be used to develop a wide range of products, services, experiences and strategy. It is an approach that can be applied by anyone.

This book is an indispensable Design Thinking reference guide for:
- Architects, industrial designers, interior designers, UX and web designers,
- service designers, exhibit designers, design educators and students, visual communication designers, packaging and fashion designers, all types of designers
- Engineers and Marketing professionals
- Executives and senior business leaders
- Decision makers in R&D of products, services, systems and experiences
- School teachers and school students

Chapters describe in easy to understand language:
- History of Design Thinking
- What is Design thinking
- Why use Design Thinking
- Who can use Design Thinking
- How to create spaces for effective Design Thinking
- Design Thinking process in detail
- 150 Design Thinking methods described step by step.

This book is the most extensive reference available to Design Thinking. Design Thinking is fun.

contents

contents

contents

contents

Chapter 1
History of
Design Thinking

history of design thinking

Design Thinking has evolved over a period of twenty to thirty years and incorporates ideas from a number of design methodologies and movements. The term first emerged in the 1980s with the rise of human-centered design

In the 1960s efforts were made to develop the field that has become known as Design Research to better inform the practice of design. The notion of design as a "way of thinking" was explored by Herbert A. Simon in his 1969 book The Sciences of the Artificial. It was further explored in Robert McKim's 1973 book Experiences in Visual Thinking. Rolf Faste expanded McKim's work in the 80s and 90s in his teaching at Stanford, defining and popularizing the idea of "design thinking" as a way of creative action that was adapted for business purposes by IDEO through his colleague David M. Kelley.

Peter Rowe's 1987 book Design Thinking was the first popular usage of the term "Design Thinking" in the literature on design. The 1992 article by Richard Buchanan titled "Wicked Problems in Design Thinking" expressed a broader view of Design Thinking.

Through the 1980s it was recognized that design needed to focus on understanding the needs and designs of people as well as business. Design Thinking incorporates some ideas from the user centered design movement that developed during this period. By the 1990s David Kelley of IDEO, Larry Leifer and Terry Winograd were amongst the founders of what is now known as the Design Thinking movement.

In 2005, SAP co-founder Hasso Plattner made a personal donation of U.S. $35 million to fund the d.school, which is officially named "Hasso Plattner Institute of Design at Stanford. that has pioneered the teaching of Design Thinking. The approach is now taught at a number of leading business schools such as the Rotman School in Toronto and at Harvard as well as many design schools.

I have listed here some of the important contributions to the field with dates and contributors.

380 BC Plato's Republic contains some of the roots of participatory design.

3rd century BC Porphry of Tyros develops mind maps.

1877 Georg von Mayr invents radar charts.

1879 Louis Emile Javal develops eye tracking.

1880 John Venn invents Venn Diagrams

1890s Credit Agricole pioneer co-creation methods.

1909 E.B. Titchener invented the word empathy in an attempt to translate the German word "Einfühlungsvermögen".

1921 Robert Bruere first uses the terms primary research and secondary research.

1928 Margaret Mead develops ethnographic field studies.

1929 Bonislaw Malinowski develops ethnographic field studies.

1940s 2nd World War from which came operational research methods and management decision-making techniques

1940 Robert Merton develops focus groups.

1942 Gordon Allport, may have been the first to describe diary studies.

1943 Kelly Johnson invents the term Skunkworks.

1944 Alex Bavelas develops Fly on the wall method.

1948 Edward Tolman invents Cognitive Maps
1950 Herman Kahn Rand develops Scenarios method.

1950s Development of creativity techniques

1953 Term brainstorming was popularized by Alex Faickney Osborn in the 1953 book Applied Imagination

1957 Walt Disney Corporation develop activity maps method.

1958 Michael Polanyi uses the term Tacit Knowledge.

1960s Designers explore models for design methodology, and "design research" to better understand and improve design processes and practices This movement marked the beginning of a debate over the process and methodology of design.

1960 Affinity diagram was devised by Jiro Kawakita

1960 Allan Collins, Northwestern University USA develops mind maps.

1961 Gordon The first creativity books start to appear

1962 The First 'Conference on Design Methods,.

1962 Archer, L. Bruce. Systematic Method for Designers.

1962 Ernest Becker Behavioral Maps

1963 Osborn, Alex F. Applied Imagination: Principles and Procedures of Creative Thinking. New York: Scribner,

1964 Alexander The first design methods or methodology books start appearing:

1965 Archer, L. Bruce. Systematic Method for Designers. Council of Industrial Design, H.M.S.O.

1965 SWOT Analysis developed by Albert Humphrey Stanford University

1967 Francis J Aguiler develops PEST Analysis.

1968 Kaoru Ishikawa develops fishbone diagram.

1968 Professor Bernd Rohrbach pioneers 635 Brainstorming Method

1969 Simon, Herbert (1969). The Sciences of the Artificial. Cambridge: MIT Press.

1969 Bill Gaver Royal College of Art cultural probes
1970 Jones, John Christopher. Design Methods. New York: John Wiley & Sons

1970s John Chris Jones,"**In the 1970s I reacted against design methods. I dislike the machine language, the behaviorism, the continual attempt to fix the whole of life into a logical framework."**

1973 Robert McKim's publishes Experiences in Visual Thinking The class McKim creates, "ME101: Visual Thinking,"in the design program at Stanford University is still taught today.

1979 Bruce Archer "**There exists a designerly way of thinking and communicating that is both different from scientific and scholarly ways of thinking and communicating, and as powerful as scientific and scholarly methods of inquiry when applied to its own kinds of problems**."

1980s The term first emerged prominently in the with the rise of human-centered design. Rolf Faste building on McKim's work in his teaching at Stanford,

1980 Bryan Lawson, How Designers Think: The Design Process Demystified.

1981 George Doran develops Smart Goals Method.

1981 Koberg, Don, and Jim Bagnall. The All New Universal Traveller: a Soft-systems Guide To: Creativity, Problem-solving and the Process of Reaching Goals. Los Altos, CA: Kaufmann

1981 The American Society of Mechanical Engineers conference on Design Theory and Methodology.
The rise of human-centered design and the rise

of design-centered business management.

1982 Cross, Nigel. "Designerly Ways of Knowing." Design Studies 3.4 (1982): 221-27.

1983 Schön, Donald. The Reflective Practitioner: How Professionals Think In Action. New York: Basic Books, 1983.

1983 Lyn Shosack develops service blueprinting method.

1984 Jay Conrad Levinson guerilla ethnography

1985 Edward de Bono Six Thinking Hats.

1986 Six Sigma emerges to streamline the design process for quality control and profit.

1987 Peter Rowe professor at the Harvard Graduate School of Design, book Design Thinking was the first significant usage of the term "Design Thinking" in literature. Rowe, G. Peter (1987). Design Thinking. Cambridge: The MIT Press. ISBN 978-0-262-68067-7.

1988 Rolf Faste, director of the design program at Stanford, publishes "Ambidextrous Thinking,"

1988 Whiteside, Bennet, and Holtzblatt Contextual Inquiry

1990s Human-centered design evolves from a technology driven focus to a human one.

1991 The consulting company IDEO. Their

design process, is influenced by the Stanford curriculum.

1991 Rowe popularized the phrase "design thinking" referring to the ways in which designers approach design problems,

1991 Mood boards first used by Terence Conran.

1992 Richard Buchanan's article "Wicked Problems in Design Thinking," Design Issues, vol. 8, no. 2, Spring 1992. adopts a broader view of Design Thinking

1994 Rolf Faste, "Ambidextrous Thinking", Innovations in Mechanical Engineering Curricula for the 1990s, American Society of Mechanical Engineers, November 1994

1994 Matthew Van Horn invents the term Wireframe the term in New York.

1995 Ikujiro Nonaka expands the ideas of Michael Polanyi on tacit versus explicit knowledge.

1997 David Kelley contributed to the book the article The Designer's Stance through an interview by Bradley Hartfield, **"It might help to pose two caricatures two hypothetical extremes. One is engineering as problem solving; the other is design as creating. "**

"the designer wants to create a solution that fits in a deeper situational or social sense." "design is messy. Engineering ... is not supposed to be messy. The designer can handle the messiness and ambiguity and is willing to trust intuition." " Successful design is done in teams." David Kelley

1999 The term Critical Design was first used in Anthony Dunne's book "Hertzian Tales"

1999 IDEO Design Thinking approach was the featured on ABC's Nightline in 1999 in an episode called "The Deep Dive."

2000s Debate about the hijacking and exploitation of design thinking by business educators.

2000 Brandt and Grunnet develop Empathy Tools.

2000 The Rotman School of Management develops a new model for business education based on Dean Roger Martin's integrative thinking for solving wicked problems.

2002 Florida, Richard L. The Rise of the Creative Class: and How It's Transforming Work, Leisure, Community and Everyday Life. New York, NY: Basic, 2002.

2002 William McDonough Cradle to Cradle.

2000 Bodystorming Buchenau and Fulton.

2003 Misuse Scenario method developed by Ian Alexander.

2005 The Hasso Plattner Institute of Design or the d.school is established at Stanford. 2005, SAP co-founder Hasso Plattner made a donation of U.S. $35 million to fund the d.school, which is named the "Hasso Plattner Institute of Design" at Stanford."

2006 Lawson, Bryan. "How Designers Think." Oxford UK: Architectural Press Elsevier, 2006

2006 Pink, Daniel H. A Whole New Mind: Why Right-brainers Will Rule the Future. New York: Riverhead, 2006

2006 Jeff Howe uses the term Crowd Sourcing.

2007 Cross, Nigel. Designerly Ways of Knowing. London UK and Boston MA: Birkhauser Verlag AG, 2007.

2007 The d-school at the HPI in Potsdam, Germany, was founded and took up operation

2007 Martin, Roger L. The Opposable Mind: How Successful Leaders Win through Integrative Thinking. Boston, MA: Harvard Business School, 2007.

2008, the HPI at Potsdam and Stanford University launched a joint research program on innovation, which is jointly led by Leifer and Christoph Meinel.

2009 Tim Brown of IDEO, and is the author of Change by Design: How Design Thinking

Transforms Organizations and Inspires Innovation

2009 Design Thinking authored by Plattner, Meinel, and Weinberg

2009 Roger Martin, Dean of the Rotman School of Management in Toronto, authors The Design of Business: Why Design Thinking is the Next Competitive Advantage

2009 Brown, Tim. "The Making of a Design Thinker." Metropolis Oct. 2009: 60-62. Pg 60: **"David Kelley... said that every time someone came to ask him about design, he found himself inserting the word thinking to explain what it is that designers do. The term design thinking stuck."**

2010 Lockwood, Thomas. Design Thinking: Integrating Innovation, Customer Experience and Brand Value. New York, NY: Allworth, 2010

2011 Faste, Rolf. "The Human Challenge in Engineering Design." International Journal of Engineering Education, vol 17, 2001.

2011 Dorst discusses how a core element of expert design is framing dealing with the paradoxes that arise from conflicting considerations in order to create value.

2011 A number of schools begin teaching design thinking in classrooms and community projects

2011 Cross, N (2011) Design Thinking: Understanding How Designers Think and Work, Berg, Oxford and New York.

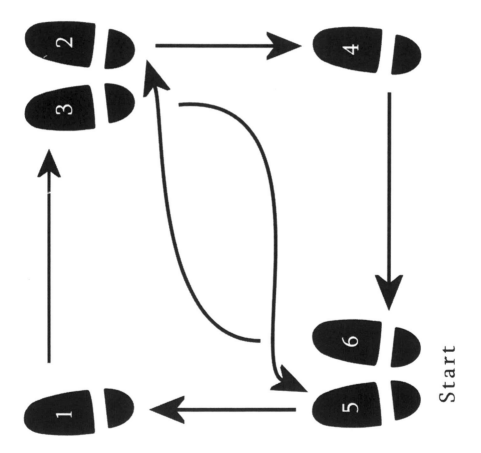

Start

RELATED DESIGN MOVEMENTS

YEAR	DESIGN MOVEMENT	DESIGN APPROACHES	PEOPLE
2010s	Design Thinking	Experience design	David Kelley
		Creative class	Tim Brown
			Roger Martin
			Bruce Nussbaum
			Rolf Faste
2000s	Service Design	Human Centered Design	Lucy Kimbell
1990s	Process Methods	Meta Design	Ezio Manzini
			William Rause
			Richard Buchanan
1980s	Cognitive Reflections	User Centered Design	Don Norman
			Donal Schon
			Nigel Cross
			Peter Rowe
			Bryan Lawson
1970s			Robert McKim
1960s	Design Science	Participatory Design	Horst Rittel
		Design Methods	Herbet Simon
			Bruce Archer
1950s	Creativity Methods	Brainstorming	Alex Osborn

Chapter 2
What is Design Thinking?

what is design thinking?

INTRODUCTION

Design Thinking is a people centered way of solving difficult problems. It follows a collaborative, team based cross disciplinary process. It uses a toolkit of methods and can be applied by anyone from the most seasoned corporate designers and executives to school children

Design Thinking is an approach that seeks practical and innovative solutions to problems. It can be used to develop products, services, experiences and strategy. It is an approach that allows designers to go beyond focusing on improving the appearance of things to provide a framework for solving complex problems. Design Thinking combines empathy for people and their context with tools to discover insights. It drives business value. Companies such as GE, Target, Procter and Gamble IDEO and Intuit have successfully applied this approach to design.
Design Thinkers observe users and their physical environments, interact with them with prototypes, and feed the outcomes of their experiences back into the design. In this chapter I will explore what Design Thinking is about.

In this chapter we will discuss what Design Thinking is and how it differs from a traditional approaches to design. We will discuss some of the characteristics of Design Thinking and some ideas that underlie each of these characteristics:

I will discuss how design thinking is:
1.   People focused
2.   Collaborative
3.   About building doing and testing things.
4.   That it is an iterative process
5.   That it has an agile perspective.
6.   That it follows a tested and successful process
7.   That it has a wide range of tools and methods that can help overcome traditional problems with design process to create more usable and innovative designs.

Design Thinking starts by thinking about people rather than by thinking about things. It is important to stand in those people's shoes, to see through their eyes, to uncover their stories, to share their worlds. Start each design by identifying a problem that real people are experiencing. Use the methods in this book selectively to gain empathy, understanding. and to inform your design. Good process needs to be supported by talented and skilled and collaborative people on your design team. Design Thinking is an approach to designing products, services, architecture, spaces and experiences that seeks to overcome some of the problems that have been associated with design since the beginning of the industrial revolution.

These problems include:

1. That the finished design often reflects the perspective of the designer more than the perspective of the group of people who may use the design.
2. That design problems have been becoming slowly more complex and that a solution must involve the knowledge of specialists in many areas beyond the expertise of the designer.
3. That designer training has evolved form art training which has stressed satisfying the designer's need for creative expression more than the needs and desires of the people who may use the design.
4. That the designer's training has not stressed collaboration of the designer with others during the design process to find a balanced design.
5. That designers tend to be stronger at creative thinking rather than analytical thinking but that analytical and creative thinking are required to find the most successful balanced solution.
6. That the design process used by designers needs to be more agile and adaptive to deal with increasing uncertainty, complexity and change.

In this chapter we will discuss why design thinking can help address these issues

"The "Design Thinking" label is not a myth. It is a description of the application of well-tried design process to new challenges and opportunities, used by people from both design and non-design backgrounds. I welcome the recognition of the term and hope that its use continues to expand and be more universally understood, so that eventually every leader knows how to use design and design thinking for innovation and better results. " *Bill Moggridge, 2010.*

CORE ATTRIBUTES OF DESIGN THINKING

Ambiguity	Being comfortable when things are unclear or when you do not know the answer	Design Thinking addresses wicked = ill-defined and tricky problems.
Collaborative	Working together across disciplines	People design in interdisciplinary teams.
Constructive	Creating new ideas based on old ideas, which can also be the most successful ideas	Design Thinking is a solution-based approach that looks for an improved future result.
Curiosity	Being interested in things you do not understand or perceiving things with fresh eyes	Considerable time and effort is spent on clarifying the requirements. A large part of the problem solving activity, then, consists of problem definition and problem shaping.
Empathy	Seeing and understanding things from your customers' point of view	The focus is on user needs (problem context).
Holistic	Looking at the bigger context for the customer	Design Thinking attempts to meet user needs and also drive business success.
Iterative	A cyclical process where improvements are made to a solution or idea regardless of the phase	The Design Thinking process is typically non-sequential and may include feedback loops and cycles (see below).
Non judgmental	Creating ideas with no judgment toward the idea creator or the idea	Particularly in the brainstorming phase, there are no early judgments.
Open mindset	Embracing design thinking as an approach for any problem regardless of industry or scope	The method encourages "outside the box thinking" ("wild ideas"); it defies the obvious and embraces a more experimental approach.

Core Attributes of Design Thinking from Baeck & Gremett, 2011

ABDUCTIVE THINKING

What is it?
With abductive reasoning, unlike deductive reasoning, the premises do not guarantee the conclusion. Abductive reasoning can be understood as "inference to the best explanation" Abductive reasoning typically begins with an incomplete set of observations and proceeds to the likeliest possible explanation for the set. It's goal is to explore what could possibly be true.

"A person or organization instilled with that discipline is constantly seeking a fruitful balance between reliability and validity, between art and science, between intuition and analytics, and between exploration and exploitation. The design-thinking organization applies the designer's most crucial tool to the problems of business. That tool is abductive reasoning." *Roger Martin*

Who invented it?
Charles Sanders Peirce originated the term and argued that no new idea could come from inductive or deductive logic.

Why use this method?
1. Abductive reasoning does its best with the information available, even if it is incomplete.
2. Einstein's work, was not just inductive and deductive, but involved a creative leap of imagination of abductive reasoning.
3. Roger Martin has argued that organizations that are able to harness abductive reasoning will have a competitive advantage this century.

Challenges
1. Abductive reasoning is used more often by designers than by scientists, engineers and managers. Designers have not developed skills in communicating the thought process of abductive reasoning in a way that is easily understood by deductive thinkers although it is a valid method of addressing complex problems.
2. Supporters of design thinking in business suggest that abduction is marginalized in the modern corporation but is necessary for innovation.

When to use this method
1. Abductive reasoning is necessary for addressing ill defined changing complex problems which are increasingly the types of problems being addressed by organizations and design teams.

References
1. Lipton, Peter. (2001). Inference to the Best Explanation, London: Routledge. ISBN 0-415-24202-9.
2. Thagard, Paul and Cameron Shelley. "Abductive reasoning: Logic, visual thinking, and coherence." Waterloo, Ontario: Philosophy Department, Univerisity of Waterloo, 1997. 2005.

DEDUCTIVE THINKING

What is it?
The process of reasoning from one or more general statements (premises) to reach a logically certain conclusion. Deductive reasoning is one of the two basic forms of valid reasoning. It begins with a general hypothesis or known fact and creates a specific conclusion from that generalization.

Who invented it?
Aristotle 384–322bce, Plato 428–347bce, and Pythagoras 582–500 bce

Why use this method?
1. To solve problems

Challenges
1. For deductive reasoning to be sound, the original hypothesis or generalization also must be correct. A logical deduction can be made from any generalization, even if it is not true. If the generalization is wrong, though, the specific conclusion can be logical and valid but still can be incorrect.
2. Managers, engineers and scientists tend to use deductive logic rather than abductive logic. With uncertain,ill defined and changing or complex problems abductive reasoning may be more effective.

How to use this method
Guidelines for logical and valid deduction:
1. All premises must be true.
2. All expressions used in the premises must be clearly and consistently defined.
3. The first idea of the major premise must reappear in some form as the second idea in the specific case.
4. No valid deductive argument can have two negative premises.
5. No new idea can be introduced in the conclusion.

References
1. Vincent F. Hendricks, Thought 2 Talk: A Crash Course in Reflection and Expression, New York: Automatic Press / VIP, 2005, ISBN 87-991013-7-8
2. Philip Johnson-Laird, Ruth M. J. Byrne, Deduction, Psychology Press 1991, ISBN 978-0-86377-149-1jiii

INDUCTIVE THINKING

What is it?
Inductive thinking is a kind of reasoning that constructs or evaluates general propositions that are derived from specific examples. Inductive reasoning contrasts with deductive reasoning, in which specific examples are derived from general propositions.

Who invented it?
Aristotle 384–322bce,

SHOSHIN

What is it?

The phrase shoshin means beginner's mind. It refers to having an attitude of full of openness, enthusiasm, and fresh perspectives in learning something new, eagerness, and lack of preconceptions even at an advanced level, like a child.

Shoshin also means "correct truth" and is used to describe a genuine signature on a work of art. It is use to describe something that is perfectly genuine.

"In the beginner's mind there are many possibilities, but in the expert's there are few"
Shunryu Suzuki-Roshi

Where did it originate?

1. Shoshin is a term from Zen Buddhism and Japanese martial arts.

Why use this method?

1. Sometimes expertise can create closed mindedness.
1. Our assumptions can stand in the way of creating new ideas. A beginner is not aware of biases that can stand in the way of a good new idea.
2. Our experience is an asset but our assumptions may be misconceptions and stereotypes,
3. Innovation often requires looking at a problem in a new way.
4. Beginner's minds can help make breakthroughs
5. Shoshin can transform a routine task into something more enjoyable and less stressful.
6. Observe and engage users without value judgments.
7. Question your assumptions. Ask why?
8. Be curious and explore.
9. Search for patterns and connections no one else has seen.
10. Be open and listen

How to use this method

1. Withhold judgement. Do not suggest that an idea will not work or that it has negative side-effects. All ideas are potentially good so do not judge them until afterwards.
2. Observe and Listen
3. Ask why several times
4. Be curious
5. Look for new connections

CONTEXT

What is it?
Context is the environment situation or circumstances that surround a product or service in use.
The five w's of context
1. Who: Those who we design for
2. What: Human interactions and perceptions
3. Where: Physical location or path of activities.
4. When: The time or elapsed time.
5. Why: The purpose or meaning of the activity.
after Abowd & Mynatt 2000

Who invented it?
The word first appeared in Late Middle English around 1375 and meant a joining together, scheme, structure or to join by weaving.

Why use this method?
1. Every design is intended to accomplish goals, in a particular environment or context. Understanding the context is necessary in order to create a successful design.

Challenges
1. A product or service may be used in diverse contexts.
2. A design can affect the context.
3. A designer needs to experience the context to create a successful design. This may be difficult, time consuming or expensive.

When to consider context
1. Define goals
1. Know Context
2. Know User
3. Frame insights
4. Generate Concepts
5. Create Solutions

How to use this method
1. Define contextual problem to address
2. Contextual inquiry
3. Discover insights
4. Create possible solutions
5. Create vision and scenarios
6. Prototype and test in context
7. Refine
8. Prototype and test in context
9. Deliver.

Resources
1. Camera
2. Note pad
3. Pens
4. Digital voice recorder

References
1. Albrecht Schmidt, Michael Beigl, and Hans-Werner Gellersen. There is more to context than location. Computers and Graphics, 23(6):893—901, 1999.
2. Peter Tarasewich. Towards a comprehensive model of context for mobile and wireless computing. In Proc. of AMCIS 2003, pages 114—124, 2003.

FRESH EYES

Why use this method?

1. Outside people have a different perspective that may allow them to contribute new ideas and see problems with existing ideas and directions.
2. Outsiders may have experiences from other industries that can help solve problems
3. Outside people may be aware of other people who can contribute something valuable.
4. They may ask different questions.
5. They may have relevant experience that is lacking in your design team.

"Innovation comes from people meeting up in the hallways or calling each other at 10:30 at night with a new idea, or because they realized something that shoots holes in how we've been thinking about a problem. It's ad hoc meetings of six people called by someone who thinks he has figured out the coolest new thing ever and who wants to know what other people think of his idea." *Steve Jobs*

CROSS POLLINATION

1. Cross-pollination helps grow ideas.
2. To solve complex problems, designers need to incorporate a wide range of styles, skills, and perspectives,
3. A team may lack diversity and not understand the perspective of end users.
4. The more we cross pollinate with other disciplines, the stronger our designs become.
5. Use cross disciplinary teams.
6. Share ideas and observations with people outside your organization.
7. Trael can help your design team get exposed to new ways of looking at a problem.
8. Diversity including race, culture, gender, and income can help cross pollinate your design with different perspectives that may reflect your customer's perspectives.
9. Read outside your field.
10. Talk to people in different industries
11. Design thinking involves understanding your customers' needs, and building your products and services and experiencing life in their context.

EVERYONE IS CREATIVE

Design Thinking process involves many stakeholders in working together to find a balanced design solution. The designer is a member of the orchestra. The customer is involved throughout the design process and works with the design team to communicate their needs and desires and to help generate design solutions that are relevant to them.

The many methods used help the design team to understand the diverse perspectives of the many stakeholders. It takes some courage for a designer to listen and recognize the point of view of the stakeholders. Managers, designers, social scientists, engineers marketers, stakeholders and others collaborate creatively to design.

The process is one of co-creation and the designer is a listener and a facilitator. Everyone adds value to the design. Design thinking is not just for professional designers. Everyone can contribute. Many schools are now teaching Design Thinking to children as an approach that can be applied to life.

CROSS-DISCIPLINARY APPROACH

Design Thinking combines the wisdom and skills of many disciplines working in close and flexible collaboration. Each team member requires disciplinary empathy allowing them to work collaboratively with other discipline members.

"Many complex design problems facing society today require cross-disciplinary approaches that integrate diverse perspectives into a collective whole. Here, the term "cross-disciplinary" is used to characterize a collection of practices such as multidisciplinary, interdisciplinary, and transdisciplinary. These involve thinking and working across technical and non-technical considerations, negotiating among different perspectives and territories of expertise, and innovation and transformative processes." *Robin Adams*

References

1. Ausburg, Tanya. Becoming Interdisciplinary: An Introduction to Interdisciplinary Studies. 2nd edition. New York: Kendall/Hunt Publishing, 2006.
2. Klein, Julie Thompson. Interdisciplinarity: History, Theory, and Practice. Detroit: Wayne State University, 1990.
3. Gunn, Giles. "Interdisciplinary Studies." Gibaldi, J., ed. Introduction to Scholarship in Modern Language and Literatures. New York: Modern Language Association, 1992. pp 239-240.

CURIOUSITY

Curiosity is having an interest in the world Curiosity is related to exploration, learning and innovation. Curiosity is one of the main driving forces behind human progress such as a caveman experimenting with fire. High levels of curiosity in adults are connected to greater analytic ability, problem-solving skills and overall intelligence. Creativity is about exploring the unknown and curiosity can be the entry point into this exploration.

Children learn about the world through curiosity. A curious mind dives beneath the surface to understand the process. Curiosity will stretch the boundaries of your ideas. Curious people look at a challenge from multiple perspectives. Curious people find new paths to solutions. The more exploration of the unknown, the more likely it will be that you will discover a new and better way of doing something. Curiosity plants seeds. Curiosity allows a designer to make new connections and find inspiration in new places. The tools of Design Thinking such as observation methods, prototyping and interviewing allow curiosity to be applied in a systematic way. Curiosity helps create new insights which are the starting point for innovation.

"Around here, however, we do not look backwards for very long. We keep moving forward, opening up new doors and doing new things, because we're curious and curiosity keeps leading us down new paths."
Walt Disney

Image Copyright Everett Collection, 2012
Used under license from Shutterstock.com

OPTIMISM

Design Thinking is driven by the optimistic belief that we can create positive change. Creativity requires optimism, believing that all problems have a solution. A willingness to try new things, experiment, prototype, give up on old ideas or ways of doing things. It is a generative activity. The word is derived from the Latin word optimum, meaning "best." Being optimistic, means that you believe that you will discover the best possible solution to a design problem. To create anything new requires a belief that there is a better way. Some people will tell you why your idea will not work.

Some types of replies that kill optimism and progress:
1. We tried that before.
2. It costs too much
3. Let's get back to reality
4. That's not our problem
5. Now's not the right time.
6. It's impossible.
7. Quit dreaming.
8. We haven't got time for research
9. It's too radical
10. Let's put that one on the back burner for now.
11. We know what our customers want
12. I always follow my secretary's advice on color. She likes green.
13. It will never fly Orville
14. Let's give it more thought.
15. I do not like the idea.
16. We are the experts
17. That's not my job.
18. We'll be a laughingstock
19. We've always done it this way.

DESIGN THINKING ADDRESSES HUMAN NEEDS

Design Thinking method seeks to understand Design Thinking takes a people-centric approach. Design Thinking seeks to uncover unmet needs and desires and respond with innovative design solutions. By not referencing existing products services and experiences this approach can lead to design solutions that are differentiated or unique and have a competitive advantage. Here is a list of some human needs that you could consider when developing a design solution.

"There's a hexagram in the I Ching, The Well, that says, "...the well is the symbol of that social structure which, evolved by mankind in meeting its primitive needs, is independent of all political forms. Political structures change, as do nations, but the life of man with its needs remains eternally the same this cannot be changed. The key to designing for eternity is to design for unchanging needs. "
Jim Lewis

Physical Sustenance
1. Air
2. Food
3. Health
4. Movement
5. Physical Safety
6. Rest / sleep
7. Shelter
8. Touch
9. Water

Security
1. Consistency
2. Order/Structure
3. Peace
4. Peace of mind
5. Protection
6. Safety
7. Stability
8. Trusting

Leisure/Relaxation
1. Humor
2. Joy
3. Play
4. Pleasure

Affection
1. Appreciation
2. Attention
3. Closeness
4. Companionship
5. Harmony
6. Intimacy
7. Love
8. Nurturing
9. Sexual Expression
10. Support
11. Tenderness
12. Warmth

Understanding
1. Awareness
2. Clarity
3. Discovery
4. Learning
5. Stimulation

Autonomy

1. Choice
2. Ease
3. Independence
4. Power
5. Self-responsibility
6. Space
7. Spontaneity

Meaning

1. Aliveness
2. Challenge
3. Contribution
4. Creativity
5. Effectiveness
6. Exploration
7. Integration
8. Purpose

Mattering

1. Acceptance
2. Care
3. Compassion
4. Consideration
5. Empathy
6. Kindness
7. Mutual Recognition
8. Respect
9. To be heard, seen
10. To be known, understood
11. To be trusted
12. Understanding others

Community

1. Belonging
2. Communication
3. Cooperation
4. Equality
5. Inclusion
6. Mutuality
7. Participation
8. Partnership
9. Self-expression
10. Sharing

Sense Of Self

1. Authenticity
2. Competence
3. Creativity
4. Dignity
5. Growth
6. Healing
7. Honesty
8. Integrity
9. Self-acceptance
10. Self-care
11. Self-knowledge
12. Self-realization
13. Mattering to myself

Transcendence

1. Beauty
2. Celebration of life
3. Communion
4. Faith
5. Flow
6. Hope
7. Inspiration
8. Mourning
9. Peace (internal)
10. Presence

Sources: MarshallRosenberg, ManfredMax-Neef, Miki and Arnina Kashtan

EMPATHY

What is it?

Empathy is sometimes defined as 'standing in someone else's shoes' or 'seeing through someone else's eyes'. It is The ability to identify and understand another's situation, feelings and motives. In design it may be defined as: identifying with others and, adopting their perspective. Empathy is different to sympathy. Empathy does not necessarily imply compassion. Empathy is a respectful understanding of what others are experiencing and their point of view.

Who invented it?

E.B. Titchener invented the word in 1909 in an attempt to translate the German word "Einfühlungsvermögen".

Why use this method?

1. Empathy is a core skill for designers to design successfully for other people.
2. Empathy is needed for business success.
3. Empathy is needed for products and services to be adopted by the people we design for.
4. Empathy builds trust.

Challenges

1. Increasing use of teams
2. Rapid pace of globalization
3. Global need to retain talent

When to use this method

1. Define intent
2. Know Context
3. Know User
4. Frame insights
5. Explore Concepts
6. Make Plans
7. Deliver Offering

How to use this method

1. Put yourself in contact and the context of people who you are designing for.
2. Ask questions and listen to the answers.
3. Read between the lines
4. Observe.
5. Listen
6. Ask questions.
7. Restating what you think you heard.
8. Recognize that people are individuals.
9. Notice body language. Most communication is non verbal
10. Withhold judgement when you hear views different to your own.
11. Take a personal interest in people

References

1. Miyashiro, Marie R. (2011). The Empathy Factor: Your Competitive Advantage for Personal, Team, and Business Success. Puddledancer Press. p. 256. ISBN 1-892005-25-5.ment and Psychopathology 20: 1053—1080.

THE VALUE OF STORYTELLING

What is it?

A powerful story can help ensure the success of a new product, service or experience. Storytelling can be an effective method of presenting a point of view. Research can uncover meaningful stories from end that illustrate needs or desires. These stories can become the basis of new designs or actions and be used to support decisions. Research shows that our attitudes, fears, hopes, and values are strongly influenced by story. Stories can be an effective way of communicating complex ideas and inspiring people to change.

Who invented it?

1. Storytelling is one of the most ancient forms of human communication.

Why use this method?

1. The stories help to get buy-in from people throughout the design process and may be used to help sell a final design.
2. Real life stories are persuasive.
3. They are different to advertising because they are able to influence a design if uncovered from users during the early research phases and provide authenticity.

Challenges

1. A story with too much jargon will lose an audience.
2. Not everyone has the ability to tell vivid stories.
3. Stories are not always generalizable

How to tell an effective story

1. Meet information needs for your audience
2. Answer in your story: What, why, when, who, where, how?
3. Offer a new vantage point
4. Tell real world stories
5. Evoke the future
6. Be authentic
7. Share emotion
8. Communicate transformations
9. Communicate who you are.
10. Describe actions
11. Show cause and effect Describe conflicts and resolution.
12. Speak from your experience.
13. Describe how actions created change
14. Omit what is irrelevant.
15. Reveal meaning
16. Share your passion
17. Be honest
18. Be real
19. Build trust
20. Show connections
21. Transmits values
22. Share a vision
23. Share knowledge
24. Your story should differentiate you.
25. Use humor
26. Foster collaboration.
27. Engage the audience
28. Craft the story for your audience.
29. Pose a problem and offer a resolution
30. Use striking imagery
31. The audience must be able to act on your story.

DIVERSITY

A diverse design team will produce more successful design than a team that lacks diversity. Innovation needs a collision of different ideas experiences, cultures and approaches.

What is it?
Diversity means different genders, different ages, be from different cultures, different socioeconomic backgrounds and have different outlooks to be most successful.

Why use this method?
1. To attract good people
2. It broadens the customer base in a competitive environment.
3. Diversity brings better decision making and improved problem solving, greater creativity and innovation,
4. Diversity helps an organization to reach new customers.
5. Diversity provides organizations with the ability to compete in global markets

References
1. Harvey, Carol P.; M. June Allard (2012). Understanding and Managing Diversity (5th ed.). New Jersey: Pearson Education, Inc.. pp. xii-393. ISBN 0-13-255311-2.

How to use this method
1. Everything from organizational symbols, rituals, and stories serve to maintain the position of power held by the dominant group.
2. View employees as individuals.
3. Seek recommitment from key participants.
4. Articulate the benefits of diversity.
5. Link your mission to diversity.
6. Identify other diversity models.
7. Develop a realistic action plan.
8. Develop criteria to measure success.
9. Create a safe environment for diversity
10. Set achievable goals for bringing about organizational diversity.
11. Articulate desired outcomes
12. Measures change.

DESIGN THINKING HELPS OVERCOME ETHNOCENTRISM

What is it?
Ethnocentrism is a characteristic of human behavior that can stand in the way of creating effective design solutions. As designers are working increasingly on global projects ethnocentrism is becoming something which needs to be more carefully considered. Ethnocentrism is judging another culture only by the values and standards of one's own culture. Ethnocentrism leads to misunderstanding others. We falsely distort what is meaningful and functional to other peoples through our own tinted glasses

Who invented it?
William G. Sumner first used the term

Why use this method?
1. Ethnocentrism can lead to failed design efforts.
2. Ethnocentrism can lead to conflicts.

Challenges
1. It is useful to recognize ethnocentrism when designing across cultures and to make efforts to reduce it's impact on the outcomes of a project.

When to use this method
1. Define intent
2. Know Context
3. Know User
4. Frame insights
5. Explore Concepts

To reduce ethnocentrism
1. Recognize that we do not understand, that we are falsely assuming something that is not the case and is out of context.
2. Control our biases and to seek more valid and balanced understanding.
3. Ask "How are the behaviors meaningful and functional to the people being studied?"
4. When we encounter ethnocentrism being promoted by particular groups, we can ask ourselves and those around us "Why are they doing this?" What function does promoting ethnocentrism

References
1. Ankerl, G. Coexisting Contemporary Civilizations: Arabo-Muslim, Bharati, Chinese, and Western. Geneva: INU PRESS, 2000, ISBN 2-88155-004-5
2. Reynolds, V., Falger, V., & Vine, I. (Eds.) (1987). The Sociobiology of Ethnocentrism. Athens, GA: University of Georgia Press.
3. Shimp, Terence. Sharma, Shubhash. "Consumer Ethnocentrism: Construction and Validation of the CETSCALE. Journal of Marketing Research. 24 (3). Aug 1987.

DESIGN THINKING IS EXPERIENTIAL

Design Thinking focuses on the quality of the user experience

Learning about an experience is possible once we make it real. Designers engage with people to understand and address their needs and gain insights about their lives. Humans react to real prototypes they can touch, see, smell, taste, hear and interact with, in their natural environment or context A prototype allows a designer to understand an experience from another person's perspective. Make a series of prototypes, test them with real people and improve them.

Answer these three questions
1. Who are the users?
2. How do they use it?
3. Does it work?

References
1. Steve Diller, Nathan Shedroff, Darrel Rhea (2005): Making Meaning: How Successful Businesses Deliver Meaningful Customer Experiences. New Riders Press ISBN 0-321-37409-6
2. Aarts, Emile H. L.; Stefano Marzano (2003). The New Everyday: Views on Ambient Intelligence. 010 Publishers. p. 46. ISBN 978-90-6450-502-7.
3. Moon, J. (2004). A Handbook of Reflective and Experiential Learning:Theory and Practice. London: Routledge Falmer. p. 126.
4. McCarthy, P. R., & McCarthy, H. M. (2006). When Case Studies Are Not Enough: Integrating Experiential Learning Into Business Curricula. Journal Of Education For Business, 81(4), 201-204.

PEOPLE AND HUMAN VALUES

Design thinking identifies and addresses human needs. Design Thinking attempts to balance business requirements, human needs, the application of technologies and environmental stainability.

Designers research how the end user has adapted their environment with their own designs or workarounds.

Human needs are investigated throughout the design process and the solution is refined through repetitive iterative steps with physical prototypes.

Design Thinking adapts the solution to the end user through understanding the end user.

UNRECOGNIZED NEEDS

The methods of Design Thinking are capable of identifying and developing design solutions to meet human needs sometimes even before people know that they have needs. Testing prototypes with real people and observing their interactions and responses can lead designers to innovative solutions that are not yet recognized.

How do you do it?

The ISO standard (ISO 9241-210, 2010) describes 6 key principles that will ensure a design is user centred:

1. The design is based upon an explicit understanding of users, tasks and environments.
2. Users are involved throughout design and development.
3. The design is driven and refined by user-centred evaluation.
4. The process is iterative.
5. The design addresses the whole user experience.
6. The design team includes multidisciplinary skills and perspectives.

Some Questions to ask:

1. Who are the users?
2. What are the users' tasks and goals?
3. What are the users' experience levels?
4. What functions do the users need from the design?
5. What information will be needed by end-users?,
6. In what form do they need it?
7. How do users think the design should work?
8. What are the extreme environments?
9. Is the user multitasking?
10. Does the interface utilize different inputs modes such as touching, spoken, gestures, or orientation?

COLLECTIVE INTELLIGENCE

What is it?

Collective intelligence is a type of shared intelligence that emerges from the collaboration of many people and is expressed in consensus decision making

Who invented it?

William Morton Wheeler 1911

How to use this

Collective intelligence requires four conditions to exist.

1. **Openness** Sharing ideas, experiences and perspectives
2. **Peering** People are free to share and build on each other's ideas freely.
3. **Sharing** knowledge, experiences ideas.
4. **Acting Globally** The internet has no geographical boundaries and may access new markets, ideas and technology.

"Good design begins with honesty, asks tough questions, comes from collaboration and from trusting your intuition." Freeman Thomas

References

1. Szuba T., Computational Collective Intelligence, 420 pages, Wiley NY, 2001
2. Glenn, Jerome C. Collective Intelligence One of the Next Big Things, Futura 4/2009, Finnish Society for Futures Studies, Helsinki, Finland
3. Leimeister, Jan Marco (2010). Collective Intelligence
4. Kaiser, C., Kröckel, J., Bodendorf, F. (2010). Swarm Intelligence for Analyzing Opinions in Online Communities. Proceedings of the 43rd Hawaii International Conference on System Sciences, pp. 1–9.
5. Thomas W. Malone, video interview, Putting collective intelligence to work on a global threat, The Globe and Mail, Sept 4, 2012
6. Thomas W. Malone, Anita Williams Woolley, Defend Your Research: What Makes a Team Smarter? More Women, Harvard Business Review (HBR), June 2011
7. Peter Gloor, Coolfarming, How to encourage innovation and inspire breakthrough products, interview in The Bulletin, September 2010
8. Thomas W. Malone, interview, Exploring Humanity's Evolving 'Global Brain', Dot Earth, The New York Times, December 3, 2012

COLLABORATION

Design Thinking is collaborative. The process involves designers collaborating with experts such as anthropologists, engineers, business people, customers and end-users. This collaboration forces designers to adopt other people's perspectives. The final design becomes more balanced than a design created by a designer working alone.

Designers use methods such as observation, interviews, affinity diagrams and empathy mapping to understand the needs and desires and opinions of these diverse groups of people.

Design thinking involves teamwork.
Design education evolved from art education. One of the important differences between an artist and a designer is that a designer does not have one client. Thousands or millions of people may purchase or use an end design. For an artist their creative self expression is a primary goal of their activity. A designer has the same need for self expression but it must be balanced with additional responsibilities to a large number of end users, to a client or employer and to the environment so a designer must be careful to find the best balance between responsibility and self expression. Collaboration helps find that balance.

Solving complex problems is easier for a designer if they understand multiple perspectives and explore the views of others.

MULTIDISCIPLINARY DESIGN

The greater the number of disciplines in a design team the greater the collective experience and the better the chance of finding an effective balance between applied technology, human values, business success and environmental sustainability.

The design thinking approach allows a more effective collaboration between people from different disciplines than was possible with past processes. The different thinking approaches of different disciplines made communication difficult and often ineffective.

CROSS DISCIPLINARY DESIGN

It is not enough to have a number of disciplines represented on a design team. You need to have a number of T Shaped thinkers to provide the glue to hold the team together and facilitate cross disciplinary collaboration. For a team of 12 people have at least 3 T shaped people and use methods that encourage effective collaboration and communication as are described in the methods chapter of this book.

"Teamwork is the ability to work together toward a common vision. The ability to direct individual accomplishments toward organizational objectives. It is the fuel that allows common people to attain uncommon results." *Andrew Carnegie*

34

ACTION ORIENTED

Many companies today suffer from people who participate in discussion in meetings but do not follow through effectively with actions. Design Thinking methods are focussed on actions and creating real physical progress rather than discussion. Design Thinking is experiential and involved improvisation like a caveman experimenting with fire.

At the beginning there are no bad ideas. The design direction is discovered through a cyclic process of brainstorming, making fast inexpensive models from available materials and then asking people to interact with the models. The process is continually hands on and means rolling your sleeves up and getting your hands dirty by trying things, making things and interacting rather than being a spectator.

GET PHYSICAL

Make simple physical prototypes of your ideas as early as possible. Constantly test your ideas with people. Do not worry about making prototypes beautiful until you are sure that you have a resolved final design. Use the prototypes to guide and improve your design. Do a lot of low cost prototypes to test how Your Ideas physically work. using cardboard, paper, markers, adhesive tape, photocopies, string and popsicle sticks. The idea is to test your idea, not to look like the final product. Expect to change it again. Limit your costs to ten or twenty dollars. Iterate, test and iterate. Do not make

the prototype jewelry. It can stand in the way of finding the best design solution. In the minds of some a high fidelity prototype is a finished design solution rather than a tool for improving a design. You should make your idea physical as soon as possible. Be the first to get your hands dirty by making the idea real.

GET YOUR HANDS DIRTY

Design thinking deliberately takes an action oriented approach. This means that you should initiate physical actions yourself early in the project and continually as the project proceeds. Getting your hands dirty means
1. Low fidelity prototyping
2. Never go into a meeting without a physical prototype.
3. Makes the prototypes yourself.
4. Interacting with end users and other stakeholders
5. Using role playing methods to physically prototype user scenarios and interaction ideas.
6. Physically testing your ideas
7. Immersing yourself physically in the context that you are designing for
8. Experiment
9. Test your ideas with real people.
10. Iterate
11. Refine
12. Explore
You should do this even before a solution is apparent.

BE VISUAL

Design Thinking is an effective approach for solving ambiguous, complex and changing problems. The solving of such problems often involves communicating ideas which are hard to describe in words. Visual mapping methods, images and sketches can help make complex ideas easier to understand and share.

You can use visual techniques even if you are not good at drawing. Take pictures of user interactions with your camera or phone. Explore some of the mapping methods described in the Methods chapter of this book. Use Venn diagrams, experience journeys, perceptual maps and radar charts to make information easier to comprehend.

These visual methods are good ways of communicating connections and relationships.

"A picture shows me at a glance what it takes dozens of pages of a book to expound."
Ivan Turgenev "Fathers and Sons "1862

FUTURE ORIENTED

Design Thinking is a future oriented approach to designing. Most organizations base their new designs on what exists. Design Thinking allows an organization to change for the better. It allows an organization to move from being a follower to being a leader in the market.

To do this you need to base your designs on

unmet end user needs rather than on products and services that already exist in a market. Design Thinking provides a variety of tools that make this possible from observation and interviewing to backcasting,

EVIDENCE BASED METHODS

Evidence-Based Design is the process of basing design decisions on credible research to achieve the best possible outcomes. Evidence based design emphasizes the importance of basing decisions on the best possible data for the best possible outcomes

Why use this method?
1. Evidence Based Design provides real evidence that improves outcomes and help with the clients bottom line.
2. The design is no longer based just on the designer's opinion

How to use this approach
1. Define the problem that you are trying to solve.
2. Start with people. Identify the group of people that the design solution will be useful for.
3. Use an integrated multidisciplinary approach.
4. Use a human centric approach
5. Consider the business case and return on investment.
6. Design to measurable outcomes and to involve end users.
7. Use strategic partnerships to accelerate innovation,

8. Use simulation and testing to understand the end user's perspective
9. Communicate with and involve the stakeholders in the design process.

References
1. Kirk Hamilton D., Four Levels of Evidence-Based Practice, The AIA Journal of Architecture, November 2006
2. Webster L., Steinke C., Evidence-based design. A new direction for health care, Design Quarterly, Winter 2009
3. A Practitioner's Guide to Evidence-Based Design by Debra D. Harris, PhD, Anjali Joseph, PhD, Franklin Becker, PhD, Kirk Hamilton, FAIA, FACHA, Mardelle McCuskey Shepley, AIA, D.Arch [3]
4. Evidence-Based Design for Multiple Building Types by D. Kirk Hamilton (Author), David H. Watkins (Author)
5. Chris E. Stout,Randy A. Hayes, The evidence-based practice: methods, models, and tools for mental health professionals, John Wiley and Sons, January 2005

EMBRACE MISTAKES

A strength of design thinking is that the process uses abductive as well as deductive and inductive styles of thinking.

Abductive thinking which is the style of reasoning most likely to develop new innovative ideas and solutions makes reasonable assumptions based on incomplete information. With this mode of thinking it is inevitable that some experiments directions will result in unexpected results. These unexpected results may be viewed as mistakes or as part of a learning process to find the best solution.

If you follow an iterative process mistakes can lead you to a success that no one else has achieved.

"I have not failed. I've just found 10,000 ways that will not work." "Just because something doesn't do what you planned it to do doesn't mean it's useless."" To have a great idea, have a lot of them."" I start where the last man left off." *Thomas A. Edison*

ITERATION

Design Thinking follows an iterative process. Iterative design is aimed at refining a design based on learning from user interaction.

Iterative design is a cyclic process of prototyping, testing, and refining a product, system service, experience or process. Following testing the most recent iteration of a design with end users, changes and refinements are made. This process is intended to improve the quality and functionality of a design. In iterative design, interaction with the design is used as a form of research for informing and evolving a project, as successive versions, or iterations of a design are created.

Iterative design is the best approach when desiring to design products or systems that are user friendly and functional well.

The designer makes a prototype, tests and refines the design. The design improves from one iteration to the next and slowly eradicates use problems.

Why use this approach?

Iterative design will ensure a product or process is the best solution possible. When applied early in the development stage, significant cost savings are possible.
Other benefits to iterative design include:
1.   Problems are discovered early when it is possible to fix them.
2.   It involves end users so the solutions are real and relevant.
3.   The designer focuses on those problems that are most relevant to the end user.
4.   This approach enables the design team to continually improve the process.

How to use this method
1.   Understand
2.   Observe
3.   Synthesize
4.   Prototype
5.   Test/Assess
6.   Iterate (Repeat for Refinement)
7.   Implement

References
1.   Nielsen, J. "Iterative User Interface Design". IEEE Computer vol.26 no.11 pp 32-41.
2.   Kruchten, P. From Waterfall to Iterative Development - A Challenging Transition for Project Managers. The Rational Edge, 2000.

"Remember, it is the achievement of the objectives that is important, not the production of artifacts or the completion of activities. Be careful not to confuse the ends (objectives) with the means (artifacts and activities)."
Source: "Managing Iterative Software Development Projects", Kurt Bittner, Ian Spence, Addisson Wesley.

CONTINUOUS LEARNING

Design Thinking is an ongoing learning process that seeks to incorporate the lessons learnt into a continuous improvement of design. It incorporates ideas drawn from the Japanese management philosophy of Kaisen, Japanese for "improvement", or "change for the better" which focus upon continuous improvement of products and processes
Like Kaisen Design Thinking stresses
1.   Teamwork
2.   Individual team member responsibilities
This is a useful approach when trying to solve changing, ambiguous complex problems. Kaisen has helped Japanese companies such as Toyota become global leaders.

CULTURE OF PROTOTYPING

Low fidelity prototyping is a quick and cheap way of gaining insight and informing decision making without the need for costly investment. Simulates function but not aesthetics of proposed design. Prototypes help compare alternatives and help answer questions about interactions or experiences.

Why use this approach?
1.   Provides the proof of concept
2.   It is physical and visible
3.   Inexpensive and fast.
4.   Useful for refining functional and perceptual interactions.
5.   Assists to identify any problems with the design.
6.   Helps to reduce the risks

7.   Helps members of team to be in alignment on an idea.
8.   Helps make abstract ideas concrete.
9.   Feedback can be gained from the user

WORK QUICKLY
The methods of design thinking have been developed to reach a successful design solution in the minimum amount of time at the minimum cost stressing human-centred exploration and fast and iterative prototyping

MAKE INEXPENSIVE MISTAKES FAIL FAST LEARN FAST
Design Thinking makes successful designs by making mistakes early in inexpensive prototypes and learning through end user and stakeholder feedback. Prototypes are conceived and constructed in order to learn. We retain the features that are working and discover areas where the design can be improved. A process built around prototyping is an effective way of reaching an effective design solution in the most efficient way.

Designers must be willing to make mistakes in order to reach a successful solution. The environment should not punish exploration and iterative failures. Design Thinkers are searching for validity. They are problem solvers.

The price of failures rises as the project proceeds. It saves cost to fail early.

"You never learn by doing something right 'cause you already know how to do it. You only learn from making mistakes and correcting them." *Russell Ackoff*

"An architect's most useful tools are an eraser at the drafting board and a wrecking ball at the site." *Frank Lloyd Wright*

TOOLS

Design Thinking process is facilitated by a large number of design methods or tools. Some tools are described in chapter 7 The tools allow a designer to make informed design decisions that are not only about physical things but also about complex interfaces, systems, services and experiences. organizations that employ designers need to create design that balances the requirements of complex ecosystems of products, environments, services and experiences both physical and virtual. They will enable you to design products, systems buildings, interfaces and experiences with confidence that you have created the most informed design solutions for real people that is possible. These tools help designers think in four dimensions instead of three. Designing experiences has the added dimension of time. These methods help the design team understand the response of customers to a proposed design and so reduce the subjectivity by providing evidence for design decisions.

The wide range of methods contained in this book will help you close the gap between your clients and organizations and the people that you are designing for to help you create more

considered, informed, repeatable, innovative, empathetic design solutions that people need but may not yet know that they want. Different design practitioners can select different methods for their toolkit and apply them in different ways. There is no best combination.

References

1. Curedale , Robert A. Design Methods 1 200 ways to apply design thinking Edition 1 November 2013 ISBN-10:0988236206 ISBN-13:978-0-9882362-0-2

2. Curedale , Robert A. Design Research Methods 150 ways to inform design Edition 1 January 2013 ISBN-10: 0988236257 ISBN-13: 978-0-988-2362-5-7

3. Curedale , Robert A Design Methods 2 200 more ways to apply design thinking Edition 1 January 2013 ISBN-13: 978-0988236240 ISBN-10: 0988236249

4. Curedale , Robert A 50 Brainstorming Methods Edition 1 January 2013 ISBN-10: 0988236230 ISBN-13: 978-0-9882362-3-3

5. Curedale , Robert A 50 Selected Design Methods to inform your design Edition 1 January 2013 ISBN-10:0988236265 ISBN-13:978-0-9882362-6-4

6. Curedale , Robert A Mapping Methods for Design Edition 1 April 2013 ISBN-10: 0989246817 ISBN-13: 978-0-9892468-1-1

PRIMARY RESEARCH

What is it?
Primary research also called as field research is collecting data that is created during the time of study. Primary research techniques include, questionnaires, interviews and direct observations.

Who invented it?
Robert W. Bruere of the Bureau of Industrial Research 1921 may have been the first to use the term

Why use this method?
You can collect this information yourself. There may be no secondary research available. It may be more reliable than secondary research. It may be more up to date than secondary research

Challenges
1. May be more expensive than secondary research.
2. Information may become obsolete
3. Large sample can be time-consuming

When to use this method
1. Define intent
2. Know Context
3. Know User
4. Frame insights
5. Explore Concepts
6. Make Plans
7. Deliver Offering

How to use this method
Methods such as:
1. Diaries
2. E-mail
3. Interviews
4. News footage
5. Photographs
6. Raw research data
7. Questionnaires
8. Observation

Resources
1. Camera
2. Notebook
3. Pens
4. Digital Voice recorder
5. Diaries
6. E-mail

References
1. Creswell, John. Research Design: Qualitative, Quantitative, and Mixed Methods Approaches. 3rd ed. Sage publications, 2008. Print.
2. Rubin, Herbert and Irene Rubin. Qualitative Interviewing: The Art of Hearing Data. 2nd edition. Thousand Oaks, CA: Sage Publications, 2004. Print.
3. Fink, Arlene. How to Conduct Surveys: A Step-by-Step Guide. 4th ed. Thousand Oaks, CA: Sage Publications, 2008. Print.
4. Sanger, Jack. Compleat Observer? A Field Research Guide to Observation. New York: Routledge, 1996. Print.

SECONDARY RESEARCH

What is it?

Secondary research is research that is existing and has been collected by others. Secondary research is the most widely used method for data collection. Secondary research accesses information that is already gathered from primary research.

Who invented it?

Robert W. Bruere of the US Bureau of Industrial Research 1921 may have been the first to use the term secondary research.

Why use this method?

1. Ease of access
2. Low cost
3. May be the only resource, for example historical documents
4. useful for studying trends.

Challenges

1. Secondary resources always have some bias.
2. Secondary research has been collected in the past so it may not be as current as primary research.
3. May not be aligned with research goals
4. Lack of consistency of perspective
5. Biases and inaccuracies
6. Data affected by context of its collection

When to use this method

1. Define intent
2. Know Context
3. Know User
4. Frame insights
5. Generate Concepts
6. Create Solutions
7. Implement solutions

How to use this method

1. Define goals.
2. Define the context of the problem to be researched.
3. Frame research questions.
4. Develop procedure.
5. Select and retrieve appropriate data.
6. Analyze the data.
7. Review your findings by comparing them with other studies.
8. Summarize your insights.

Resources

1. Books
2. Internet
3. Online search engines
4. Magazines
5. E-books
6. Bibliographies
7. Biographical works
8. Commentaries, criticisms
9. Dictionaries, Encyclopedias
10. Histories;
11. Newspaper articles
12. Web site

References

1. Secondary Research: Information Sources and Methods. David W. Stewart, Michael A. Kamins Sage Publications, Inc; 2nd edition (December 18, 1992) ISBN-10: 0803950373 ISBN-13: 978-0803950375

QUALITATIVE RESEARCH

What is it?
Seeks to understand people in the context of their daily experiences. Uses ethnographic methods including observation and interviews. Seeks to understand questions like why and how. Obtains insights about attitudes and emotions. Often uses small sample sizes. Seeks to see the world through the eyes of research subjects. Methods are flexible. Used to develop an initial understanding.

Who invented it?
Bronisław Malinowski 1922

Why use this method?
Methods commonly used by designers to gain empathy for the people they are designing for.

Challenges
1. Concerned with validity
2. Subjective
3. Hard to recreate results
4. People may behave differently to the way they say they behave
5. Experiences can not be generalized.

How to use this method
1. Define research question
2. Select research subjects and context to study.
3. Collect data
4. Interpret data.
5. Study data for insights
6. Collect more data
7. Analyze data

Resources
1. Camera
2. Video camera
3. Note pad
4. Pens
5. Digital voice recorder
6. White board
7. Post-it-notes
8. Blank cards

References
1. Holliday, A. R. (2007). Doing and Writing Qualitative Research, 2nd Edition. London: Sage Publications
2. Denzin, N. K., & Lincoln, Y. S. (2011). The SAGE Handbook of qualitative research (4th ed.). Los Angeles: Sage Publications.
3. Malinowski, B. (1922/1961). Argonauts of the Western Pacific. New York: E. P. Dutton.

QUANTITATIVE RESEARCH

What is it?
Quantitative research uses mathematical and statistical methods. Sample sizes are often large. Findings may be expressed as numbers or percentages. Uses methods such as surveys and questionnaires. Asks questions like "How many?" Used to recommend a final course of action.

Who invented it?
The Royal Statistical Society founded in 1834 pioneered the use of quantitative methods.

Why use this method?
1. High level of reliability
2. Minimum personal judgement.
3. It is objective.

Challenges
1. Methods are static. Real world changes.
2. Structured methods
3. Difficult to control the environment
4. Can be expensive if studying a large numb Er of people.

How to use this method
1. Research design
2. Devise ways to measure hypothesis
3. Select subjects and context
4. Undertake research
5. Process data
6. Analyze data
7. Conclusions

References
1. Bernard, H (1994) Research Methods in Anthropology: Qualitative and Quantitative Approaches, London, Sage
2. Creswell, J. W. (2009). Research design: Qualitative, quantitative, and mixed methods approaches (3rd ed.). Thousand Oaks, CA: Sage.

DESIGN ETHNOGRAPHY

What is it?
Ethnography is a collection of research methods that includes observing and interviewing people. Design ethnography helps create better more compelling and meaningful design. Ethnographers study and interpret culture, through fieldwork.

Who invented it?
Bronisław Malinowski 1922 was an important pioneer of methods used today by designers.

Why use this method?
1. To inform the design and innovation processes rather than basing your designs on intuition.
2. To ensure that your design solutions resonate with the people that you are designing for,

Challenges?
1. People may behave differently when they are in groups or alone.
2. Researchers should be aware that their research affects the people that they are studying.

When to use this method
1. Define intent
2. Know Context
3. Know User
4. Frame insights
5. Explore Concepts
6. Make Plans
7. Deliver Offering

How to use this method
There are many different ethnographic techniques. Some of the general guidelines are:
1. Listen
2. Observe.
3. Be empathetic and honest.
4. Do research in context, in the environments that the people you are studying live or work.
5. Influence your subject's behavior as little as possible with your presence.
6. Beware of bias.
7. Take photos and notes.
8. Have clear goals related to understanding and prediction.
9. Study representative people

Resources
1. Note pad
2. Pens
3. Post-it-notes
4. Video camera
5. Camera
6. Voice recorder
7. White board
8. Dry-erase pens.

References
1. Erickson, Ken C. and Donald D. Stull (1997) Doing Team Ethnography : Warnings and Advice. Sage, Beverly Hills.
2. Westbrook, David A. Navigators of the Contemporary: Why Ethnography Matters. (2008). Chicago: University of Chicago Press.

GUERILLA ETHNOGRAPHY

What is it?
Guerrilla ethnography is a collection of low cost responsive and flexible creative research methods. Examples include man on the street interviews, rapid iterative prototypes. remote usability testing. and empathy maps.

Who invented it?
Jay Conrad Levinson 1984

Why use this method?
1. Guerrilla methods are fast,
2. Guerrilla methods are less expensive.
3. Provide direction and data rather than opinions and speculation.
4. Uncover how people think and behave.
5. Provides sufficient insight to make more informed design decisions and guide design decisions.

Challenges?
1. Sometime the information gathered is more like a compass for design decisions rather than a road map.

When to use this method
1. Know Context
2. Know User
3. Frame insights

How to use this method
1. Start by defining an activity, context, and time frame to focus on.
2. Create a plan.
3. Recruit from online sources like Facebook, Mechanical Turk, Ethnio, Craigslist, Twitter, or friends and family.
4. Observe real people in real-life situations
5. Capture Data
6. Reflection and Analysis
7. Brainstorming for solutions
8. Develop prototypes of possible solutions
9. Evaluate and refine the prototypes. Test several iterative refinements.
10. Ask for them to show and tell
11. Listen for pain points and seek opportunities.
12. Do not lead the user to the "right" path
13. Allow for exploration and discovery
14. Make simple prototypes of your favored designs. Only build what you need. No more.

References
1. Holtzblatt, K., Wendell, J.B., & Wood, S. 2005. Rapid Contextual Design: A How-to guide to key techniques for user-centered design. San Francisco: Morgan-Kaufmann.

AGILE DESIGN

What is it?
Agile software development is a group of software development methods based on iterative collaboration between cross-functional teams. It features methods that help rapid and flexible response to change. Iterative methods are favored that involve stakeholders.

Agile manifesto 2001:
1. Individuals and interactions over processes and tools
2. Working software over comprehensive documentation
3. Customer collaboration over contract negotiation
4. Responding to change over following a plan

Who invented it?
Bernie Dimsdale at IBM 1957

Challeng es
Opponents of the use of this method claim weaknesses of the methods are :
1. Claimed universality
2. Claimed infallibility
3. Ritual activity
4. Has it's own jargon
5. The administration minimize diversity of opinion

When to use this method
1. Define intent
2. Know Context
3. Know User
4. Frame insights
5. Generate Concepts
6. Create Solutions
7. Implement solutions

How to use this method
Twelve principles underlie the Agile Manifesto:
1. Satisfied customers
2. Welcome change at all stages of design.
3. Working software is delivered often.
4. Working software measures progress
5. Sustainable development,
6. Close, regular cooperation between business people and developers
7. Face-to-face conversation where possible
8. Use motivated people,
9. Attention to good design
10. Simplicity
11. Self-organizing teams
12. Regular adaptation to changing circumstances.

References
1. Beck, Kent; et al. (2001). "Manifesto for Agile Software Development". Agile Alliance.
2. Shore, J., & Warden S. (2008). The Art of Agile Development. O'Reilly Media, Inc.

GET INSPIRATION IN NEW PLACES

What is it?
Everyone tends to adopt a particular perspective over time. We can help overcome our tendency not to explore new types of solutions by looking for inspiration in new places.

How to use this method
Here are some ways that many creative people find inspiration.

1. Walk your dog
2. Read a book
3. Travel
4. Surf the internet
5. Talk to some people.
6. Be inspired by history
7. Go to bed and think about it again in the morning.
8. Get some exercise.
9. Do a mind map
10. Brainstorm
11. Take a field trip to a museum Switch desks with someone
12. Look at other industries
13. Be inspired by anything and everything in your surroundings
14. Be inspired by people.
15. Be inspired by architecture
16. Be inspired by ethnic culture
17. Create an inspiration board
18. Exhibits and shows
19. Movies
20. Everyday things
21. Explore
22. Meditate
23. Go shopping
24. Visit a bookstore
25. Explore a new place
26. Talk to a child
27. Observe people
28. Landscape
29. Alternative cultures and their arts;
30. Listen to your senses
31. Music
32. Be inquisitive, ask questions
33. Be a good listener
34. Shapes
35. Relationships
36. Find what works best for you.
37. Visit an Art Gallery
38. Visit a Foreign Food Store
39. Hop on a Bus
40. Wander through some Antique Stores
41. Keep an inspiration notebook
42. Use your phone to collect things that you find interesting, notes and images
43. Album Art
44. Drawing and sketching
45. Modeling clay
46. Explore Pinterest
47. Shopping but not buying
48. Play a game
49. Go outside and enjoy nature
50. Learn something new
51. Do continuing education
52. Visit a car show
53. Go to a conference
54. Talk to an expert
55. Go to a public lecture
56. Research history
57. Ask a question on a social network

ACTIVE LISTENING

What is it?
Active listening is a communication method where the listener repeats what they understand to the speaker.

Who invented it?
Thomas Gordon coined the term
Carl Rogers 1980

Why use this method?
1. The ability to listen is an important skill for a designer to demonstrate empathy.

Challenges
1. Listening and hearing or understanding are not the same
2. People give meaning to what they hear.
3. Listening constructs meaning from verbal and non verbal observations.

When to use this method
1. Know Context
2. Know User

How to use this method
1. The listener observes the speakers body language.
2. This helps the listener understand the speaker's message
3. The listener paraphrases the speakers words to demonstrate understanding of the message.
4. The listener summarizes the issues.

Active listening skills include
1. Posture showing engagement
2. Eye contact
3. Environment that does not distract
4. Appropriate gestures and facial expressions.

References
1. Reed, Warren H. (1985). Positive listening: learning to hear what people are really saying. New York: F. Watts. ISBN 0-531-09583-5
2. Atwater, Eastwood (1981). I Hear You. Prentice-Hall. p. 83. ISBN 0-13-450684-7.
3. Novack DH, Dube C, Goldstein MG. Teaching medical interviewing. A basic course on interviewing and the physician-patient relationship. Arch Intern Med 1992;152:1814–2.

DESIGN FOR ALL SENSES

What is it?

Anglo Saxon design culture concentrates on the sense of vision but we use five senses to make buying decisions and to use products

Human beings have a multitude of senses. Sight, hearing, taste, smell , and touch. While the ability to detect other stimuli beyond those governed by the traditional senses exists, including temperature , kinesthetic sense , pain, balance , and acceleration.

Who invented it?

In the time of William Shakespeare, there were commonly reckoned to be five wits or five senses.[29] At that time, the words "sense" and "wit" were synonyms,[29] so the senses were known as the five outward wits.[30] [31] This traditional concept of five senses is common today, and Extrasensory perception is often called the sixth sense.

The traditional five senses are enumerated as the "five material faculties" (pañcanna indriy na avakanti) in Buddhist literature. They appear in allegorical representation as early as in the Katha Upanishad (roughly 6th century BC), as five horses drawing the "chariot" of the body, guided by the mind as "chariot driver".

Why consider five senses?

1. Smell triggers memory, Smell is the only sense that becomes fully developed before birth and is critical to the way we experience the world.
2. Smell and taste have an impact on behavior, perception and health.
3. The most successful design please all or senses

ACTIONABLE INSIGHTS

What is it?

Design Thinking provides insights that are based on unrecognized or unmet needs. An insight is a new point of view based on an understanding of the way of thinking and behavior. An insight occurs by mentally connecting two or more things that have not been connected before. These things may be things that many people have seen or experienced but not connected before. A goal of Design Thinking is to build actionable insights

Why use this method?

1. Insights that are based on unrecognized or unmet needs. add competitive advantage. that may be greater than obtained by imitating competitor's products
2. An insight provides the foundation for innovation.
3. An insight is necessary to create something better than what exists today.

Challenges

1. An insight should be based on evidence

How to use this method

1. Many design methods reveal design insights
2. Methods that may reveal insights include observation, interviews and other ethnographic methods.

References

1. Sternberg, Edited by Robert J.; Davidson, Janet E. (1996). The nature of insight (Reprint. ed.). Cambridge, MA; London: The MIT Press. ISBN 0-262-69187-6.
2. Gilhooly, KJ; Murphy, P (1 August 2005). "Differentiating insight from non-insight problems". Thinking & Reasoning 11 (3): 279–302
3. Segal, Eliaz (1 March 2004). "Incubation in Insight Problem Solving". Creativity Research Journal 16 (1): 141–148.
4. Smith, C. M.; Bushouse, E., Lord, J. (13 November 2009). "Individual and group performance on insight problems: The effects of experimentally induced fixation". Group Processes & Intergroup Relations 13 (1): 91–99
5. Bradley, Nigel, (2007), Marketing Research: Tools and Techniques, Oxford: Oxford University Press. ISBN 978-0-19-928196-1

Chapter 3
Why use Design Thinking?

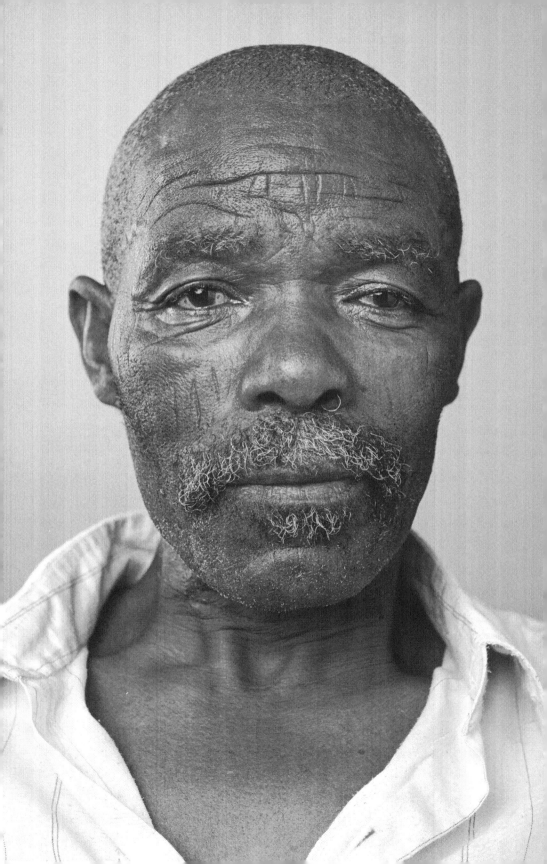

Why use design thinking?

Design Thinking is an approach to designing products, services, architecture, spaces and experiences that seeks to overcome some of the problems that have been associated with design since the beginning of the industrial revolution.

These problems include:

1.   That the finished design often reflects the perspective of the designer more than the perspective of the group of people who may use the design.
2.   Design problems have been becoming slowly more complex and that a solution must involve the knowledge of specialists in many areas beyond the expertise of the designer.
3.   Designer training has evolved form art training which has stressed satisfying the designer's need for creative expression more than the needs and desires of the people who may use the design.
4.   Designer's training has not stressed collaboration of the designer with others during the design process to find a balanced design.
5.   Designers tend to be stronger at creative thinking rather than analytical thinking but that analytical and creative thinking are required to find the most successful balanced solution.
6.   The design process used by designers needs to be more agile and adaptive to deal with increasing uncertainty, complexity and change.

In this chapter we will discuss why design thinking can help address these issues
Design Thinking is a people centered way of solving difficult problems. Design thinking is an approach that can be used to solve complex, ambiguous, uncertain and changing problems. These types of problems are known as "wicked problems" It is an adaptive approach suited to today's business environment. The design processes of the past have each had some weaknesses. Corporations have concentrated on business success and failed to address human needs and desires as successfully as they could. Human centered design has concentrated on people but had not been as focussed on business issues. Eco design seeks to produced environmentally sustainable design but the products and services produced have not always been as desirable and successful from a business perspective as they could be. Design Thinking seeks to find a better balance between Business, Technology, Human values and environmental sustainability by taking a team based approach drawing on the complimentary skills, education and experiences of a group of professionals. It is a more integrative approach that draws on collective intelligence to produce results that are greater than the results possible by individuals working alone or using a less integrative team process.
In this chapter I will discuss some of the reasons that Design Thinking has become widely adopted by many businesses whose future survival depends on consistent innovation.

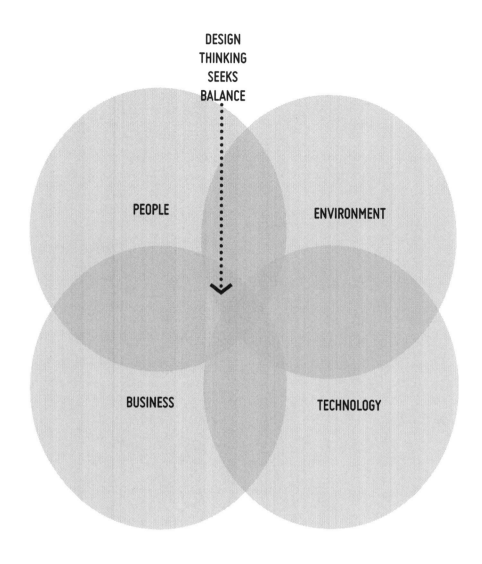

DESIGN
THINKING
SEEKS
BALANCE

PEOPLE

ENVIRONMENT

BUSINESS

TECHNOLOGY

The design processes of the past have each had some weaknesses. Corporations have concentrated on business success and failed to address human needs and desires as successfully as they could. Human centered design has concentrated on people but had not been as focussed on business issues. Eco design seeks to produced environmentally sustainable design but the products and services produced have not always been as desirable and successful from a business perspective as they could be. Design Thinking seeks to find a better balance between Business, Technology, Human values and environmental sustainability by taking a team based approach drawing on the complimentary skills, education and experiences of a group of professionals. It is a more integrative approach that draws on collective intelligence to produce results that are greater than the results possible by individuals working alone or using a less integrative team process

BALANCED DESIGN

What is it?
Design Thinking seeks to find an optimal balance between four factors.
1. **Business needs**, including return on investment, growth, price point, competitive advantage cash flow.
2. **Technology**. Selection of appropriate manufacturing methods and processes, materials and engineering approaches.
3. **People's needs and desires.** This includes the usability, and aesthetics.
4. **Environmental factors**. This includes environmental sustainability.

Why create balanced design?
Designers have often in the past oriented designs towards people's needs and desires but been less successful balancing business, environmental and technological factors. Many businesses have oriented their goals towards business factors. Companies that find a sustainable balance between these factors develop a competitive advantage over companies that tend to be oriented towards one factor.

When to use this method
1. Define goals
1. Know Context
2. Know User
3. Frame insights
4. Generate Concepts
5. Create Solutions

How to use this method
1. Balanced design is more likely to evolve if the design and management team has diversity of nationality, gender, age, occupation and culture.
2. Companies that have individual VPs with specialization in each of these areas are more likely to be successful.

WICKED PROBLEMS

Design thinking focusses on solutions to problems, It may be better than traditional design processes at addressing what have been called "Wicked Problems". Wicked problems are are ill-defined or tricky, not wicked in the sense of evil. The iterative prototype and testing based approach does not assume a solution from the outset but experiments and tries alternative solutions and proceeds to refine the designs on the basis of successful testing.

Super wicked problems

K. Levin, proposed an additional type of problem called the "super wicked problem"He defined super wicked problems as having the following additional characteristics:

1. There is limited time.
2. No central decision maker.
3. The people who are trying to solve a problem are the same people who are causing the problem.
4. Policies discount the future irrationally.

An example of a super wicked problem is global warming.

Rittel and Webber specified ten characteristics of wicked problems in 1973:

1. "There is no definitive formulation of a wicked problem
2. Wicked problems have no stopping rule.
3. Solutions to wicked problems are not true-or-false, but better or worse.
4. There is no immediate and no ultimate test of a solution to a wicked problem.
5. Wicked problems do not have an enumerable set of potential solutions,
6. Every wicked problem is essentially unique.
7. Every wicked problem can be considered to be a symptom of another problem.
8. The existence of a discrepancy representing a wicked problem can be explained in numerous ways. The choice of explanation determines the nature of the problem's resolution.
9. The planner has no right to be wrong
10. Wicked problems have no given alternative solutions."

Source: Rittel and Webber

THE CONVERGENCE OF DESIGN AND BUSINESS

"I would argue that to be successful in the future,businesspeople will have to become more like designers — more 'masters of heuristics 'than 'managers of algorithms'.For much of the 20th century,they moved ahead by demonstrating the latter capability. This shift creates a huge challenge,as it will require entirely new kinds of education and training, since until now,design skills have not been explicitly valued in business. The truth is,highly skilled designers are currently heading-up many of the world's top organizations they just do not know they are designers,because they were never trained as such. The second implication is that we need anew kind of business enterprise. This new world into which we are delving will require us to tackle mysteries and develop heuristics —and that will require a substantial change in some of the fundamental ways we work. Traditional firms will have to start looking much more like design shops on a number of important dimensions."

Source: Rotman Magazine
Roger Martin The Design of Business (Winter 2004)

How to use this method

1. Roger Martin predicts businesses will need to use more abductive thinking in the future to be successful
2. He suggests that businesses will need to adopt new collaborative and iterative methods
3. He suggests that businesses will move from ongoing tasks and permanent assignments toward a project based model where assignments may be changing.
4. He suggests that businesses will move towards solving "wicked problems.

Source: Rotman Magazine
Roger Martin The Design of Business (Winter 2004)

INFORMED DESIGN

Design Thinking attempts to make decisions based on the best available evidence to build meaningful design solutions. This makes the design development process more likely to reach successful design solutions. Rather than a designer placing some sketched on the wall and suggesting to a client or manager that the designer feels one concept is intuitively better, the whole design team is involved in gathering and weighing evidence and corroboratively making more balanced decisions. which are driven by an understanding of the end user's perspectives. Design decisions are based on evidence rather than intuition.

INTEGRATIVE THINKING

A decision-making process in which an individual balances tensions between opposing variables. Design thinking promotes integrative thinking by using methods that discourage conventional thinking.

" **Integrative thinkers consider the problem as a whole, rather than breaking it down and farming out the parts. Finally, they creatively resolve tensions without making costly trade-offs, turning challenges into opportunities.**"
Roger Martin

Who invented it?
Integrative Thinking is a field in Applied Mind Science which was originated by Graham Douglas in 1986

References
1. Martin, R. L. (2007). The Opposable Mind: How Successful Leaders Win Through Integrative Thinking. Boston: Harvard Business School Press.

Why use Integrative Thinking?
Conventional Thinkers
1. "Focus only on obviously relevant features.
2. Consider one-way linear relationships between variables, in which more A produces more B.
3. Break problems into pieces and work on them separately or sequentially.
4. Make either or choices; settle for best available options."

Integrative Thinkers
1. Seek less obvious but potentially relevant factors
2. Consider multidirectional and nonlinear relationships among variables.
3. See problems as a whole examining how the parts fit together and how decisions affect one another
4. Creatively resolve tensions among opposing ideas; generate innovative outcomes.

How to use this method
In general, integrative thinking follows a four-step process.
1. The first step (salience) seeks to define the relevant aspects of a problem.
2. The second step (causality) seeks to determine the relationships between related and seemingly unrelated parts of the problem.
3. The third step (architecture) involves the creation of a model that outlines the relationships defined in the previous two steps.
4. The fourth step (resolution) outlines the decision and how it was reached. The process is similar to a feedback

Source Roger Martin

COMPLEXITY AMBIGUITY VOLATILITY UNCERTAINTY

What is it?

Organizations view their current and future state as being increasing a state of change, volatility, ambiguity and uncertainty. Organizations need ways to be more responsive and flexible. Design Thinking is a more agile way of solving organizational problems.

Why use Design Thinking?

By taking a more thoughtful and organized approach to considering these factors Design Thinking Methods offer organizations the promise of more stability and effectiveness in their strategy and implementation of design.

References

1. Sterman, J.D. (1994). "Learning in and about Complex Systems", System Dynamics Review, 10(2-3): 291-330.
2. Anderson, Edward G and Nitin R. Joglekar. (2012). The Innovation Butterfly: Managing Emergent Opportunities and Risks During Distributed Innovation. Springer (Understanding Complex Systems Series)"
3. Wolf, Daniel (2007). Prepared and Resolved: The Strategic Agenda for Growth, Performance and Change. dsb Publishing. p. 115. ISBN 0-9791300-0-X.

When to use this method

1. Define goals
1. Know Context
2. Know User
3. Frame insights
4. Generate Concepts
5. Create Solutions

How to use this method

The methods of design Thinking can be applied to help an organization to help build clarity by:

1. Anticipate the issues that shape conditions
2. Understand the consequences of issues and actions
3. Appreciate the interdependence of variables
4. Prepare for alternative realities and challenges
5. Interpret and address relevant opportunities
6. Sense making
7. Planning and readiness
8. Responsiveness

"Some things benefit from shocks; they thrive and grow when exposed to volatility, randomness, disorder, and stressors and love adventure, risk, and uncertainty. Yet, in spite of the ubiquity of the phenomenon, there is no word for the exact opposite of fragile. Let us call it antifragile. Antifragility is beyond resilience or robustness. The resilient resists shocks and stays the same; the antifragile gets better." *Nassim Nicholas Taleb Antifragile: Things That Gain From Disorder 2012*

CHANGE

Design Thinking leverages different perspectives to respond to change. Just as ecological diversity enables more living species to service in a changing ecosystem Design Thinking responds to a changing world by leveraging diverse teams and diverse views.

Some ways in which the world is changing:

1. Access to information
2. Continuing education
3. Growth of Asian economies
4. human centered design
5. Low cost competition
6. Mobility
7. Multiple cultures
8. Outsourcing
9. Personalization
10. Regional characteristics
11. Smaller organizations
12. Social networking
13. Strategic contribution
14. Telework
15. The cloud
16. The crowd
17. The nature of an expert
18. The service economy
19. The value of design

What is it?

Design is change. The rate of change in the world is increasing. Changes in an organization can result from changes in global markets, new competitors, new technology, government legislation and customer feedback. Changes can be planned or unplanned. Planning for change is not a choice but a necessity.

Why manage change?

1. Productivity declines when change is poorly managed
2. Some resistance to change is inevitable.
3. Change creates conflict
4. Change involves risk
5. It is natural to resist change

Challenges

1. Change can create resentment.
2. Not everyone reacts the same way to change. Some people prefer stability and others prefer change.
3. Change involves loss.
4. Needs and fears should be addressed when planning for change.

When to consider change

1. Define goals
2. Know Context
3. Know User
4. Frame insights
5. Generate Concepts
6. Create Solutions

How to manage change

1. Adjust your mindset from viewing change as a problem to an opportunity.
2. Keep sight of the long term vision
3. Have organizational structures that create long term solutions and short term solutions.
4. Be open to learning.
5. Provide others with information.
6. Be inclusive when discussing change.
7. Improve your ability to respond to change.
8. Communicate the desired changes and the need for change.
9. People undergoing change react in a cycle of emotions going through shock, denial, anger, bargaining, depression, testing, acceptance.
10. Involve the people resisting change in the in designing and implementing change.
11. Offer incentives for change.
12. Manage expectations realistically
13. Be consistent

References

1. Marshak, R.J. (2005). Contemporary challenges to the philosophy and practice of organizational development. In David L. Bradford and W. Warner Burke. Reinventing organizational development: New approaches to change in organizations. San Francisco, CA: Pfeiffer.

DESIGNING ACROSS CULTURES

What is cross-cultural design?

1. Companies are expanding their customer basis globally
2. Design Thinking approach helps usability and user experience across cultural boundaries

Why use cross-cultural design?

1. User experience attributes are influenced by Culture
2. Influences human interaction

The Design Thinking process helps designers work across cultures. By 2048 it is predicted that the economy of China will be twice the size of the economy of the United States. It is becoming increasingly necessary for designers to understand cultural differences when reaching design decisions.

The Design Thinking process utilizes ethnographic tools including observation and interviewing to help inform designers of cultural differences so that they can make informed decisions.

How do you do cross-cultural design?

1. User - centered design in the target culture and countries
2. User studies with local people
3. Usability tests

INNOVATION

The goal of design thinking is to understand, observe, and identify what customers want in a product, service or experience.

Design Thinking seeks to answer the following three questions:
1.   Who should be the target users?
2.   What do they need?
3.   How do you know?

Design Thinkers observe users in the context of their physical environments,interact with them with prototypes, and use their learning to create better designs.

By focusing on unmet needs rather than competitors products Design Thinking is capable of creating consistently repeatable innovation customer value and market opportunity through developing design solutions that do not currently exist in the market.

SYSTEMS SERVICES AND EXPERIENCES

The traditional skills taught at design schools such as sketching work well for designing physical objects and environments.Today 90% of US workers work in the service industries. Skills like sketching are less effective in describing changing, ambiguous and complex systems, experiences and services.

Design Thinking methods such as customer journey maps help designers to cross disciplinary boundaries to design less tangible or physical services and experiences that change over time.

Physical products today are often designed as part of an ecosystem of products, services and experiences. It is services and experiences that drive most value for customers and businesses. Design Thinking provides tools to navigate these relationships between physical products and nonphysical services and experiences to make informed decisions driven by customer needs.

EXPERIMENTAL APPROACH

For Design Thinkers, experimentation is a way of life. Design thinking encourages collective ownership, experimentation and risk.

"The methodology, guides the designer's work through phases and steps that involve observations, ideation, and experimentation.

When we visited IDEO and the d.School at Stanford University it became clear that experimentation needn't wait for a nod from an executive. Experimentation is a way of life. As our group made its way past the blocks of foam core, bins of knick-knacks, and the ubiquitous roles of duct tape, I came to understand that experiments and prototypes are designed for learning, not convincing.

Tom Kelly, the General Manager of IDEO suggests lowering the bar on prototypes of ideas. In his book, co-authored with Jonathan Littman, The Ten Faces of Innovation, Kelley and Littman refer to the power of "low-fidelity prototypes." At IDEO, one frequently hears the adage, "Fail often to succeed sooner." *Jay G. Cone*

"I have not failed. I have merely found ten thousand ways that will not work."
Thomas Edison

RISK

It is impossible to avoid risk when developing new products, services and experiences. Design Thinking gives us the tools to effectively manage risk by basing design decisions on an understanding of the point of view of customers.

References

1.   ISO/DIS 31000 (2009). Risk management Principles and guidelines on implementation. International Organization for Standardization.
2.   Alexander, Carol and Sheedy, Elizabeth (2005). The Professional Risk Managers' Handbook: A Comprehensive Guide to Current Theory and Best Practices. PRMIA Publications. ISBN 0-9766097-0-3.
3.   Gorrod, Martin (2004). Risk Management Systems : Technology Trends (Finance and Capital Markets). Basingstoke: Palgrave Macmillan. ISBN 1-4039-1617-9.
4.   Hopkin, Paul "Fundamentals of Risk Management 2nd Edition" Kogan-Page (2012) ISBN 978-0-7494-6539-1

BIAS

Design Thinking reduces the bias in decisions that can result in poor decisions and solutions by exploring multiple perspectives of stakeholders and by designing with teams that have diversity in the form of gender, age, education and culture.

CONTINUOUS LEARNING

The process of Design Thinking is a process of continuous learning. "The methodology, guides the designer's work through phases and steps that involve observations, ideation, and experimentation.

It uses the Japanese concept of Shoshin

Shoshin means beginner's mind. It refers to having an attitude of full of openness, enthusiasm, and fresh perspectives in learning something new, eagerness, and lack of preconceptions even at an advanced level, like a child.

Shoshin also means "correct truth" and is used to describe a genuine signature on a work of art. It is use to describe something that is perfectly genuine.

"In the beginner's mind there are many possibilities, but in the expert's there are few"
Shunryu Suzuki-Roshi

DISRUPTIVE SOLUTIONS

The focus of the Design Thinking methods on uncovering and creating solutions to unmet user needs means that this approach has the potential to create disruptive market solutions.

In particular industries such new products and services have happened every 20 to 25 years. An example is the invention of digital watches. This disruptive new technology changed the face of watchmaking and moved the center of that industry from Switzerland to Asia in the 1970s.

Other examples were the invention of the bag less vacuum cleaner by James Dyson or the commercial electric light bulb by Thomas Edison.

References
1. Anthony, Scott D.; Johnson, Mark W.; Sinfield, Joseph V.; Altman, Elizabeth J. (2008). Innovator's Guide to Growth – Putting Disruptive Innovation to Work. Harvard Business School Press. ISBN 978-1-59139-846-2.
2. Christensen, Clayton M., Baumann, Heiner, Ruggles, Rudy, & Sadtler, Thomas M. (2006). "Disruptive Innovation for Social Change" Harvard Business Review, December 2006.
3. Danneels, Erwin (2006). "From the Guest Editor: Dialogue on The Effects of Disruptive Technology on Firms and Industries". Journal of Product Innovation Management 23 (1): 2—4.

Chapter 4
Who can use
Design Thinking?

who can use design thinking?

Design Thinking is a technique for everyone and any problem. Design Thinking process involves many stakeholders in working together to find a balanced design solution. The designer is a member of a type of design orchestra. The customer is involved throughout the design process and works with the design team to communicate their needs and desires and to help generate design solutions that are relevant to them.

The many methods used help anyone to understand the diverse perspectives of the many stakeholders. It takes some courage to listen and recognize the point of view of the stakeholders. Managers, designers, social scientists, engineers marketers, stakeholders customers and others can collaborate creatively to apply Design Thinking to everyone's benefit.

The process is one of co-creation and the designer is a listener and a facilitator. Everyone adds value to the design. Design thinking is not just for professional designers. Everyone can contribute. Many schools are now teaching Design Thinking to children as an approach that can be applied to life.

characteristics of design thinkers

d.school Bootcamp Bootleg (2009)	d.school Bootcamp Bootleg (2010)	Tim Brown (2008)	Baeck & Gremett (2011)	Comment
Focus on human values	Focus on human values	Empathy	Empathy	"Focus on human values" includes empathy for users and feedback from them.
Create clarity from complexity	Craft clarity	Integrative thinking	Ambiguity Curiosity Holistic Open mindset	All these items refer to styles of thinking. "Clarity" refers to producing a coherent vision out of messy problems. Baeck & Gremett focus on attitudes of the Design Thinker.
		Optimism		Only mentioned by Tim Brown, but seems to be regarded as a universal characteristic of Design Thinkers.
Get experimental and experiential	Embrace experimentation	Experimentalism	Curiosity Open mindset	Experimentation is an integral part of the designer's work.
Collaborate across boundaries	Radical collaboration	Collaboration	Collaborative	Refers to the collaboration between people from different disciplines (having different backgrounds and viewpoints).
Show, do not tell Bias toward action	Show, do not tell Bias toward action			Emphasizes action, for example, by creating meaningful prototypes and confronting potential users with them.
Be mindful of process	Be mindful of process			Emphasizes that Design Thinkers need to keep the overall process (which is regarded as a core element of Design Thinking, in mind with respect to methods and goals.

Source: Gerd Waloszek, SAP AG, SAP User Experience — September 1, 2012

LIST OF DESIGN THINKING SKILLS

1. Learn from failure
2. Research skills
3. Interviewing skills
4. Empathy skills
5. Point of view synthesis
6. Prototyping skills
7. Problem identification
8. Mind full of design process
9. 2d and 3d visual expression skills
10. Acting and storytelling skills
11. Incremental and radical inventiveness
12. Make evaluations and provide feedback
13. Ability to synthesize ideas from data
14. Human centered ness – empathy
15. Value diverse perspectives
16. Action orientation
17. Ability to synthesize insights
18. Anthropology skills
19. Ability to make claims and judgements
20. Demonstrate skills used in each role (cross pollinator)
21. Ability to understand, observe, define)
22. Ability to implement

Source: Foundations of innovation teacher guide overview henry ford learning Institute version 2.0 April 2010

1. Team oriented
2. Collaborative
3. Agile perspective
4. Comfortable with ambiguity
5. Curious
6. Optimistic
7. Integrative thinking
8. Shoshin
9. Solution focused
10. Tool skills
11. Experimental
12. Innovative
13. Creative
14. Risk taker
15. Open to new ideas
16. T. shaped
17. Beginners mindset
18. Abductive thinker
19. Convergent and divergent thinking skills
20. Analytical thinker
21. Creative thinker
22. Critical thinker
23. Not ethnocentric
24. Considers context
25. Uses other perspectives and positions
26. Assesses audience
27. Justifies conclusions
28. Able to evaluate sources
29. Recognizes bias
30. Able to think reflectively
31. Qualifies assertions
32. Questions assumptions
33. Understands own biases

CONVERGENT THINKING

What is it?
Convergent thinking is a tool for problem solving in which the brain is applies a mechanized system or formula to some problem, where the solution is a number of steps from the problem. This kind of thinking is particularly appropriate in science, engineering, maths and technology.

Convergent thinking is opposite from divergent thinking in which a person generates many unique, design solutions to a design problem. Divergent thinking is followed by convergent thinking, in which a designer assesses, judges, and strengthens those options. Divergent thinking is what we do when we do not know the answer, when we do not know the next step

Who invented it?
Hudson 1967,
Joy Paul Guilford

Why use this method?
1. Convergent thinking leads to a single best answer, leaving no room for ambiguity.
2. Focuses on recognizing the familiar, reapplying techniques, and accumulating stored information

Challenges
1. Divergent and convergent thinking need to be used together to solve many problems.
2. Designers and business managers are working on many problems which require divergent thinking due to changing complex environments.
3. Traditional management and engineering education stresses convergent thinking.

When to use this method
1. Explore Concepts
2. Make Plans

How to use this method
Some of the rules of convergent thinking are:
1. Follow a systematic approach, find the patterns affinities and structure in a group of ideas.
2. Use methods to evaluate ideas, assess qualitative and quantitative measures of ideas,
3. Take care to consider everything take your time.
4. Do not expend too much time in looking for the perfect solution of a complex ill defined problem,
5. Assess risks and have a contingency plan.

References
1. Cropley, Arthur (2006). "In Praise of Convergent Thinking". Creativity Research Journal 18: 391–404.

DIVERGENT THINKING

What is it?

The design process is a series of divergent and convergent phases. During the divergent phase of design the designer creates a number of choices. The goal of this approach is to analyze alternative approaches to test for the most stable solution. Divergent thinking is what we do when we do not know the answer, when we do not know the next step. Divergent thinking is followed by convergent thinking, in which a designer assesses, judges, and strengthens those options.

Who invented it?

Hudson 1967,
Joy Paul Guilford

Why use this method?

1. To an extent the number of choices created and compared during the divergent phases of design help determine the quality of the finished design.

Challenges

1. Use when objectives are changing or ill defined.
1. Divergent and convergent thinking need to be used together to solve many problems.
2. Designers and business managers are working on many problems which require divergent thinking due to changing complex environments.

When to use this method

3. Frame insights
4. Explore Concepts
5. Make Plans

How to use this method
Some of the rules for divergent thinking are:

1. Reframe the problem
2. See the problem from different perspectives,
3. Connect with and have empathy with the people that you are designing for.
4. Defer negative criticism.
5. Generate lots of ideas.
6. Combine and modify ideas,
7. Be imaginative,
8. Do not be afraid to break paradigms

Resources

1. Pens
2. Paper
3. White board
4. Dry erase markers
5. Post it notes.

References

1. Wade, Carole; Tavris, Carol (2008). Invitation to Psychology. Upper Saddle River, NJ: Pearson – Prentice Hall. pp. 258. ISBN 0-13-601609.

CROWD FUNDING

What is it?

Crowdfunding is asking a large group of people to donate an amount of money for a project in exchange for a reward.

There are three types of crowdfunding:

1. Equity-based crowdfunding
2. Donation-based crowdfunding
3. Debt-based crowdfunding

Who invented it?

In 1997, fans financed a U.S. tour for the British rock group Marillion,

Why use this method?

1. Relatively low risk for designer and founder.
2. Allows designers to create and make their own products.
3. Fast and efficient.

Challenges

1. Intellectual property protection can be more complicated.
2. Platforms may limit the funds that you can receive.
3. New regulations and tax considerations
4. Clearly articulate what it is you're trying to accomplish in a way that inspires people to want to back it.
5. Define a compelling reward for the members of the crowd.

When to use this method

1. Deliver Offering

How to use this method

Instructions for Kickstarter.com:

1. A designer visits a site and proposes an idea
2. The community reviews the proposal,
3. The idea is accepted or rejected.
4. The designer launches their project.
5. The designer creates a video to communicate the idea.
6. The designer structures a reward for backers.
7. This is often one of what is being created.
8. In film, dance or theater the reward may be a ticket.

References

1. The Geography of Crowdfunding, NET Institute Working Paper No. 10-08, Oct 2010
2. Ordanini, A.; Miceli, L.; Pizzetti, M.; Parasuraman, A. (2011). "Crowd-funding: Transforming customers into investors through innovative service platforms". Journal of Service Management 22 (4): 443.

CROWD SOURCING

What is it?
Crowd sourcing involves out sourcing a task to a dispersed group of people. It usually refers to tasks undertaken by an undefined public group rather than paid employees.
Types of crowd sourcing include:
1. Crowd funding
2. Crowd purchasing
3. Micro work

The incentives for crowd sourcing can include: immediate payoffs, delayed payoffs, and social motivation, skill variety, task identity, task autonomy, direct feedback from the job

Who invented it?
Jeff Howe first used the term in a June 2006 Wired magazine article "The Rise of Crowd sourcing"

Why use this method?
1. Crowd sourcing can obtain large numbers of alternative solutions.
2. It is relatively fast
3. Inexpensive.
4. Diverse solutions.
5. group of people is sometimes more intelligent than an individual

Challenges
1. A faulty results caused by targeted, malicious work efforts
2. Ethical concerns
3. Difficulties in collaboration and team activity of crowd members.
4. Lack of monetary motivation

When to use this method
1. Define intent
2. Know Context
3. Know User
4. Frame Insights
5. Explore Concepts
6. Make Plans
7. Deliver Offering

How to use this method
1. Define your problem
2. Define your use of the crowd
3. Identify incentives.
4. Identify mechanism to reach the crowd.
5. Inspire your users to create
6. Distribute brief to the crowd
7. Analyze results.
8. Create preferred design solution.
9. Repeat above stages as necessary to refine the design.

Resources
1. A social or other network
2. Crowd sourcing site or interface
3. A mechanism to reach the crowd.
4. An incentive for the crowd.
5. A crowd

References
1. Jeff Howe (2006). "The Rise of Crowd sourcing". Wired.
2. Howe, Jeff (2008), "Crowd sourcing: Why the Power of the Crowd is Driving the Future of Business", The International Achievement Institute.

THE VALUE OF DIVERSITY

A diverse design team will produce more successful design than a team that lacks diversity. Innovation needs a collision of different ideas and approaches.

What is it?

Diversity means different genders, different ages, be from different cultures, different socioeconomic backgrounds and have different outlooks to be most successful.

Why use this method?

1. To attract good people
2. It broadens the customer base in a competitive environment.
3. Diversity brings substantial potential benefits such as better decision making and improved problem solving, greater creativity and innovation, which leads to enhanced product development, and more successful marketing to different types of customers. Diversity provides organizations with the ability to compete in global markets

References

1. Harvey, Carol P.; M. June Allard (2012). Understanding and Managing Diversity (5th ed.). New Jersey: Pearson Education, Inc.. pp. xii-393. ISBN 0-13-255311-2.

How to use this method

1. Everything from organizational symbols, rituals, and stories serve to maintain the position of power held by the dominant group.
2. View employees as individuals.
3. Seek recommitment from key participants.
4. Be open-minded. Recognize, and encourage employees to recognize, that one's own experience, background, and culture are not the only ones with value to the organization.
5. Articulate the benefits and motivations for becoming a more diverse organization.
6. Develop a definition of diversity that is linked to organizational mission.
7. Identify other organizations, both locally and nationally, that might serve
8. as models for diversity efforts.
9. Develop a realistic action plan for diversity efforts that takes into account ongoing operations and competing priorities.
10. Develop criteria to measure success. In other words, begin to build an evaluation plan.
11. Create a safe environment for candid and honest participation
12. Set relevant, pragmatic and achievable goals for bringing about organizational diversity.
13. Articulate expected outcomes and measures of change.

WAYS TO ASSIST TEAM CREATIVITY

What is it?

1. Improved research and employee education to provide skills that are needed for innovation. Research shows a clear link between skill levels of a workforce and the extent to which firms are creative.
2. Innovation occurs when participants understand rewards from their participation. There needs to be methods of motivating innovation. Connect innovation performance to career opportunities or rewards so that employees are rewarded for being creative.
3. Everyone should be aware of how innovation creates value
4. Senior management needs to be engaged in the innovation process
5. There should be an environment of trust and idea support, Emotional safety between coworkers to allow workers to express ideas.
6. Encourage Openness,
7. Encourage considered risk taking. Ask new questions
8. Seek innovation in the business model.
9. Listen to new voices. Have a process that involves and respects young designers.
10. Work from the future back. Exploit change. Develop an effective trend research process
11. Look for inspiration in new places.
12. Manage a portfolio of opportunities
13. Build small work teams during ideation phase. 4 or 5 people cross-disciplinary, diverse groups.
14. Engage and give responsibility to all team members
15. An environment that encourages experimentation and does not punish mistakes.
16. Human resources training. Hire Personalities that have a need to create.
17. Reach outside the organization to Universities, other companies, and suppliers. Foster new creative partnerships. Use the capabilities of customers and users to assist the innovation process Create mechanisms for knowledge transfer from outside the company.
18. Audit of current capabilities, an action plan and transformation roadmap Identify gaps in current methods
19. Create a diverse workforce and diverse teams. Improve cross cultural understanding
20. Use creativity tools and Innovation methods
21. Develop unique selling propositions
22. Develop a formal innovation philosophy
23. The project goals need to be clearly articulated at the beginning of the project and concepts need to be constantly reviewed against the goals
24. Prototype and test concepts in many different ways. Reduce risk by low cost experiments.   Learn from prototypes and experiments revise and refine the concept

25. Have Regular team meetings. Weekly and daily. Describe clear goals and continuously describe and discuss roles and deliverables of individual team members from the beginning of the project.
26. Develop permanent project spaces
27. Rotate meetings to different discipline areas so that team members are able to see the cultures of other disciplines
28. Reduce hierarchical leadership structure of teams.
29. Customer visit teams Involve your customers in the design. Customer brainstorming.
30. Crowdsourcing- Use the internet to invite finished product ideas and designs. Understand how users will adopt a new product.
31. Monitor disruptive new technologies and trends and have a formal process of developing designs integrating those trends
32. Develop an advanced concept incubator
33. Create a physical environment or workspace that supports innovation

References

1. Amabile, Teresa M.; Barsade, Sigal G; Mueller, Jennifer S; Staw, Barry M., "Affect and creativity at work," Administrative Science Quarterly, 2005, vol. 50, pp. 367–403.
2. Craft, A. (2005). Creativity in Schools: tensions and dilemmas. Routledge. ISBN 0-415-32414-9.
3. Dorst, K.; Cross, N. (2001). "Creativity in the design process: co-evolution of problem—solution". Design Studies 22 (5): 425–437. doi:10.1016/S0142-694X(01)00009-6
4. Florida, R. (2002). The Rise of the Creative Class: And How It's Transforming Work, Leisure, Community and Everyday Life. Basic Books. ISBN 0-465-02476-9.
5. DeGraff, J.; Lawrence, K. (2002). Creativity at Work. Jossey-Bass. ISBN 0-7879-5725-9.
6. Robinson, Andrew (2010). Sudden Genius?: The Gradual Path to Creative Breakthroughs. Oxford: Oxford University Press. ISBN 978-0-19-956995-3.
7. O'Hara, L. A. & Sternberg, R. J.. "Creativity and Intelligence". In ed. Sternberg, R. J. Handbook of Creativity. Cambridge University Press.
8. Pink, D. H. (2005). A Whole New Mind: Moving from the information age into the conceptual age. Allen & Unwin.

STAKEHOLDERS

What is it?

Identify the people who will be affected by the design, It is likely that you will not be able to identify all stakeholders early in a project.

1. Power (high, medium, low)
2. Support (positive, neutral, negative)
3. Influence (high or low)
4. Need (strong, medium, weak)

Why use this method?

1. Stakeholder analysis helps to identify:
2. Stakeholder interests
3. Ways to influence other stakeholders
4. Risks
5. Key people to be informed during the project
6. Negative stakeholders as well as their adverse effects on the project

How to use this method

1. Create a stakeholder map through one or more brainstorming sessions with your team. This can be updated during the design project

The following list identifies some of the most commonly used methods for stakeholder mapping:

2. Mitchell 1997 proposed a classification of stakeholders based on power to influence,
3. Fletcher, Guthrie 2003 defined a process for mapping stakeholder expectations based on value hierarchies
4. Cameron, Crawley 2010 defined a process for ranking stakeholders based on needs and the relative importance of stakeholders to others
5. Savage, Nix 1991 defined a way to classify stakeholders according to potential for threat and potential for cooperation.
6. Turner, Kristoffer and Thurloway, 2002 developed a process of identification, assessment of awareness, support, influence leading to strategies for communication and assessing stakeholder satisfaction,

References

1. Fletcher, A., et al. (2003). "Mapping stakeholder perceptions for a third sector organization." in: Journal of Intellectual Capital 4(4): 505 – 527.

2. Mitchell, R. K., B. R. Agle, and D.J. Wood. (1997). "Toward a Theory of Stakeholder Identification and Salience: Defining the Principle of Who and What really Counts." in: Academy of Management Review 22(4): 853 - 888.

3. Savage, G. T., T. W. Nix, Whitehead and Blair. (1991). "Strategies for assessing and managing organizational stakeholders." In: Academy of Management Executive 5(2): 61 – 75.

4. Cameron, B.G., T. Seher, E.F. Crawley (2010). "Goals for space exploration based on stakeholder network value considerations." in: Acta Astronautica doi:10.1016/j.actaastro.2010.11.003.

5. A. M. Hein; A. C. Tziolas; R. Osborne (2011), "Project Icarus: Stakeholder Scenarios for an Interstellar Exploration Program", JBIS, 64, 224-233

6. Turner, J. R., V. Kristoffer, et al., Eds. (2002). The Project Manager as Change Agent. London, McGraw-Hill Publishing Co.

7. Weaver, P. (2007). A Simple View of Complexity in Project Management. Proceedings of the 4th World Project Management Week. Singapore.

8. Hemmati, M., Dodds Γ., Enayti, J.,McHarry J. (2002) "Multistakeholder Procesess on Governance and Sustainability. London Earthscan

9. Mendelow, A. (1991) 'Stakeholder Mapping', Proceedings of the 2nd International Conference on Information Systems, Cambridge, MA (Cited in Scholes,1998).

CREATIVITY

Everyone can be creative. Some traits of the most creative personalities are:

1. Open to new experiences
2. Independent and self reliant
3. Willingness to risk
4. Sense of humor or playfulness
5. Enjoys experimentation
6. Personal courage
7. Preference for complexity
8. Goal orientation
9. Internal control
10. Original
11. Persistence
12. Curiosity
13. Vision
14. Acceptance of disorder. Tolerant of ambiguity
15. Motivated, has vitality and enthusiasm
16. Competitive
17. Less inhibited, less formal and unconventional
18. Rejects authority
19. Perseveres and is thorough
20. Critical, less contented, dissatisfied
21. Likes to collect things such as books, music, designed objects, travel experiences
22. Is widely informed, has wide interests

References

1. Amabile, Teresa M.; Barsade, Sigal G; Mueller, Jennifer S; Staw, Barry M., "Affect and creativity at work," Administrative Science Quarterly, 2005, vol. 50, pp. 367—403.
2. Craft, A. (2005). Creativity in Schools: tensions and dilemmas. Routledge. ISBN 0-415-32414-9.
3. Dorst, K.; Cross, N. (2001). "Creativity in the design process: co-evolution of problem—solution". Design Studies 22 (5): 425—437. doi:10.1016/S0142-694X(01)00009-6
4. Florida, R. (2002). The Rise of the Creative Class: And How It's Transforming Work, Leisure, Community and Everyday Life. Basic Books. ISBN 0-465-02476-9.
5. DeGraff, J.; Lawrence, K. (2002). Creativity at Work. Jossey-Bass. ISBN 0-7879-5725-9.
6. Robinson, Andrew (2010). Sudden Genius?: The Gradual Path to Creative Breakthroughs. Oxford: Oxford University Press. ISBN 978-0-19-956995-3.
7. O'Hara, L. A. & Sternberg, R. J.. "Creativity and Intelligence". In ed. Sternberg, R. J. Handbook of Creativity. Cambridge University Press.
8. Pink, D. H. (2005). A Whole New Mind: Moving from the information age into the conceptual age. Allen & Unwin.

T SHAPED PEOPLE

What is it?
Having skills and knowledge that are both deep and broad.
The vertical bar on the T represents the depth of related skills in a single field, and the horizontal bar represents the ability to collaborate across disciplines other than one's own

Who invented it?
David Guest, "The hunt is on for the Renaissance Man of computing," The Independent (London), September 17, 1991

Tim Brown, CEO of the IDEO design consultancy defended this approach to résumé assessment as a method to build interdisciplinary work teams for creative processes.

Challenges
1. When people come out of school, they're often I-shaped
2. If someone is a really popular member of a project team they are probably good collaborators.

WHY EMPLOY T SHAPED PEOPLE?

1. People who are T-shaped are well-rounded and versatile. They are better able to contribute their ideas to a discussion and are able to take on a variety of roles.
2. T-shaped people, free to take on different roles as work changes, are far more valuable than those trapped in rigid silos of scope and responsibility.
3. Work is more cross-functional, requires more collaboration and sharing, and relies less on how things were done in the past.
4. Organizations are realizing that when people are assigned to or choose roles to play in an organization they are often more creative and efficient than when they are confined to the duties prescribed by a title or position.
5. Many companies are experimenting with putting people into role-based work. Google, for example, often assigns engineers to a team where they work out, with the team members, the role they will play. The same happens routinely at IDEO, the well-known design firm in Palo Alto, California.
6. We do not know what these skills, experiences, and activities are; they change constantly and they are interdependent on others in our team.
7. Procter & Gamble, Nike, Apple are examples of companies that employ t shaped people.
Source Tim Brown

Chapter 5
Design Thinking spaces

design thinking spaces

The design of a space can support innovation and project success. The design thinking approach can be non-linear and messy. Your team can be working in a project space for a considerable time during a project. Space influences behaviour. There are some simple tools and actions that you can take to make the space comfortable and a productive work environment.

Here are some principles to consider when designing spaces for innovation activities: a stressful or even depressing work environment doesn't give one the mood to think of doing things differently. The employee would only look forward to the end of the day. Peoples needs drive the best design spaces. In this chapter I have some suggestions for creating productive design thinking working spaces that will help your team.

"We shape our buildings; thereafter, they shape us."
Winston Churchill

MOBILE WHITE BOARDS

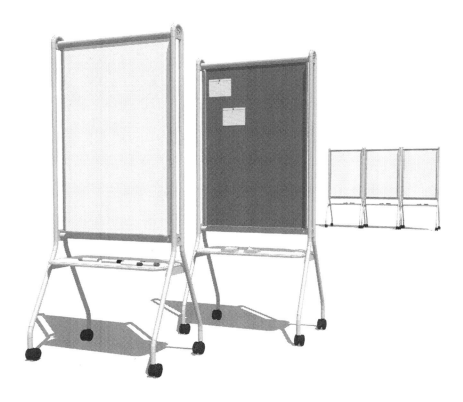

Mobile white boards are one of the most useful tools for conducting design thinking activities. The reverse side of the white board can have a pin board. The white boards can be placed in a row for a larger group or used individually in different locations for a number of smaller groups

PRESENTATION SPACES

1. Lightweight, comfortable, readily moveable chairs perhaps on wheels can maximize a relatively small footprint and be arranged in multiple configurations
2. Show your work in progress and let people comment.
3. Surround yourself with the material that your team is working on.
4. Mobile large white boards 6 ft x 4 ft and pin boards.
5. Presentation boards can be hung from a picture rail or on wheels.
6. Mobile boards can have a magnetic white board on one side and a pin board on the reverse side.
7. Keep boxes of colored pins and magnets in the space.
8. A laptop-sized surface for each attendee
9. Walls can be used for projection, writing, or pinning up information in areas visible to everyone
10. Acoustic privacy should be ensured.
11. Large walls can be used as display spaces.
12. Use work tools that are easily accessible
13. Think of every vertical surface as a potential space for displaying work
14. Select furniture than can be used in multiple ways or has been designede for multiple purposes for example a mobile storage cart that can double as a stool.
15. Use flexible technologies such as wifi that allow relocation of services such as internet and power connections.
16. Have a projector Projector and screen

TACTICAL SPACES

1. Team rooms should offer the flexibility to be arranged to suit the project at hand
2. Seating should allow all participants to see one another and read body language
3. Select furniture with wheels that allows it to be moved so that you can quickly change from working in large groups to working in small groups.
4. Small tables can be used for breakouts or grouped into a common surface
5. Ample writing and display areas, as well as surfaces for laying things out, support the need for visual cues and reference materials
6. Tables should be power and internet enabled
7. Acoustic shielding is key

Source: Adapted from Haworth recommendations

MOBILE TABLES

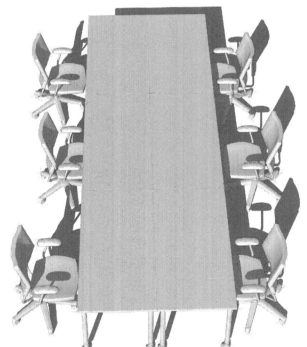

Mobile tables can be used together as one large table for group brainstorming sessions or can be placed around the room for smaller working group sessions.

COLLABORATIVE SPACES

Have a team space where the history of project work is on display to reduce the need for rework

1. Build spaces that support different types of collaboration.
2. Consider physical and virtual collaboration.
3. Spaces should be flexible for unplanned collaboration.
4. Position individual works paces around group spaces for flexibility
5. Provide comfortable group areas for informal interactions and information sharing.
6. Consider technologies that allow remote team members to interact with the team
. as though they were located in the same space.
7. Provide a large area of vertical displays such as walls white boards, pin boards, foam core boards, projection surfaces, that allow users to actively and flexibly interact with the information

Source: Adapted from Haworth recommendations

FLEXIBLE SPACES

Design Thinking spaces need to be flexibly configured in order to support spontaneous exchanges of information. The spaces need to support different modes of work where people can work individually or collaborate in small or large groups. The team should be confident to reconfigure their space and experiment spontaneously as they see the need arising.

1. Lightweight, comfortable, readily moveable chairs on wheels can maximize a small space and be arranged in multiple ways
2. Consider movable partitions to adjust privacy. This is sometimes achieved with curtains.
3. Design spaces for multiple functions
4. Select furniture that can move and be adapted in different ways. For example a storage cube on wheels with a cushion on top can be used as a stool and for storage.
5. Create a flexible hub for large and small group activities
6. Encourage the team to reconfigure the furniture to their changing needs.
7. Allow for flexible privacy. Consider the needs of videoconferencing.

Source: Adapted from Haworth recommendations

IMPROMPTU SPACES

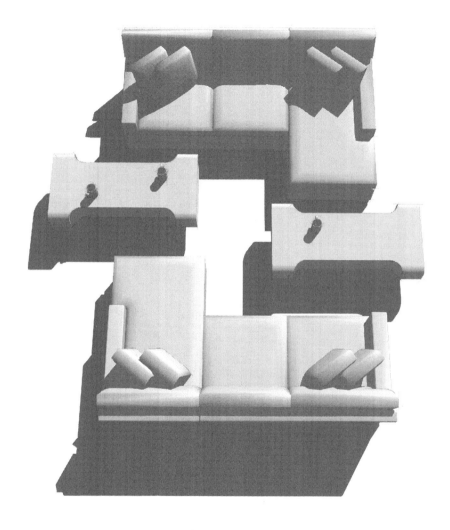

Impromptu spaces to sit and connect throughout the building encourage short conversations and idea sharing

STRATEGIC THINKING SPACES

1. Seating should allow all participants to see one another, and people should have control over how far apart they sit
2. The space should allow for frequent movement and sit-to-stand action
3. Seating should be comfortable to encourage relaxing.
4. No barriers should be placed between people, unless they need horizontal surfaces for writing or references
5. Good visual and acoustic shielding from outside will limit distractions within and outside the space

Source: Adapted from Haworth recommendations

SOCIAL SPACES

1. Open and relaxed areas for informal conversations are important components for successful innovation spaces.
2. Because these include a wide range of spaces, from reception areas and lounges to coffee bars and multipurpose rooms, each environment must be considered individually
3. Impromptu spaces to sit and connect throughout the building encourage short conversations and idea sharing
4. Domestic furniture can be used for a less formal atmosphere.
5. Flexibility in multipurpose spaces requires furniture that allows them to be arranged to suit a variety of activities
6. Have a refreshment area for coffee with a refrigerator.
7. Provide comfortable furniture that supports social interactions such as lounge chairs, and cafe tables.
8. Locate casual collaboration areas in close proximity to work areas so it's easy to take a break, swap stories, etc.
9. Provide welcoming areas for guests with appropriate views into the space and work in progress
10. If your culture can bear it, add in a little music as people enter to perk people up.
11.

Source: Adapted from Haworth recommendations

FOAM CORE PIN BOARDS

An inexpensive and flexible method of creating temporary mobile surfaces for affinity diagrams and other group activities is to use sheets of one quarter inch foam core. The boards can be used in groups or individually. Thumb tacks can be used to pin cards to the surfaces. Post it notes can be used and repositioned on the surfaces. The material comes in white and black.

INSPIRING SPACES

Creating something new is fundamental to all knowledge work, and inspiration is especially important for those charged with product and service development and other areas of organizational innovation. Stimulating, engaging spaces can jump-start and sustain creative thinking. "Creating an environment that ignites imagination has a lot to do with creating small moments of surprise and curiosity,"

Provide for abundant natural lighting and views
Include natural elements and materials throughout the space
Consider color carefully in terms of its ability to excite or sooth
Provide settings that are casual, informal, and comfortable

Allow for artwork and meaningful objects throughout the space that can support individuals and culture.
1.   The colors and other aspects should support creativity.

EQUIP YOURSELF WELL

1.   A space that accommodates 20 people comfortably.
2.   Make your work tools large enough to be easily visible in the environment.
3.   Acoustic privacy from outside noise
4.   Visual privacy for confidential discussions from outside spaces.
5.   Adjoining space where team members can conduct personal telephone conversations
6.   Adequate light and ventilation for tasks..
7.   Large Mobile magnetic white boards with 300 to 500 colored magnets.
8.   Networking capability for computers for each participant
9.   Data connections and power connections should allow repositioning of team members. This can be achieved by using a network of floor connections or hubs.
10. Wireless internet
11. Two speaker phones in accessible positions
12. 4x6", and 3x5" blank cards
13. Chord management
14. Individual table that can be repositioned to create one large table or tables for groups of 1 or 4.
15. Large Wall Clock:
16. Laser printer that can print 11" x 17" format
17. Space to hang winter clothing for cold locations.
18. Lockable space for personal things such as a filing cabinet or drawers.
19. Large wall calendar
20. Fridge Space for refreshments like coffee.
21. Video camera and tripod.
22. Digital still camera.

Source: Adapted from Haworth recommendations

MOBILE SEATING AND STORAGE

Flexible seating and storage units

COMFORTABLE SPACES

1. A good size for a design thinking space is a space that accommodates 20 people comfortably.
2. Design spaces to accommodate a variety of postures
3. Spaces for quite concentration should have less visual stimulation than environments for high activity.
4. Create environments that encourage socialization and collaboration and interaction and a sense of belonging to a team and an organization.
5. Provide choice and control for your team members
6. Provide spaces outside the team room for people to get away and socialize.
7. Provide spaces that reflect your values.

Source: Adapted from Haworth recommendations

MENTAL SPACE

1. Do something different. Travel farther. See a different kind of movie. Study paintings, logos, photographs, websites. Go on a walk. Listen more. See more Let yourself make mistakes. Try something new.

PLAN FOR CASUAL INTERACTION

Managers once discouraged, even forbade, casual interactions among employees. Today we know that chance encounters and conversations on the job promote cooperation and innovation, and companies craft their floor plans and cultures with this in mind. Open floor plans, or indeed any type of design, can either encourage or discourage informal interactions, depending on a complex interplay of physical and social cues. The most effective spaces bring people together and remove barriers while also providing sufficient privacy that people do not fear being overheard or interrupted.

"Our building which is Steve Jobs's brainchild, is another way that we try to get people from different departments to interact. Most buildings are designed for some functional purpose, but ours is structured to maximize inadvertent encounters. At its center is a large atrium, which contains the cafeteria, meeting rooms, bathrooms and mailboxes. As a result everyone has strong reasons to go there repeatedly during the course of the workday. It's hard to describe just how valuable the resulting chance encounters are"

Source: Ed Catmull President Pixar 2008 Harvard Business Review.

SPACES AT PIXAR

1. Empower your creative employees. Give your team control over every stage of the creative process and to make decisions. Pixar's Directors offer advice on projects but the production leaders decide what to use.

2. Create a peer culture. Creativity at Pixar involves many people working together to solve many problems. A movie contains tens of thousands of ideas.

3. Encourage people to help each other produce their best work.

4. Give everyone the freedom to communicate with anyone. People from any department are able to approach people from any other department without going through "proper channels"

5. Encourage new hires to have the confidence to speak. Understand that we haven't got all the answers and we want everyone to question why we are doing something that doesn't make sense to them.

6. Trust people to solve problems without getting permission.

7. Get people in different disciplines to treat one another as peers.

8. Craft a learning environment. Develop the mind set that all employees are continually learning and it is fun to learn together.

9. Have project Post mortems that stimulate discussion. Vary the way that you do postmortems. List the top five things that you would do again and the top five things that you wouldn't.

10. Make a safe environment for everyone to offer ideas.

11. Constantly work to employ better technology at every stage.

12. Arrange meetings so that there are always fresh eyes.

13. Stay close to innovations happening in the academic community.

14. The building is designed to encourage inadvertent encounters. The mailboxes, cafeteria, meeting rooms and bathrooms are at the center of the building. Chance encounters are valuable.

15. Have a regular injection of outsiders who will challenge the status quo. Bring in people with fresh perspectives.

16. Use data to analyze your performance.

Source: adapted from "How Pixar Fosters collective creativity" by Ed Catmull President Pixar 2008 Harvard Business Review

SPACES AT GOOGLE

1. "Have a group of half a dozen different people interview new employees. Select interviewers from different backgrounds including management and the candidate's potential future work colleagues.

2. Pamper your employees. Google offer first-class dining facilities, gyms, laundry rooms, massage rooms, haircuts, carwashes, dry cleaning, commuting buses.

3. Share offices with several disciplines so that people can communicate directly on a continual basis face to face. Put teams in day to day physical proximity.

4. Make every project a team project.

5. Communicate. Each Google worker e-mails a snippet once a week to his work group describing what he has done in the last week.

6. Use and test your own products. One of the reasons for Gmail's success is that it was beta tested within the company for many months

7. Encourage creativity. Google engineers can spend up to 20 percent of their time on a project of their choice. One of our not-so-secret weapons is our ideas mailing list: a company wide suggestion box where people can post ideas ranging from parking procedures to the next killer app.

8. Strive to reach consensus. Modern corporate mythology has the unique decision maker as hero. We adhere to the view that the "many are smarter than the few," and solicit a broad base of views

before reaching any decision.

9. Do not be evil. As in every organization, people are passionate about their views. We foster to create an atmosphere of tolerance and respect, not a company full of yes men.

10. Data drive decisions. At Google, almost every decision is based on quantitative analysis. We've built systems to manage information, not only on the Internet at large, but also internally. We have a raft of online "dashboards" for every business we work in that provide up-to-the-minute snapshots of where we are

11. Communicate effectively. Every Friday we have an all-hands assembly with announcements, introductions and questions and answers. (Oh, yes, and some food and drink.)

12. Discourage"techno arrogance." Engineers are competitive by nature and they have low tolerance for those who aren't as driven or as knowledgeable as they are. But almost all engineering projects are team projects; having a smart but inflexible person on a team can be deadly."

Source :Eric Schmidt and Hal Varian
Google: 10 golden rules

Eric Schmidt is CEO of Google. Hal Varian is a Berkeley professor and consultant with Google.

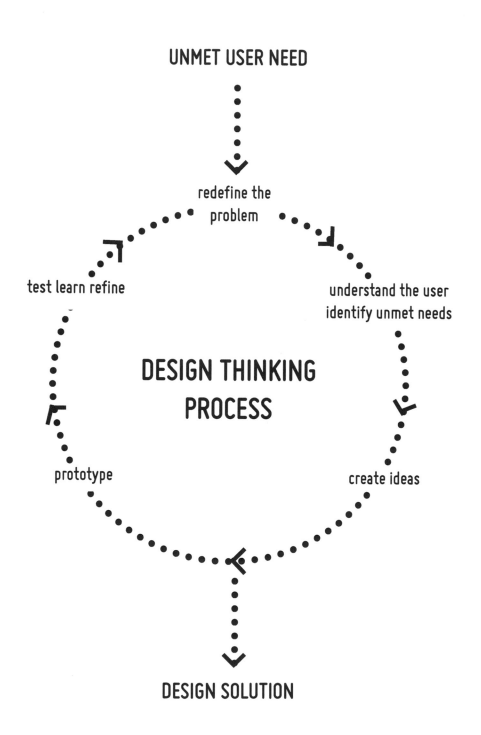

UNMET USER NEED

redefine the problem

test learn refine

DESIGN THINKING PROCESS

understand the user identify unmet needs

prototype

create ideas

DESIGN SOLUTION

Chapter 6
Design Thinking process

design thinking process

This chapter describes a model for the design thinking process. Different design organizations have developed slightly different process models. The chart on the following pages shows how a number of organizations that have adopted a Design Thinking approach describe their own process stages.

The Design Thinking model I describe in this chapter is based on a synthesis of the various design thinking models and my own experiences designing products and services. It has eight phases

1. **Writing a design proposal.** The notes here are meant to assist designers who are new to writing proposals. I included them because I have often been asked about this phase of the design process in online discussions and little is published that is useful for working designers. The model described is a fee for time model which is the most common model used in industrial design. The planning and estimating phase will be different for a design manager working internally in an organization for planning an internal design development.
2. **Building a team** In this section I describe some of the characteristics that are desirable for a cross functional team and a number of team building exercises.
3. **Define the intent.** In this section I describe activities that can help you identify and focus your objectives and goals in the design development.
4. **Get to know the people and context.** These activities are amongst the most important for Design Thinking. The activities described will help you understand the perspectives of the people that you are designing for. This is sometimes called empathy.
5. **Interpret and synthesize.** This section will help your team make sense of the research that you have gathered.
6. **Generate ideas.** This section describes a number of team based methods for creating ideas and possible design solutions.
7. **Prototype and refine.** It is important to create physical models as soon as possible and work with your end users to interact with the prototypes and provide your design team with feedback that will allow you to improve your design through iterative chnages and retesting of your prototypes.
8. **Test improve and Implement solutions.** In this phase your team will turn your ideas into finished products, services and experiences.

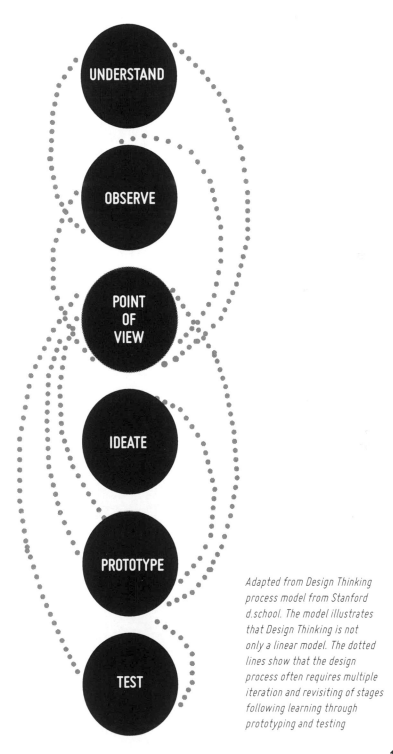

UNDERSTAND

OBSERVE

POINT
OF
VIEW

IDEATE

PROTOTYPE

TEST

Adapted from Design Thinking process model from Stanford d.school. The model illustrates that Design Thinking is not only a linear model. The dotted lines show that the design process often requires multiple iteration and revisiting of stages following learning through prototyping and testing

DESIGN THINKING PROCESS MODELS

	Hayes 1989	Amabile 1989	Plattner 2009 Design Thinking	Kolko 2007	IDEO Kelley 2002	Treffinger 1992	Roozenburg 1995
		task presentation	understand		understand	mess finding	function
	identify the problem	preparation	observe	research	observe	data finding	analysis
	problem representation		point of view	synthesis		problem finding	synthesis
	planning the solution	idea generation	ideate	ideation		idea finding	
	execute the plan		prototype	refinement	visualize		simulation
	evaluate the plan	idea validation	test		evaluate and refine	solution finding	evaluation
	evaluate the solution	outcome assessment		reflection	implement	acceptance finding	decision

DESIGN THINKING PROCESS MODELS

	Wikipedia Herbert Simon	IDEO Toolkit	Tim Brown IDEO	d.school D-School HPI	d.school Bootcamp Bootleg HPIModes	Baeck & Gremett 2011	Mark Dziersk Fast Company
Understand the problem	define	discovery	inspiration	understand	empathize: observe, engage, immerse	define the problem to solve	define the problem
observe users	research			observe		look for inspiration	
interpret the results		interpretation		point of view	define problem statement		
generate ideas	ideation	ideation	ideation	ideate	ideate	ideate	create many options
prototype experiment	prototype	experimentation	implementation	prototype	prototype	generate prototypes	refine directions repeat
test, implement, improve	objectives/ choose implement learn	evolution		evolution	test refine and improve solutions	solicit user feedback	pick the winner, execute

Source: this page adapted from Gerd Waloszek, SAP AG, SAP User Experience 2012

SOME SAMPLE QUESTIONS FOR A PRODUCT DESIGN CLIENT BRIEF

General
1. What are your contact details?
2. Why is this product being developed?
3. What specific outcomes do we want to achieve?
4. What standards does the product need to conform to?
5. How will the product be used?
6. What is the positioning strategy?
7. What national and international standards does the product need to comply with?
8. Who will approve payment of the invoices?
9. What is your budget?
10. Who will approve the work?

Market
1. Who are the intended users?
2. Age gender, culture, location?
3. Who are your competitors?
4. Have you done an intellectual property search?
5. What is your brand?
6. What is your pricing strategy?

Manufacturing
1. Who will manufacture the product?
2. What are the preferred materials?
3. What are the preferred manufacturing processes?
4. What is the anticipated release date
5. Will it be released at a particular show or event?
6. What are the anticipated annual manufacturing quantities
7. What batch quantities will it be manufactured in?
8. What is the preferred location of manufacturing?
9. Do you have preferred manufacturing vendors?

Distribution
1. What are the preferred distribution channels?
2. How should the product be packaged?
3. Who will maintain the product?
4. How will the product be transported?
5. How will the product be stored?
6. Where will the product be distributed?
7. Are there any other considerations?

THE PROJECT BRIEF

One of the most difficult areas to find useful information is the activity of preparing a client project proposal. A proposal with terms helps create certainty about the agreement and help minimize the risk of legal disputes. A proposal helps you cover all the important matters and to not overlook things. A proposal helps avoid mismatched expectations between a designer and client. They help you enforce your agreement, get paid, comply with the law and provide good service. It is important that a brief should be carefully prepared by the designer in order to provide a client with defined expectations and a budget and structure for the proposed design services. I have put together some guidelines based on my experience which can support a successful design process. A poorly conceived design proposal can lead to budget and time overruns, and an unhappy client.

Laws and considerations vary by locality and industry. Design proposals are legally binding documents. Design projects often involve changes of direction and rework. The material here are meant as general considerations only for design proposals on the basis of charge on an hourly basis. Some design professions including architecture commonly charge clients on a different basis. Seek qualified advice and get a local attorney to review your proposal and terms before presenting them to a client. Do not enter into royalty agreements lightly and make sure if you do that you are dealing with a reliable client and make sure that you have a good contract.

A proposal should contain at least the following
1. Cover letter
2. Statement of brief based on comprehensive briefing information supplied by the client
3. The body of the proposal containing descriptions of phases, tasks and deliverable for each phase
4. A estimated summary of costs and design hours and elapsed time for each phase
5. Total estimated costs and times
6. Terms and conditions
7. Some one page case studies of similar projects undertaken in the past if available.

ASK QUESTIONS

It is important before preparing a design brief that a designer asks questions that may effect the duration of the work, the tasks and deliverables and the cost to the client. If these questions are not asked then rework may be needed later in the project to correct a designers incorrect assumptions. This may add cost which may not have been calculated into the client's budget.

When preparing your proposal summarize the answers given to the client to your briefing questions in your introductory pages. If the client needs to change their brief during a project this is usually managed by a change order where the designer refers to the initial brief and the requested change and provides an estimate for the additional work required for the change.

TASKS AND DELIVERABLES

A proposal is broken down into a number of phases. These phases may vary depending on the area of design. Typically they are something like this

1. Observation
2. Ideation
3. Fast Prototyping
4. Refining
5. Implementation

The proposal should contain an overview of what is expected to happen in that phase. In each phase it is important for the designer to define clearly what it is intended will be delivered to the client in terms of tasks undertaken and physical or virtual deliverables. If this is done carelessly a client may say that more concepts were expected for the cost or exploration of more factors were expected.

A task may be defined as what factors will be explored. For a product designer these may include exploration of human factors, materials, finishes or processes.

A deliverable is the product of one or more tasks. Anything that requires action on your part to produce:

A description of a physical deliverable in the case of sketches may be defined as 10 colored perspective view sketches, letter sized. One sketch each for ten different concepts. A web designer may define deliverables as wireframes. Allow a review meeting at the end of each phase up to three hours duration

CREATE A BUDGET AND PLAN

What is it?
A Gantt chart is a bar chart that shows the tasks of a project, the start time and the time from start to completion of each task.

This method is used widely in industry to ensure that activities are completed on time and on budget.

Who invented it?
Henry Gantt first published in "Organizing for Work 1919.

Why use this method?
1. Use to track a design project
2. Use to ensure that tasks are completed on time.

How to use this method
1. Identify the tasks
2. Identify the milestones in the project.
3. Identify the time required for each task.
4. Identify the order and dependencies of each task.
5. Identify the tasks that can be undertaken in parallel
6. Draw a horizontal time axis along the top or bottom of a page.
7. Draw a list of tasks in order down the left hand side of the page in the order that they should be undertaken.
8. Draw a diamond for tasks that are short in duration such as a meeting
9. For longer activities draw a horizontal bar indicating the planned duration.

FEES AND EXPENSES

Fees and expenses are usually quoted in the form of a table.

An estimate for the number of design hours and the estimated duration of the work for each phase. The duration and the design hours are usually different because the duration depends on the number of other projects on which the designer is working and on factors such as client approval. Provide totals of estimates for the whole project.

The first phase is often quoted at a fixed price and later phases are estimated which may be revised if necessary before the commencement of each phase. In the United states a deposit is usually required for 30% or 50% of design hours prior to commencement of each phase. Clients who do not intend to pay fees will always seek to avid paying a deposit so it is my advice not to proceed without a deposit.

Expenses are usually quoted separately to design time. They typically may include things like travel, accommodation, art supplies, and research costs. There is normally a markup on the designer's costs when they are passed on to the client. A designer may provide a budget estimate at the start of the project or simply state that they will be charged as incurred.

TERMS AND CONDITIONS

Terms and conditions usually include but are not limited to payment terms, limits of liability,force majeure, intellectual property right management, ownership of digital files, passing of title and risk. A set of terms and conditions carefully drafted and reviewed by an attorney may protect the designer and their client in many unforeseen situations.

AUTHORIZATION TO PROCEED

You should not start a project before a person who is legally able to represent your client's organization signs a statement that they have reviewed your proposal and terms and conditions and agrees to them and authorizes you to proceed. You should not start a project before you have received a deposit.

ASSEMBLE A TEAM

What is it?
Selecting the right team may be the most important single factor for predicting project success or failure. A cross disciplinary team is able to tackle complex problems that cannot be solved by a single individual. Organizations are increasingly relying on teams to achieve higher levels of innovation, by using teams combining multiple perspectives from different areas of expertise.

Why use this method?
1. Collaborative cross disciplinary teams outperform individuals.
2. Interdisciplinary teams that work together in highly collaborative ways, building on each others insights and knowledge.
3. Small, nimble teams with hybrid skills are able to adapt to changing circumstance and requirements..

Challenges
1. Collaboration is not always easy to achieve in cross disciplinary teams.
2. Managed conflict may be necessary to allow the best ideas to float to the top.
3. Teams where no conflict is permitted may be less innovative.
4. Some cultures are less supportive of creative conflict.
5. Level of knowledge sharing, lack of feedback, expectations, rewards and incentives, motivation and self identity can effect team performance.

6. Too many I shaped people may hinder collaboration. Large traditional organizations have mainly I shaped people.
7. "A Renaissance team of T and I-shaped thinkers is a potentially volatile cocktail. Its value is too precious to be put at risk by even a single individual, regardless of how otherwise talented." *Bill Buxton*

How to use this method
How do you select the team?
1. Hire people who do not require predictability and stability in order to be effective.
2. Hire people with strong interpersonal skills.
3. Select people with the capacity for abstract thinking, yet they also have a strong grounding in physical materials and tools.
4. Select people who have a history of getting their hands dirty as they were growing up, deeply involved in things such as fixing bicycles or cars.
5. You do not need jacks-of-all-trades.
6. You need a mixture of "T" Shaped people and "I" shaped people.
7. Startups need more T shaped people.
8. Having some T shaped people on any team helps the team dynamics
9. T shaped people can bridge different perspectives and fill gaps within the team and to take on new skill-sets quickly.
10. I shaped people keep you in touch with the latest techniques, thinking and opportunities in specific areas.
11. **"If you think you know the core**

competencies needed for a team, list them on a bunch of Post-it notes, and have each person on the team write the name of the "go-to" person on the team who has the most depth in that area. If you do not have strong consistency in the responses, Houston, you probably have a problem. "*Bill Buxton*

12. Do not put someone else like you on the team. You need people who fill the gaps of your skill set.

13. Have at least three T shaped people on your team with equal levels of competence and creativity in three domains: business, people, and technology.

14. Test and select for I shapedness and form a team of both I shaped and T shaped people.

15. Identify the core competencies you need for the team and then write the "go-to" team member for each competency. Address any gaps.

16. Brilliant candidates who lack social skills will weaken the team.

Source: Bill Buxton on July 13, 2009 Bloomberg

T SHAPED PEOPLE

A T Shaped person has skills and knowledge that are both deep and broad. They have a primary area of expertise as well as skills to a lesser extent in other areas. They are different from a generalist or a jack of all trades The vertical bar on the T represents the depth of related skills and expertise in a single field, whereas the horizontal bar is the ability to collaborate across disciplines with experts in other areas and to apply knowledge in areas of expertise other than one's own. Tim Brown used the term to describe people who were inquisitive about and empathetic with other skills "We need people fluent in one language but literate in many" T shaped people are sometimes called Generalizing specialists

I SHAPED PEOPLE

I shaped people have a deep understanding of their discipline, but not of any other disciplines. I shaped people are people who have narrow, but expert skills in one specific area. A researcher who has spent his entire life in science in one area may be an I shaped person. When people come out of school, they're often I shaped.

Who invented it?

The term T shaped was first used by David Guest in"The hunt is on for the Renaissance Man of computing," The Independent (London), September 17, 1991 The term was popularised by Tim Brown of IDEO in'Strategy By Design' FastCompany article

References
1. Angus Bannerman, "Want to plan campaigns? Best get your 'I's crossed," Marketing Week, October 2, 2003
2. David Guest, "The hunt is on for the Renaissance Man of computing," The Independent (London),
3. Dave Amber, "Researchers Seek Basics Of Nano Scale," The Scientist, August 21, 2000

TEAM BUILDING EXERCISES

What are team building exercises?
A team building exercise is a short exercise at the beginning of a Design Thinking project that helps the design team work productively together as quickly as possible. The duration of an exercise is usually less than 30 minutes. I describe some examples of exercises in the following chapter.

They are an important component of collaborative or team based design. The Design Thinking approach recognizes the value of designers working productively as members of a diverse cross-disciplinary teams with managers, engineers, marketers and other professionals.

References
1.　Altogether Now by Lorraine L. Ukens Jossey Bass/Pfieffer, San Francisco, CA,
2.　Building Team Spirit by Barry Heermann McGraw Hill Companies, United States,
3.　CEO Tools by Kraig Kramers Gandy Dancer Press, United States,
4.　Team games for trainers by CarolyN Nilson McGraw Hill, Inc, New York, NY, 1993

Why use team building exercises?
When a designer works with others in a new team it is important that the group works as quickly as possible in a creative constructive dialogue. An icebreaker is a way for team members to quickly start working effectively;y together. It is a worthwhile investment of half an hour at the beginning of a project and can be fun. Ice breakers help start people thinking creatively, exchanging ideas and help make a team work effectively. For meetings in a business setting in which contribute.

When use team building exercises
1.　When team members do not know each other
2.　When team members come from different cultures
3.　When team needs to bond quickly
4.　When team needs to work to a common gaol quickly.
5.　When the discussion is new or unfamiliar.
6.　When the moderator needs to know the participants.

SHARE WHAT YOU KNOW

1. In the project kick off meeting ask every team member to introduce themselves and to describe in 3 minutes what experience they have that may be relevant to the project.
2. The moderator can list areas of knowledge on a white board.

IDENTIFY WHAT YOU KNOW AND WHAT YOU NEED TO KNOW.

Arrange a project kick-off meeting.
Invite your team and important stakeholders.
On a white board or flip chart create two lists.
Ask each person to introduce themselves and describe what they know or have experienced that may be useful for implementing the project. Brainstorm with your group the areas that are unknown and how that information may be obtained.

Methods for filling the gaps include interviews, user observation and focus groups or inviting experts to visit to answer questions.

Formulate a research plan and assign responsibilities, tasks and deliverables with dates.

1. Ask your team to brainstorm the areas where knowledge needs to be gathered to progress the project.
2. Identify how the information needed to undertake the project can be gathered and assign team members to relevant tasks to gather the needed information with dates

KICK OFF MEETING

What is it?
A kick off meeting is the first meeting of a design project with the project team. In a kick off meeting project roles and responsibilities, objectives and rules, schedule and processes are defined.

Why use this method?
1. Useful for getting all team members in alignment.
2. Opportunity to energize design team.

Challenges
1. Requires planning

Resources
1. Project space
2. Whiteboard
3. Dry erase markers
4. Notebooks
5. Pens

When to use this method
1. Define intent

How to use this method
Appoint a project manager

Invite stakeholders

Sample agenda:
1. Introductions of stakeholders
2. Overview and background.
3. Project objectives
4. Project plan and timeline
5. Deliverables
6. Project management process
7. Project space
8. Weekly meetings
9. Reporting
10. Communication plan
11. Change control
12. Contact list
13. Status reports
14. Issues
15. Set expectations
16. Project resources
17. Meeting minutes
18. File location and distribution
19. Project team and their roles
20. Risk management
21. Meeting summary
22. Action items
23. Meeting questions and answers

IDENTIFY THE UNMET NEEDS AND DESIRES

Unmet needs are the needs that a person hasn't satisfied. A need is where something is required or necessary.

Some ways to discover unmet needs and desires:
1. Talk to end users
2. Observe end users
3. Talk to experts
4. Talk to peers
5. Talk to extreme users
6. Immerse yourself in the user's context.

1. **Ask people what is their biggest problem**
   Related questions,
   ◦ "What causes the problem?"
   ◦ "What are the impacts of the problem?"
   ◦ "How important is the problem?"
   ◦ "What is your solution to the problem?"
   ◦ "What are possible solutions?"
2. **Probe about workarounds** – How do people adapt their environment to solve problems that they have?
3. **Ask what their single biggest obstacle is to achieve what they are trying to achieve** How can you help them?
4. **Ask what's changing in their world** What are the trends?
5. **Observe people**
6. Can you see problems they have that they perhaps do not even recognize are problems?
7. **Ask other stakeholders**
8. **Study their competitors**

DEVELOP A STRATEGY

Answer these five questions:
1. "What are our broad aspirations for our organization and the concrete goals against which we can measure our progress?
2. Across the potential field available to us, where will we choose to play and not play?
3. In our chosen place to play, how will we choose to win against the competitors there?
4. What capabilities are necessary to build and maintain to win in our chosen manner?
5. What management systems are necessary to operate to build and maintain the key capabilities?

The trick is to have five answers that are consistent with one another and actually reinforce one another."

Five Questions to Build a Strategy
by Roger Martin May 26, 2010

DEFINE YOUR TARGET AUDIENCE

Creating a projected user models will keep the development team rooted to a realistic user requirements and minimizes user frustration with the real product. Having a deep understanding of users can help development team better understand the wants & needs of the targeted customers. This will help the development team relate better with the target user. Understanding user tasks helps in developing design solutions that will ensure that the user expectations are met & avoid design errors and customer frustration.

Use research methods such as interviewing, observation, empathy maps and user experience maps to better understand your audience.

Market segmentation is basically the division of market into smaller segments. It helps identify potential customers and target them.

The division of market is carried out by using one of the five segmentation strategies

1. Behavior segmentation
2. Benefit segmentation
3. Psychographic segmentation
4. Geographic segmentation
5. Demographic segmentation

1. What is your target' groups goals emotions, experiences, needs and desires?
2. Information collected from just a few people is unlikely to be representative of the whole range of users.

3. What are the user tasks and activities?
4. How will the user use the product or service to perform a task?
5. What is the context of the user?
6. Where are they? What surrounds them physically and virtually or culturally?
7. How large is your user group?

When defining your target audience consider factors such as:

1. Age
2. Gender
3. Occupation
4. Industry
5. Usual hours
6. Travel
7. Citizenship status
8. Marital state
9. Income
10. Culture
11. Occupation
12. Language
13. Religion
14. Location
15. Education
16. Nationality
17. Mobility
18. Migration
19. Mental state
20. Abilities
21. Disabilities
22. Health

IDENTIFY THE STAKEHOLDERS

1. Identify and document a list of stakeholders
2. Determine internal stakeholders
3. Identify and document external stakeholders
4. Prioritize the stakeholders by participation or importance
5. Determine stakeholders specific interests and needs
6. Evaluate stakeholder influence
7. Create a process for communicating with all stakeholders
8. Prepare a stakeholder management plan.
9. Prepare a stakeholder communication plan
10. Define responsibilities
11. Define which stakeholders will be participating at different stages in the project
12. Obtain stakeholder buy-in

IDENTIFY OPPORTUNITIES

Use methods such as opportunity mapping, perceptual mapping and problem and opportunity trees to identify areas of opportunity that are currently unmet or have few competitors.

SELECT RESEARCH METHODS

Design research is useful to understand your end users perspective and their behaviors. The Methods chapter in this book describes many commonly used methods of getting to know your users and their contexts.

DOCUMENT A RESEARCH PLAN

1. What information do you need to inform the design process?
2. Why do you want to answer this question
3. How do you plan on discovering it?
4. Who should you interview?
5. Why do you select these people?
6. How do you gain access to these people?
7. What are your biases about this topic?
8. How do you reduce bias?
9. What methods will you use to inform the design process?
10. How do you know if you can trust what you find?
11. How will you find people you can trust to help you learn?
12. How will you share the information?

DEFINE THE CONTEXT

What is it?
Context is the environment situation or circumstances that surround a product or service in use.
The five w's of context
1. Who: Those who we design for
2. What: Human interactions and perceptions
3. Where: Physical location or path of activities.
4. When: The time or elapsed time.
5. Why: The purpose or meaning of the activity.

after Abowd & Mynatt 2000

Who invented it?
The word first appeared in Late Middle English around 1375 and meant a joining together, scheme, structure or to join by weaving.

Why use this method?
1. Every design is intended to accomplish goals, in a particular environment or context. understanding the context is necessary in order to create a successful design.

Challenges
1. A product or service may be used in diverse contexts.
2. A design can affect and be affected by the context.
3. A designer needs to experience the context to create a successful design.

When to consider context
4. Define goals
1. Know Context
2. Know User
3. Frame insights
4. Generate Concepts
5. Create Solutions

How to use this method
1. Define contextual problem to address
2. Contextual inquiry
3. Discover insights
4. Create possible solutions
5. Create vision and scenarios
6. Prototype and test in context
7. Refine
8. Prototype and test in context
9. Deliver.

Resources
1. Camera
2. Note pad
3. Pens
4. Digital voice recorder

References
1. Albrecht Schmidt, Michael Beigl, and Hans-Werner Gellersen. There is more to context than location. Computers and Graphics, 23(6):893–901, 1999.
2. Peter Tarasewich. Towards a comprehensive model of context for mobile and wireless computing. In Proc. of AMCIS 2003, pages 114–124, 2003.

DEFINE INTENT

What is it?

Designs are created for a purpose. The design intent is a written statement of the creative objectives of the design. While not describing the final design solution, the design intent provides the design team with a target for their efforts. It often gives a description of the problem to be sold, information about how the solution will be used.

Why use this method?

1. A design intent statement provides a focus for design efforts throughout a project.

Challenges

1. The statement of intent should be clear and unambiguous to all team members.

When to use this method

1. Define intent

How to use this method

1. A design intent statement is best based on an understanding of a particular problem being addressed or a need identified.
2. This can be the result of research such as observation or interviews with the user group.
3. It includes information about the scope of the solution.

QUESTIONS FOR DESIGN INTENT

1. Is the problem clear?
2. Are the objectives clear?
3. Is there agreement on the design intent by all stakeholders?
4. What are the constraints?
5. Have assumptions been tested?
6. What are the risks?
7. What are the business objectives
8. What are the user objectives
9. What are the environmental objectives
10. What are the technology objectives?

"If I had sixty minutes to save the world, I would spend fifty-five minutes defining the problem and only five minutes finding the solution." *Albert Einstein*

REFRAME THE PROBLEM

What is it?
A frame of reference is a set of assumptions which we use to create meaning. The frame can include beliefs, preferences, values, culture and other ways in which we bias our understanding.

"We create frames for what we experience and the both inform and limit the way we think."

"Starting at a picnic by the lakeside in Chicago, this famous film transports us to the outer edges of the universe. Every ten seconds we view the starting point from ten times farther out until our own galaxy is visible only as a speck of light among many others. Returning to earth with breathtaking speed, we move inward—into the hand of the sleeping picnicker—with ten times more magnification every ten seconds. Our journey ends inside a proton of a carbon atom within a DNA molecule in a white blood cell."

"When you empathize, you are, essentially, changing your frame of reference by shifting your perspective to that of the other person. Instead of looking at a problem from your own point of view, you look at it from the point of view of your user."

Tina Seelig describing the Eames film Powers of Ten.

How to use this method
1. Think of the problem from different perspectives.
2. Deconstruct your assumptions and beliefs to change paradigms
3. Brainstorm the problem from different points of view.
4. Meet with stakeholders.
5. Use methods such as mind maps, customer journeys.

You can reframe:
1. A problem as an opportunity
2. A weakness as a strength
3. Unkindness as lack of understanding

References
1. Hale, K. (1998) The Language of Cooperation: Negotiation Frames, Mediation Quarterly, 16(2), 147-162
2. Watzlawick, P., Weakland, J. and Fisch, R. (1974). Change: Principles of Problem Formation and Problem Resolution, NY: Norton

DEFINE THE GOALS

What is it?
A goal is the intent or intents of the design process.

Why use this method?
1. This method helps clarify the intent of the design project.
2. "Learning strategies and self-efficacy are the most important consequences of goal orientation followed by feedback seeking, and organizational outcomes."

Source Payne

How to use this method
1. Write a detailed description of the design problem.
2. Define a list of needs that are connected to the design problem.
3. Make a list of obstacles that need to be overcome to solve the design problem.
4. Make a list of constraints that apply to the problem.
5. Rewrite the problem statement to articulate the above requirements.

Who invented it?
J.A. Eison 1970s

When to use this method
1. Define intent

Resources
1. Pen
2. Paper
3. White board
4. Dry erase markers

References
1. DeGeest, D., & Brown, K. G. (2011). The role of goal orientation in leadership development. Human Resource Development Quarterly, 22(2), 157-175.
2. Button, S. B., Mathieu, J. E., & Zajac, D. M. (1996, July). Goal orientation in organizational research: A conceptual and empirical foundation. Organizational Behavior and Human Decision Processes, 67(1), 26-48.

"If a man knows not to which port he sails, no wind is favorable."
Lucius Annaeus Seneca

DEFINE THE SCOPE AND CONSTRAINTS

Defining the scope is one of the most important stages of a project. The will not be successful if you do not understand what you will be delivering finally to your client. Prepare two lists of what is included and what will not be included in the sope of your project.

In the project scope definition, the elements within the scope and out of the scope are well defined in order to clearly understand what will be the area under the project control. Therefore, you should identify more elements in detailed manner and divide them among the scope and out of scope.

Scope creep

Scope creep often happens in a project when a client requests something be added during a project. Change orders should be created to cover the additional costs incurred by such requests.

Most of such requirements haven't been in the initial requirements. As a result, change requests need to be raised in order to cover the increasing costs of the services provider.

GATHER INSPIRATION

Many designers find inspiration from the work of other designers or from competitors products. This leads to an incestuous reworking of the same ideas and a separation from the people and context we are designing for. It leads to creating products and services that are undifferentiated, unprofitable and unsatisfying. The most creative people find inspiration from any source. The starting point of all design is making a new connection. The things that you connect may have been seen by many people but never connected.

1. Leave your studio.
2. Go for a walk
3. Talk to real people
4. Mix with new people
5. Seek diverse perspectives
6. Study history
7. Travel
8. Go to bookstores
9. Libraries
10. Museums
11. Street markets
12. Flea markets
13. Observe nature
14. Listen to stories
15. Ask questions
16. Uncover needs and desires.

Exploring new places with new people can lead to innovative new design solutions. Collect things that you find inspiring and surround yourself and your team with them when you design.

UNCOVER PEOPLE'S STORIES

What is it?

A powerful story can help ensure the success of a new product, service or experience. Storytelling can be an effective method of presenting a point of view. Research can uncover meaningful stories from end that illustrate needs or desires. These stories can become the basis of new designs or actions and be used to support decisions. Stories can be an effective way of communicating complex ideas and inspiring people to change.

Why use this method?

1. The stories help to get buy-in from people throughout the design process and may be used to help sell a final design.
2. Real life stories are persuasive.
3. They are different to advertising because they are able to influence a design if uncovered from users during the early research phases and provide authenticity.

Challenges

1. A story with too much jargon will lose an audience.
2. Not everyone has the ability to tell vivid stories.
3. Stories are not always generalizable.

Photos: photocase.com – lube

How to use this method

An effective story:

1. Meet information needs for your audience
2. Answer in your story: What, why, when, who, where, how?
3. Offer a new vantage point
4. Tell real world stories
5. Evoke the future
6. Be authentic
7. Share emotion
8. Communicate transformations
9. Communicate who you are.
10. Describe actions
11. Show cause and effect Describe conflicts and resolution.
12. Speak from your experience.
13. Describe how actions created change
14. Omit what is irrelevant.
15. Reveal meaning
16. Share your passion
17. Be honest
18. Be real
19. Build trust
20. Show connections
21. Transmits values
22. Share a vision
23. Share knowledge
24. Your story should differentiate you.
25. Use humor
26. Foster collaboration.
27. Engage the audience
28. Craft the story for your audience.
29. Pose a problem and offer a resolution
30. Use striking imagery
31. Fit the audience
32. The audience must be able to act on your story.

OBSERVE

What is it?
This method involves observing people in their natural activities and usual context such as work environment. With direct observation the researcher is present and indirect observation the activities may be recorded by means such as video or digital voice recording.

Why use this method?
1. Allows the observer to view what users actually do in context.
2. Indirect observation uncovers activity that may have previously gone unnoticed

Challenges
1. Observation does not explain the cause of behavior.
2. Obtrusive observation may cause participants to alter their behavior.
3. Analysis can be time consuming.
4. Observer bias can cause the researcher to look only where they think they will see useful information.

When to use this method
1. Know Context
2. Know User
3. Frame insights

"A few observations and much reasoning lead to error; many observations and a little reasoning lead to truth." *Alexis Carrel*

How to use this method
1. Define objectives
2. Define participants and obtain their cooperation.
3. Define The context of the observation: time and place.
4. In some countries the law requires that you obtain written consent to video people.
5. Define the method of observation and the method of recording information. Common methods are taking written notes, video or audio recording.
6. Run a test session.
7. Hypothesize an explanation for the phenomenon
8. Predict a logical consequence of the hypothesis
9. Test your hypothesis by observation
10. Analyze the data gathered and create a list of insights derived from the observations.

Resources
1. Note pad
2. Pens
3. Camera
4. Video camera
5. Digital voice recorder

References
1. Kosso, Peter (2011). A Summary of Scientific Method. Springer. pp. 9. ISBN 9400716133,

INTERVIEW

What is it?
An interview is a conversation where questions are asked to obtain information. Some methods are described in the following chapter.

Why use this method?
Contextual interviews uncover tacit knowledge about people's context that the people may not be consciously aware of. The information gathered can be detailed.

Challenges
1. Keep control
2. Be prepared
3. Be aware of bias
4. Be neutral
5. Select location carefully

Resources
6. Note pad
7. Confidentiality agreement
8. Digital voice recorder
9. Video camera
10. Digital still camera

When to use this method
1. Know Context
2. Know User
3. Frame insights

How to use this method
1. Contextual inquiry may be structured as 2 hour one on one interviews.
2. The researcher does not usually impose tasks on the user.
3. Go to the user's context. Talk, watch listen and observe.
4. Understand likes and dislikes.
5. Collect stories and insights.
6. See the world from the user's point of view.
7. Take permission to conduct interviews.
8. Do one-on-one interviews.
9. The researcher listens to the user.
10. 2 to 3 researchers conduct an interview.
11. Understand relationship between people, product and context.
12. Document with video, audio and notes.

Resources
1. Computer
2. Notebook
3. Pens
4. Video camera
5. Release forms
6. Interview plan or structure
7. Questions, tasks and discussion items
8. Confidentiality agreement

References
1. Kvale, Steinar. Interviews: An Introduction to Qualitative Research Interviewing, Sage Publications, 1996
2. Foddy, William. Constructing Questions for Interviews, Cambridge University Press, 1993

CREATE AN INTERVIEW GUIDE

How to use this method
1. Plan in advance what you want to achieve
2. Research the topic
3. Select a person to interview.
4. Meet them in their location if possible.
5. Set a place, date, and time.
6. Be sure he or she understands how long the interview should take and that you plan to record the session.
7. Start with an open-ended question. It is a good way to put the candidate at ease,
8. Tape record the interview if possible.
9. Decide what information you need
10. Think of Patton's 6 types of questions related to:
    ○ Behavior or experience.
    ○ Opinion or belief.
    ○ Feelings.
    ○ Knowledge.
    ○ Sensory.
11. Write down the information you'd like to collect through the interview. Now frame your interview questions around this information.
12. Prepare follow-up questions to ask.
13. Research the person that you are interviewing
14. Check your equipment and run through your questions.
15.
16. Use neutral wording
17. Do not ask leading questions or questions that show bias.
18. Leave time for a General Question in the End

19. The last question should allow the interviewee to share any thoughts or opinions that they might want to share, such as "Thank you for all that valuable information, is there anything else you'd like to add before we end?"

Source: adapted from The Art of Interview" by Anne Williams

References
1. Dick, Bob. Convergent Interviewing. Session 8 of "Areol-Action Research and Evaluation", Southern Cross University, 2002
2. Groat, Linda & Wang, David. Architectural Research Methods, John Wiley & Sons, Inc
3. Weiss, Robert. Learning from Strangers: The Art and Method of Qualitative Interview Studies. The Free Press
4. Seidman, I. Technique isn't everything, but it is a lot. In Interviewing as qualitative research: A guide for researchers in education and the social sciences. New York, NY: Teachers College Press
5. Foddy, William. Constructing Questions for Interviews, Cambridge University Press,

THE INTERVIEW

1. Bring your questions to the interview
2. Explore the answers but return to your list of questions to follow your guide.
3. Record details such as the subjects name contact and details
4. Take detailed notes
5. Use empathy tools to encourage your participant to share information.
6. Final question: "Is there anything you think I should have asked that I didn't?"
7. Transcribe the interview
8. Write out both sides of the conversation, both question and answer.
9. Never change what the interviewee said or how they said it.
10. Outline the important points.
11. Edit the transcript for clarity, flow, and length.
12. Tell a story Now that you've gathered all of this great information and have accurately recorded it, it is important that you find a way to effectively document and share
13. the story in a way that celebrates and accurately describes the story you were told.
14. Add details from your notes appearance and personality of your subject, ambient sounds, smells, visuals.
15. Check the facts.

Source: adapted from The Art of Interview" by Anne Williams

Resources

1. Voice recorder preferably digital, with fresh batteries and spares
2. Notebook durable cover, continuous spiral binding, interior dividers with pockets
3. Pens
4. Your contact information

"I'm strange, crazy, intelligent, wild, soft, coy, thrifty, boring, romantic, selfish, full of pride, mean, dark, sweet and most of all I'm through with this interview." *Winona Ryder*

RECRUIT PARTICIPANTS

What is it?

Finding a group of participants who are representative of your end users is one of the most challenging parts of the Design Thinking process.

You might not have the budget to be able to identify the best candidates easily. Your candidates may not show up on time or at all. They may not match your ideal candidates. It is important to carefully select your research participants so that they are as representative as possible of your end users.

Challenges

1. The participants must be representative of your end users
2. Do not underestimate the time it takes to find, contact, screen, and schedule.
3. You may need to do a lot of cold calling.
4. Incentivize if you can
5. Try to recruit participants who:
∘ Are representative
∘ Can express themselves and provide useful information
∘ Show up

How to use this method

1. Define terms and criteria for recruiting
2. Demographics like age, income, and domestic lifestyle (married? kids?),
3. Business criteria such as whether they're a current or prospective customer, and if they're a current customer, how much of the product / service do they purchase or use in a given month/quarter/year?
4. Define the incentives
5. Understand your environment
6. Decide how to recruit
∘ A recruiting company With the right information, a good recruiting company can get the best participants
∘ Find several recruiting companies you can use.
∘ Your client
∘ Friends and Family
∘ Utilize word-of-mouth recruiting
∘ The Web
7. Draft a screener
8. Recruit Participants
9. Schedule, confirm, and remind participants

DO FIELDWORK

What is it?

Field research involves a range of, methods: informal interviews, direct observation, and group interviews. Although the method generally is characterized as qualitative research, it may include quantitative research.

A field study is a study carried on in the context of people rather than in design studio or a laboratory. A field study is primary research It involves observing or interviewing people in their natural environments.

Who invented it?

Pioneers included:
James Cowles Prichard 1841
Margaret Mead, 1928
Bronisław Malinowski, 1929
Pierre Bourdieu 1958-1962

Why use this method?

1. A field study can be used to inform design and to create more successful outcomes for design by better informing the designer of the behaviors, desires and needs of the people being designed for.

Challenges

1. May be more expensive than secondary research.
2. Information may become obsolete

When to use this method

1. Define intent
2. Know Context
3. Know User
4. Frame insights
5. Explore Concepts
6. Make Plans
7. Deliver Offering

How to use this method

1. Define goals.
2. Develop plan
3. Create study materials such as question guides, release forms,
4. Prepare for site visits
5. Perform observations and interviews.
6. Analyze data
7. Develop insights
8. Make recommendations.

Resources

1. Note pads
2. Pens
3. Digital camera
4. Video camera
5. Post-it notes

References

1. Jarvie, I. C. (1967) On Theories of Fieldwork and the Scientific Character of Social Anthropology, Philosophy of Science, Vol. 34, No. 3 (Sep., 1967), pp. 223-242.
2. Marek M. Kaminski. 2004. Games Prisoners Play. Princeton University Press. ISBN 0-691-11721-7

UNDERSTAND RISKS

Risk management involves identifying, analyzing and prioritizing of risks Risks can come from uncertainty in any area connected to a design development. There are many methods for monitoring and managing risks.
Strategies to manage risk include transferring the risk to another party, avoiding the risk, reducing the negative effect or probability of the risk, or accepting the consequences of a particular risk.

How do you reduce risk?
1. Identify threats
2. Assess the vulnerability to threats
3. Determine the expected consequences of the risks
4. Identify ways to reduce the risks
5. Priorities risk reduction methods based on a strategy

References
1. Alexander, Carol and Sheedy, Elizabeth (2005). The Professional Risk Managers' Handbook: A Comprehensive Guide to Current Theory and Best Practices. PRMIA Publications. ISBN 0-9766097-0-3.
2. Hopkin, Paul "Fundamentals of Risk Management 2nd Edition" Kogan-Page (2012) ISBN 978-0-7494-6539-1

WHO TO RECRUIT

1. Find appropriate participants.
2. Find people who represent "extremes."
3. Extreme participants help to gain insights into unarticulated behaviors, desires, and needs of the average population.
4. By including both extremes of your spectrum as well as some people in the middle, the full range of behaviours, beliefs can be studied

When recruiting consider factors such as:
1. Age
2. Gender
3. Occupation
4. Industry
5. Usual hours
6. Travel
7. Citizenship status
8. Marital state
9. Income
10. Culture
11. Occupation
12. Language
13. Religion
14. Location
15. Education
16. Nationality
17. Mobility
18. Migration
19. Mental state
20. Abilities
21. Disabilities
22. Health

BENCHMARK COMPETITORS

Steps in the Benchmarking Process:
1. Determine what you will benchmark.
2. Identify the factors that interest you and how to measure those factors.
3. Select the best organizations to benchmark. Consider factors such as user satisfaction, price, technology, return on investment, market growth.
4. Measure the factors.
5. Measure your own performance for the same factors
6. Brainstorm how you can improve your own performance to surpass the performance of the benchmarked organizations.
7. Implement your improvements and methods to monitor your continued performance over time.

References
1. Benchmarking for Competitive Advantage. Robert J Boxwell Jr, New York: McGraw-Hill. p. 225. ISBN 0-07-006899-2.
2. Beating the competition: a practical guide to Benchmarking. Washington, DC: Kaiser Associates. p. 176. ISBN 978-1-56365-018-5.
3. Camp, R. The search for industry best practices that lead to superior performance. Productivity Press.
4. Bogan, C.E. and English, M.J. Benchmarking for Best Practices: Winning through Innovative Adaptation. New York: McGraw-Hill.

IMMERSE YOURSELF

Leave your design studio and visit the people who you are designing for. Go to their, workplaces, homes and social spaces. Immerse yourself in their context and you will gain an understanding of their point of view. This will help you understand their needs and desires and create designs that they will purchase and use.

References
1. Holtzblatt, K., Wendell, J.B., & Wood, S. 2005. Rapid Contextual Design: A How-to guide to key techniques for user-centered design. San Francisco: Morgan-Kaufmann.
2. Beyer, H. & Holtzblatt, K. Contextual Design: Defining Customer-Centered Systems. San Francisco: Morgan Kaufmann. ISBN 1-55860-411-1
3. McDonald, S., Monahan, K., and Cockton, G. 2006. Modified contextual design as a field evaluation method. In Proceedings of the 4th Nordic Conference on Human-Computer interaction: Changing Roles (Oslo, Norway, October 14–18, 2006). A. Mørch, K. Morgan, T. Bratteteig, G. Ghosh, and D. Svanaes, Eds. NordiCHI '06, vol. 189. ACM Press, New York, NY, 437-440.

RESEARCH

1. **Primary research** also called field research is collecting data that is created during the time of study. Primary research techniques include, questionnaires, interviews and direct observations.
2. **Secondary research** is research that is existing and has been collected by others. Secondary research is the most widely used method for data collection. Secondary research accesses information that is already gathered from primary research.
3. **Qualitative research** seeks to understand people in the context of their daily experiences. Uses ethnographic methods including observation and interviews. Seeks to understand questions like why and how. Obtains insights about attitudes and emotions. Often uses small sample sizes. Seeks to see the world through the eyes of research subjects. Methods are flexible. Used to develop an initial understanding.
4. **Quantitative research** uses mathematical and statistical methods. Sample sizes are often large. Findings may be expressed as numbers or percentages. Uses methods such as surveys and questionnaires. Asks questions like "How many?" Used to recommend a final course of action.

TALK TO VENDORS

A good vendor can help improve your design. They are part of your team. Select vendors carefully and communicate with them regularly.

TALK TO STAKEHOLDERS

Stakeholder are people who may be influenced by your design. Some stakeholders can help you design a more successful product or service. Though you may be designing for a patient in a hospital, the design may be used or effect doctors, nurses, the family of the patient, health workers, insurance workers and many other stakeholders. Create a stakeholder map and matrix to understand who you should involve in the project and how you can keep them informed and contributing positively.

PERSONA

PERSONA NAME
....

DEMOGRAPHICS
....
....
....
....

CHARACTERISTIC STATEMENT
....
....
....
....
....

GOALS
....
....
....
....

AMBITIONS
....
....
....
....

INFLUENCERS AND ACTIVITIES
....
....
....
....

SCENARIOS
....
....
....
....

OTHER CHARACTERISTICS

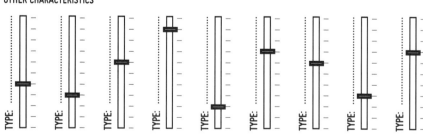

TYPE: TYPE: TYPE: TYPE: TYPE: TYPE: TYPE: TYPE: TYPE:

DEVELOP PERSONAS

What is it?
"A persona is a archetypal character that is meant to represent a group of users in a role who share common goals, attitudes and behaviors when interacting with a particular product or service Personas are user models that are presented as specific individual humans. They are not actual people, but are synthesized directly from observations of real people." *Cooper*

Who invented it?
Alan Cooper 1998

Why use this method?
1. Helps create empathy for users and reduces self reference.
2. Use as tool to analyze and gain insight into users.
3. Help in gaining buy-in from stake holders.

Challenges
1. Portigal (2008) claimed that personas give a "cloak of smug customer-centricity" while actually distancing a team from engagement with real users and their needs

References
1. Pruitt, John & Adlin, Tamara. The Persona Lifecycle : Keeping People in Mind Throughout Product Design. Morgan Kaufmann, 2006. ISBN 0-12-566251-3

How to use this method
1. Inaccurate personas can lead to a false understandings of the end users. Personas need to be created using data from real users.
2. Collect data through observation, interviews, ethnography.
3. Segment the users or customers
4. Create the Personas
5. Avoid Stereotypes
6. Each persona should be different. Avoid fringe characteristics. Personas should each have three to four life goals which are personal aspirations,
7. Personas are given a name, and photograph.
8. Design personas can be followed by building customer journeys

Resources
1. Raw data on users from interviews or other research
2. Images of people similar to segmented customers.
3. Computer
4. Graphics software

SYNTHESIS

1. Synthesis is the convergent part of the design process.
2. Ideate: Explore and many possibilities as time and resources make possible.
3. Select: Select the most promising ideas. This can be done by a voting process with a group of stakeholders and your divers team.
4. Implement: Build a series of prototypes to test.
5. Evaluate: Test your prototypes with end users. Refine the prototype design and retest until you have something that works well.

CREATE ACTIONABLE INSIGHTS

What is it?
Design Thinking provides insights that are based on unrecognized or unmet needs. An insight is a fresh point of view based on a deep understanding of the way of thinking and behavior. An insight occurs by mentally connecting two or more things that have not been connected before. These things may be things that many people have seen or experienced but not connected before. A goal of Design Thinking is to build actionable insights

Why use this method?
1. Insights that are based on unrecognized or unmet needs. add competitive advantage. that may be greater than obtained by imitating competitor's products
2. An insight provides the foundation for innovation.
3. An insight is necessary to create something better than what exists today.

Challenges
1. An insight should be based on evidence

How to use this method
2. Many design methods reveal design insights
3. Methods that may reveal insights include observation, interviews and other ethnographic methods.

USER NEED STATEMENT

The user need statement or question is the desires or needs of end users expressed in their own words.

EXAMPLES

User Need Statement
I am a farmer who has a hard time finding drinkable water for my animals.

Point of View Question
How might we create something to help the farmer find drinkable water for his animals?

POINT OF VIEW QUESTION

What is it?
A point-of-view (POV) is reframing of a design challenge into an actionable problem statement. The POV is used as the basis for design ideation. The POV defines the design intent.

"The mere formulation of a problem is far more often essential than its solution, which may be merely a matter of mathematical or experimental skill" *Albert Einstein*

Why use this method?
1. The POV helps reframe the design problem into an actionable focus for the generation of ideas.

How to use this method
1. Use field research to identify user's needs and desires
2. Break a large group into smaller groups of 4 or 5 cross disciplinary members.
3. Ask each group to analyze the list of needs and desires to create a list of insights
4. Ask each group to create a POV statement.
5. The statement should define the users, their need that will be the subject of the design project and the insight that will be the basis of the ideation exercise.
6. Each small group presents their POV statement to the larger group.
7. The larger group votes on preferred statement or brainstorms a statement.

BRAINSTORMING

Preparing for brainstorming
Come to the brainstorm session prepared.
1. Bring a lot of paper and markers.
2. Pens
3. Post-it-notes
4. Index cards
5. A flip chart
6. White board or wall
7. Video camera
8. Camera
9. One clear goal per brainstorming session.
10. Determine who will write things down and document the proceedings?
11. Allow one to two hours for a brainstorming session.
12. Recruit good people.
13. 8 to 12 people is a good number
14. Prepare brainstorm questions that you think will help guide the group.

Create a strategy
1. What do you want to achieve?
2. What problem do you want solved?
3. Define the goal
4. How will you define the problem to the participants?
5. How long will the session be?
6. How many people will be involved?
7. What will be the mix of people?
8. Will there be a follow up session?
9. Will you send out information before the session?
10. Do the participants have the information that they need?
11. Who should you invite?

12. Assemble a diverse team.
13. Do the participants have the right skills and knowledge for the task?
14. Where will the brainstorm be held?
15. Who owns the intellectual property?
16. Will the session be free of interruptions?
17. How will you record the ideas?
18. What will you do with the information?
19. What brainstorming technique will be used and is it best for your purpose?
20. Be mindful of the scope brainstorm questions. Neither too broad nor too narrow.
21. 45-60 minutes for brainstorm time. Warm up 15-30 minutes.
22. Wrap up 15-30 minutes.

Choosing a technique
1. There are many different brainstorming methods.
2. Choose a method that suites your task and participants
3. Try different methods over time to find which ones work best for you.

Refreshments
1. An army marches on it's stomach
2. Offer tea, coffee water, soda.

Facilitating

1. Encourage everyone to contribute.
2. Review the rules and ask group to enforce them.
3. Use a warm up activity of about 30 minutes duration to get your team working productively
4. Encourage an attitude of shoshin.
5. Ask participants to turn phones off or onto vibrate mode.
6. A facilitator isn't a leader.
7. Do not steer the discussion
8. Do not let particular people dominate the conversation.
9. Keep the conversations on topic.
10. Set realistic time limits for each stage and be sure that you keep on time.
11. 5. Have a brainstorm plan and stick to it.
12. The facilitator should create an environment where it is safe to suggest wild ideas.
13. Provide clear directions at the beginning of the meeting.
14. Clearly define the problem to be discussed.
15. Write the problem on the whiteboard where everyone can see it.
16. Provide next steps at the end of the meeting.
17. Select final ideas by voting.
18. Use your camera or phone to take digital pictures of the idea output at the end of your meeting.
19. Good facilitation requires good listening skills
20. The facilitator should run the white board, writing down ideas as people come up with them,
21. Prevent people from interrupting others
22. Invite quieter people to contribute.
23. Hire a facilitator if necessary.
24. Start on time.
25. End on time.
26. keep things moving
27. You can filter the best ideas after the session or get the team to vote on their preferred ideas during the session.
28. Listen
29. Write fast & be visual
30. Use humour and be playful
31. Thank the group after the session.
32. Provide next steps to the group after the meeting.
33. Keep participants engaged
34. Encourage inter activity
35. 100 ideas per hour.
36. Avoid social hierarchy
37. Organize small break-out sessions that cut across traditional office boundaries to establish teams.
38. Encourage passion.

"Ways to affect the above and reframe the brainstorm on the fly:
1. **Pose a more specific question**
2. **Rephrase a question**
3. **Follow a thread that seems promising**
4. **Shift gears and offer a whole new question**
5. **Lob in a crazy idea**
6. **Encourage people to move around, pace and play**
7. **Say something funny"**
8.

Source Hasso Plattner Institute of Design Standford University

143

RULES FOR BRAINSTORMING

1. **"Defer judgment** Separating idea generation from idea selection strengthens both activities. For now, suspend critique. Know that you'll have plenty of time to evaluate the ideas after the brainstorm.
2. **Encourage wild ideas**
3. **One conversation at a time** Maintain momentum as a group. Save the side conversations for later.
4. **Headline** Capture the essence quickly "
5. **Focus on quantity** not on quality."

Post-it voting

1. Give every participant 4 stickers and have everyone put stickers next to their favorite ideas.
2. Each person tags 3 favorite ideas
3. Cluster favorite ideas
4. Clustering of stickers indicate possible strong design directions.

Group review

Ask everyone to review the boards of ideas, and discuss the specific ideas or directions they like and why.

Source adapted from Hasso Plattner Institute of Design

The environment

1. Select a space not usually used by your team.
2. Refreshments
3. Find a comfortable quiet room
4. Comfortable chairs
5. No interruptions
6. Turn phones off
7. Go off-site. A new environment might spur creativity and innovation by providing new stimuli. Helps participants mentally distance themselves from ordinary perceptions and ways of thinking.
8. Location matters:
9. Use big visible materials for writing on
10. Keep the temperature comfortable Adequate lighting
11. Suitable external noise levels
12. A circular arrangement of seats allows participants to read body language and with no "head of the table."
13. Seats should be not too far apart
14. Have a space with a lot of vertical writing space.

Methods of arranging ideas

1. 2X2 matrix
2. Clustering
3. Continuums
4. Concentric circles
5. Timeline
6. Pyramid
7. Prioritization
8. Adoption curve

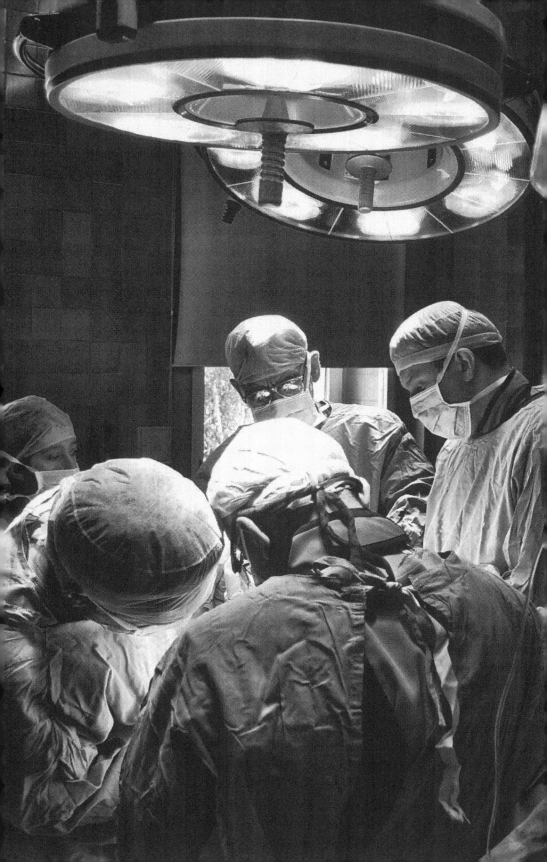

INCENTIVES FOR BRAINSTORMING

Research suggests that incentives can augment creative processes. Participants were divided into three conditions.

1. A flat fee was paid to all participants.
2. Participants were awarded points for every unique idea of their own, and subjects were paid for the points that they earned.
3. Subjects were paid based on the impact that their idea had on the group; this was measured by counting the number of group ideas derived from the specific subject's ideas.

Condition III outperformed Condition II, and Condition II outperformed Condition I at a statistically significant level for most measures.

The results demonstrated that participants were willing to work far longer to achieve unique results in the expectation of compensation.

Source: Marketing Science Vol.25, No.5, September—October 2006,pp.411

CLUSTER YOUR INSIGHTS

1. Prioritize the groups. This is sometimes done by comparing the number of ideas in each group. Or it can be done by voting.
2. Select a number of the groups for further refinement and development. This could be the top one or three groups.

3. Sort the ideas into categories of related ideas.
4. Brainstorm with your team possible ways of relating the ideas.
5. Repeat the brainstorming process by developing and refining only these top groups.

FIND THEMES

1. Pin your idea sketches or post-it notes on a wall. Each team member can briefly explain the concepts as they are being placed.
2. Look for patterns or themes of relationships between the ideas.
3. Ask your tem without talking to each other to arrange the ideas in to related groups. The relationships that unite each group can be anything that your team thinks is significant
4. Label each group by the relationship factor.

SELECT TOP INSIGHTS

1. Brainstorm with the team what are the most significant insights. You can select the top one or three insights for further development.

ESTABLISH DIFFERENTIATION

In a world awash with countless products and services it is important that your idea has some key differentiation in order to be successful. A product, service or experience that is not differentiated will compete on the basis of price and it is likely that someone somewhere will be able to make and sell the same thing at a lower price than you can.

If your product answers a strong unmet need in your target audience then the chances of it being successful for them and for you are greater. Do not draw your inspiration from competitor's products. You will split the market, cannibalize some of their customers and your potential market will be relatively small. If you have identified an unmet need through end user research then you may not have competitors and your product or service does not need to be the lowest price in order to sell.

INVESTIGATE EXISTING INTELLECTUAL PROPERTY

Many ideas have been thought of in the Past. It is easy to think that we may have been first to think of an idea when someone has already had the same idea. It may already be protected by a form of intellectual property protection such as a patent. Different countries and areas of the world have different intellectual property protection systems. If you manufacture a product service for which someone else owns the intellectual property rights they may be entitled to seek financial recompense from you. It is possible to uncover some prior intellectual property registrations yourself using tools such as the Google Patent search tool.

To do it thoroughly it is necessary to work with an intellectual protection specialist such as an IP attorney. The cost of not investigating intellectual property can be high. You can spend a lot of time and money developing an idea that cannot be manufactured or distributed.

It is important at an early stage to talk with and engage an experienced professional to determine whether your idea is original, whether it infringes existing intellectual property and how best to protect it if it can be protected and in which countries or regions.

147

CREATE SCENARIOS

What is it?

A scenario is a narrative or story about how people may experience a design in a particular future context of use. They can be used to predict or explore future interactions with concept products or services. Scenarios can be presented by media such as storyboards or video or be written. They can feature single or multiple actors participating in product or service interactions.

Who invented it?

Herman Kahn, Rand Corporation 1950, USA

Why use this method?

1. Scenarios become a focus for discussion which helps evaluate and refine concepts.
2. Usability issues can be identified early in the design process
3. The are useful tool to align a team vision.
4. Scenarios help us create a good experience for the whole experience
5. Interactive experiences involve the dimension of time.
6. Personas give us a framework to evaluate possible solutions.

Challenges

1. Generate scenarios for a range of situations.
2. Include problem situations
3. Hard to envision misuse scenarios.

When to use this method

1. Frame insights
2. Generate Concepts
3. Create Solutions

How to use this method

1. Identify the question to investigate.
2. Decide time and scope for the scenario process.
3. Identify stake holders and uncertainties.
4. Define the scenarios.
5. Create storyboards of users goals, activities, motivations and tasks.
6. Act out the scenarios.
7. The session can be videotaped.
8. Analyze the scenarios through discussion.
9. Summarize insights

Resources

1. Storyboard templates
2. Pens
3. Video cameras
4. Props
5. White board
6. Dry-erase markers

References

1. "Scenarios," IDEO Method Cards. ISBN 0-9544132-1-0
2. Carroll, John M. Making Use: Scenario-based design of human-computer interactions. MIT Press, 2000.
3. Carroll J. M. Five Reasons for Scenario Based Design. Elsevier Science B. V. 2000.
4. Carroll, John M. Scenario-Based Design: Envisioning Work and Technology in System Development.

ROLE PLAYING

What is it?

Role playing is a research method where the researcher physically acts out the interaction or experience of the user of a product, service or experience. It is a type of prototyping, a narrative or story about how people may experience a design in a particular future context. Role playing can be used to predict or explore future interactions with concept products or services.

Why use this method?

1. Role playing helps a designer gain empathy and insights into the experience of the user.
2. Useful for unfamiliar situations.
3. It is a physical activity so may uncover insights not apparent when using storyboarding
4. It helps designers empathize with the intended users and their context.
5. Is an inexpensive method requiring few resources.

Challenges

1. It is difficult to envision all the ways a product or service could be misused.
2. Some people feel self conscious when asked to role play

Resources

1. Note pad
2. Pens
3. Video camera
4. Empathy tools

How to use this method

1. Identify the situation.
2. Identify scenarios and tasks users undertake.
3. Create storyboards.
4. Assign roles.
5. Isolate moments where the users interact with the product or service.
6. Use your own intuitive responses to iterate and refine the design.
7. This method can be used to test physical prototypes.
8. You can act out the tasks in the environments or context of use.
9. You can use empathy tools such as glasses to simulate the effects of age or a wheelchair.
10. Consider typical misuse cases.
11. Discuss insights.

References

1. Greenberg, J. (1993). The role of role playing in organizational research. Journal of Management, 19(2), 221-241.
2. Duncombe, S., & Heikkinen, M. H. (1990). Role-playing for different viewpoints. The Social Studies (Washington, D.C.)

BODYSTORM

What is it?
Bodystorming is method of prototyping experiences. It requires setting up an experience – complete with necessary artifacts and people – and physically "testing" it. A design team play out scenarios based on design concepts that they are developing. The method provides clues about the impact of the context on the user experience.

Who invented it?
Buchenau, Fulton 2000

Why use this method?
1. You are likely to find new possibilities and problems.
2. Generates empathy for users.
3. This method is an experiential design tool. Bodystorming helps design ideation by exploring context.
4. It is fast and inexpensive.
5. It is a form of physical prototyping
6. It is difficult to imagine misuse scenarios

Challenges
1. Some team members may find acting a difficult task.

Resources
1. Empathy tools
2. A large room
3. White board
4. Video camera

When to use this method
1. Know Context
2. Know User
3. Frame insights
4. Explore Concepts

How to use this method
1. Select team.
2. Define the locations where a design will be used.
3. Go to those locations and observe how people interact. the artifacts in their environment.
4. Develop the prototypes and props that you need to explore an idea. Identify the people, personas and scenarios that may help you with insight into the design directions.,
5. Bodystorm the scenarios.
6. Record the scenarios with video and analyze them for insights.

References
1. Understanding contexts by being there: case studies in bodystorming. Personal and Ubiquitous Computing, Vol. 7, No. 2. (July 2003), pp. 125-134, doi:10.1007/s00779-003-0238-7 by Antti Oulasvirta, Esko Kurvinen, Tomi Kankainen

USE EMPATHY TOOLS

Empathy tools are aids or tools that help designers empathize with the people they are designing for. They can be used to test a prototype design or in activities such as role playing or body storming.

Who invented it?
Brandt, E. and Grunnet, C 2000

Why use this method?
1. To help a designer understand the experiences of people that they are designing for.

Challenges
1. Empathy tools are imperfect approximations of user experiences.

When to use this method
1. Know Context
2. Know User
3. Frame insights
4. Explore Concept

How to use this method
1. Wear heavy gloves to experience less sensitivity in your hands
2. Wear fogged glasses to experience less acute vision
3. Wear black glasses to eat to experience issues locating food and utensils.
4. Spend a day in a wheelchair.
5. Wear earplugs to experience diminished hearing

Resources
1. Wheelchair
2. Fogged glasses
3. Blackened glasses
4. Gloves
5. Earplugs
6. Crutches
7. Walking stick

References
1. Brandt, E. and Grunnet, C., "Evoking the Future: Drama and Props in User-centered Design", PDC 2000

DO A REALITY CHECK

At each milestone in a design development, the design team and important stakeholders such as customers, clients, manufacturers representatives can meet and review the design to see how real the solution is and refine the direction as necessary.

Why use this method?
1. It keeps the team honest
2. Makes sure that no important factors have been overlooked.
3. Keeps the stakeholders involved.

Challenges
1. A design project can go off course if the design team work in isolation from stakeholders.

When to use this method
1. Define intent
2. Know Context
3. Know User
4. Frame insights
5. Explore Concepts
6. Make Plans
7. Deliver Offering

How to use this method
At the conclusion of each phase of a design such as idea generation, research, prototyping and testing, production engineering a meeting of stakeholders should be arranged and a reality check made on whether the design is a real solution. This type of checklist can be worked through with the group.

Resources
1. White board
2. Dry erase markers

IDENTIFY STAKEHOLDERS FOR FEEDBACK

Stakeholders include any individuals who are influence by the design. Specifically, the project team, end users, strategic partners, customers, alliances, vendors and senior management are project stakeholders

Possible stakeholders

1. Employees
2. Shareholders
3. Government
4. Customers
5. Suppliers
6. Prospective employees
7. Local communities
8. Global Community
9. Schools
10. Future generations
11. Ex-employees
12. Creditors
13. Professional associations
14. Competitors
15. Investors
16. Prospective customers
17. Communities

REVIEW QUESTIONS

1. Does the design conform to the design intent statement?
2. Is the design achievable?
3. Have the important risks been identified?
4. Is the design a solution to an identified need or problem?
5. What is the business case?
6. Is the design consistent?
7. Is the design as simple as possible?
8. Are the components recyclable?
9. Can the design be scaled?
10. Are all features necessary?
11. Is everything documented?
12. What are the risks associated with this design?
13. Are any new risks posed by the design that have not been identified?
14. Are the interfaces identified
15. Is the design consistent with the context?
16. Have critical features and interactions been prototyped and tested?
17. Is the cost of ownership reduced?
18. Is the design easy to maintain?
19. Have all legal requirements and regulations been addressed?
20. Have the key stakeholders been identified and involved?
21. What were the assumptions?
22. Is the design usable and accessible?
23. How will the design be implemented?
24. What is the scope of the design?
25. What design alternatives were considered?

SEEK FEEDBACK

Usability testing is a technique used in user-centered interaction design to evaluate a product by testing it on users. Usability testing focuses on measuring a design's fitness for an intended purpose. Usability testing involves observation under controlled conditions to determine how well people can use the design

Who invented it?
Henry Dreyfuss was a pioneer of usability testing during the late 1940s

Why use this method?
1. To make the design easier to use.
2. Because you don't know what the end users need and want
3. One size does usually not fit all.
4. To help you design become successful.

References
1. Nielsen, J. Usability Engineering, Academic Press Inc, p 165
2. NN/G Usability Week 2011 Conference "Interaction Design" Manual, Bruce Tognazzini, Nielsen Norman Group, 2011

How to use this method
Methods include:
1. **Hallway testing** five to six people are brought in to test the product, or service. The name of the technique refers to the fact that the testers should be random people who pass by in the hallway.
2. **Remote usability** Usability evaluators, developers and end users are located in different countries and time zones, .
3. **Expert review.** Involves bringing in experts with experience in the field to evaluate the usability of a product system or service.
4. **Automated expert review** Automated expert reviews provide usability testing but through the use of programs given rules for good design and heuristics. Though an automated review might not provide as much detail and insight as reviews from people, they can be finished more quickly and consistently.
5. **A/B Testing.** Two versions (A and B) are compared, which are identical except for one variation that might impact a user's behavior.

CREATE LOW-FIDELITY PROTOTYPES

What is it?

Low fidelity prototyping is a quick and cheap way of gaining insight and informing decision making without the need for costly invest-ment. Simulates function but not aesthetics of proposed design. Prototypes help compare alternatives and help answer questions about interactions or experiences.

Why use this method?

1. May provide the proof of concept
2. It is physical and visible
3. Inexpensive and fast.
4. Useful for refining functional and percep-tual interactions.
5. Assists to identify any problems with the design.
6. Helps to reduce the risks
7. Helps members of team to be in alignment on an idea.
8. Helps make abstract ideas concrete.
9. Feedback can be gained from the user

Challenges

1. Do not create a beautiful prototype at this stage as it may seem like a finished solution to some.

"To invent, you need a good imagination and a pile of junk."
Thomas A. Edison

How to use this method

1. Construct models, not illustrations
2. Select the important tasks, interactions or experiences to be prototyped.
3. Build to understand problems.
4. If it is beautiful you have invested too much.
5. Make it simple
6. Assemble a kit of inexpensive materials
7. Preparing for a test
8. Select users
9. Conduct test
10. Record notes on the 8x5 cards.
11. Evaluate the results
12. Iterate

Resources

1. Paper
2. Cardboard
3. Foam board,
4. Post-it-notes
5. Hot melt glue

References

1. Sefelin, R., Tscheligi, M., & Gukker, V. (2003). Paper Prototyping — What is it good for? A Comparison of paper — and Computer — based Low fidelity Prototyping, CHI 2003, 778-779
2. Snyder, Carolyn (2003). Paper Prototyping: the fast and easy way to design and refine user interfaces. San Francisco, CA: Morgan Kaufmann

LOW FIDELITY PROTOTYPE KIT

Here are some suggestions for a kit of materials
to help you construct low fidelity prototypes

1. Copy paper
2. Magnets
3. Snaps
4. Masking tape
5. Duct tape (color would be ideal)
6. Tape
7. Post-it notes
8. Glue sticks
9. Paper clips, (asst colors ideal)
10. Decorative brads (square, crystal)
11. Hole punch
12. Scissors
13. Stapler (with staples)
14. Hot glue
15. Glue guns
16. Rulers
17. Pipe Cleaners
18. Colored card
19. Zip ties
20. Foam core sheets
21. Velcro
22. Rubber bands, multicolored
23. Assorted foam shapes
24. Markers
25. Scissors
26. Glue sticks
27. Tape
28. Glue guns
29. Straws
30. Paper Clips
31. Construction Paper
32. ABS sheets
33. Felt
34. Foam sheets
35. String
36. Foil
37. Butcher paper
38. Stickers
39. Pipe cleaners
40. Popsicle sticks
41. Multicolored card

TEST

The product, service or experience is tested, Improvements are made. The process is not over until the design works. The prototype may not work as well as expected, New ideas may need to be brainstormed and the prototype modified and retested

BUILD IN THE FEEDBACK
TEST AGAIN

Review you video of end users interacting with your prototype. Get feedback from as many stakeholders as possible including end users, and your design team. Brainstorm a list of insights generated. Brainstorm how the design could be improved to overcome any issues that you have seen. Refine your prototype build in the feedback and test it again. Go though this iterative process as many times as is necessary till your design works well for your intent.

References

1. Nielsen, J. (1994). Usability Engineering, Academic Press Inc, p 165
2. NN/G Usability Week 2011 Conference "Interaction Design" Manual, Bruce Tognazzini, Nielsen Norman Group, 2011
3. International Standardization Organization. ergonomics of human system interaction – Part 210 –: Human centred design for interactive systems (Rep N°9241-210). 2010, International Standardization Organization

HEURISTIC EVALUATION

Heuristic evaluation is an evaluation of by one or more experts. The experts measure the usability, efficiency, and effectiveness of the interface based on 10 usability heuristics defined by Jakob Nielsen in 1994.

Nielsen's Usability Heuristics, which have continued to evolve in response to user research and new devices, include:

1. Visibility of System Status
2. Match Between System and the Real World
3. User Control and Freedom
4. Consistency and Standards
5. Error Prevention
6. Recognition Rather Than Recall
7. Flexibility and Efficiency of Use
8. Aesthetic and Minimalist Design
9. Help Users Recognize, Diagnose, and Recover from Errors
10. Help and Documentation

MAKE A VIDEO

Record the end user interacting with existing products and services as well as your prototypes. Recording the activity in it's natural setting will help you understand the subtle and complex nature of an activity and can be used for feedback from stakeholders to refine the design direction.

Who invented it?
The first known ethnographic film was made by in 1895 by Felix-Louis Regnault who filmed a Senegalese woman making pots

Why use this method?
Joseph Schaeffer suggested that there are at least four ways that video can be useful .
1.   Videos allow for coverage of complex activities in their natural settings over an extended period of time.
2.   Videos can increase quality and reliability of observations made regarding the activity.
3.   Videos can be reviewed by researchers and participants which can help increase the scope and quality of understanding the activity.
4.   Videos can be used to establish connections between understandings and the observed activities.

The sooner and more often you invite feedback, the better that your final design will be. You do not discover the problems until you show your design to the stakeholders and ask for their feedback. Note the problems each time you get feedback and fix them. This is the process that Thomas Edison used to invent the first usable light bulb and that James Dyson used to invent the world's most successful vacuum cleaner. You can apply this iterative process to any type of design.

159

MAKE A HIGH FIDELITY PROTOTYPE

What is it?
High fidelity prototyping is a prototype that looks like and may work like the finished design. It simulates the aesthetics of proposed design.

Why use this method?
1. May provide the proof of concept
2. It is physical and visible
3. Useful for refining functional and perceptual interactions.
4. Assists to identify any problems with the design.
5. Helps to reduce the risks
6. Helps members of team to be in alignment on an idea.
7. Helps make abstract ideas concrete.
8. Feedback can be gained from the user

Challenges
1. Expensive and slow.
2. People may become attached a high fidelity prototype and not wish to change the design so it should be produced only when iteration and refinement stages are complete.
3. Producer might get too attached to prototype and it becomes jewelry because it is beautiful rather than a design tool.

How to use this method
1. Create final design through guided iterative process.
2. There are various methods for prototyping designs in different fields of design.
3. Create engineering database.
4. Build prototype
5. Preparing for a test
6. Select users
7. Conduct test
8. Record notes on the 8x5 cards.
9. Evaluate the results

Resources
1. Rapid prototyping facility
2. Model shop
3. Spray paint
4. Engineering database
5. Many other resources depending on what is being prototyped

When to use this method
1. Make plans
2. Deliver offering

REVIEW OBJECTIVES

1. Is the design approach feasible?
2. Does the design meet all of the objectives?
3. Were the weak parts of the design corrected?
4. What further testing is necessary?
5. Involve end users, vendors and other important stakeholders in the review

TEST AND EVALUATE

Testing is one of the core activities of Design Thinking

The design team checks design capabilities, requirements by testing with end users and the ability to meet these, and epitomizing the design to combine these two.

Testing is carried out with consumers through observation, focus groups and other methods.

FINALIZE YOUR PRODUCTION DESIGN

The details of this phase will depend on the type of design area that you are working in.

BUILD EXTERNAL PARTNERSHIPS

Collaboration with other organizations and individuals is becoming an integral part of the design process. Organizations benefit from their partners' insights and expertise. Many of the best ideas have emerged not through the inspiration of a single mind, but through the exchange of ideas.

"You have half of an idea, somebody else has the other half, and if you're in the right environment, they turn into something larger than the sum of their parts."

"We often talk about the value of protecting intellectual property building barricades, having secretive R&D labs, patenting everything that we have, so that those ideas will remain valuable but I think there's a case to be made that we should spend at least as much time, if not more, valuing the premise of connecting ideas and not just protecting them."
Jource UK Design Counncil, Johnson

SIGN OFF FROM ALL STAKEHOLDERS
When you believe that you have a design that can be distributed and sold, show it to all your stakeholders one last time before documenting the design for final manufacture.

MAKE YOUR PRODUCTION SAMPLES AUTHORIZE VENDORS
Manufacture first samples Review first production with vendors.

LAUNCH

At this point in the design process the product or service is launched, and the process now includes liaison with appropriate internal teams in areas such as marketing, communications, packaging and brand.

1. How can you make it impossible for this to fail?
2. Decide on your goals.
3. Prepare.
4. Make it fun and interesting
5. Set a date.

Pre-Launch
1. 3-4 weeks of pre-launch
2. Create the campaign.
3. Evoke emotion.
4. Create desire.
5. Prepare marketing materials.
6. Do something original.
7. Review what's working.
8. Create urgency.

Mid-Launch
1. Publish your blog post, send out your email announcement.
2. Post on social media and other various communication channels.
3. Listen and respond.

Post-Launch
1. Have a party!
2. Ask for feedback from first buyers
3. Deliver a bonus that wasn't expected
4. Make it memorable.
5. Review and improve.
6. Plan ahead.

Source: Adapted from Jonathan Mead "The 40 Step Checklist for a Highly Successful Launch"

DELIVER
Do final testing obtain sign off from stakeholders and launch. The design should successfully address the problem identified in the user research phase of the process.

Key activities and objectives during the Deliver stage are:

Final testing, approval and launch
Targets, evaluation and feedback loops.

SNAGGING
Identify small adaptions necessary to prepare the product or service for final distribution.

DID THE DESIGN MEET IT'S GOALS?

The information and metrics that are gathered are, of course, not always quantitative business metrics. Feedback related to problems with a product or service, or suggestions for improvements, flow back into the organization via other channels, and can be used to spin off into new projects or improvements. One example of this type of information would be feedback gathered by BSkyB from its customer service centres.

Ideas that have emerged during the design process or in post-launch feedback may be put to one side but developed later, and will then go through the design process again on its own.

MEASURE SUCCESS
1. Determine how you will measure the success
2. 2 to 3 months after release measure the success
3. Measure the success and objectively evaluate.
4. Implement metrics and measurements

Some of the ways to measure success:
1. Customer satisfaction
2. ROI is standard business measure of project profitability, over the market life of the design expressed as a percentage of initial investment.
3. Increased usage
4. Increased revenue from existing customers
5. The ability of your product to solve the problem
6. New customer acquisition
7. Product margin
8. Cash flow
9. Product Team's satisfaction
10. Improved customer retention rate
11. Increased market share
12. Satisfactory environmental impact
13. Contribution to strategic direction of the organization
14. Positioning
15. The value of the solution to the adopting user.
16. Improved position against competitors
17. Increase in inquiries
18. Quality

WHAT COULD BE IMPROVED?
Invite customers to co-create, and integrate feedback.

DEFINE NEXT VISION
The design process is never complete. Now it is time to start planning the next product or service so that you can stay ahead of the many competitors.

166

QUALITATIVE
insights

diary studies

user interviews   usability testing
                         contextual inquiry   validation
participatory design

focus groups   eye tracking
             card sorting

GOALS AND ATTITUDES   BEHAVIOURS
what people say   what people do

customer support
data analysis   automated usability
                              testing
user surveys

                                               site traffic analysis

                                               A/B testing

QUANTITATIVE
validation

Source: after Mulder

Chapter 7
Design Thinking Methods

design thinking methods

The wide range of methods contained in this chapter have been selected to help you adopt and apply a design thinking approach to design. The methods are necessary when working in multidisciplinary multinational collaboration. They include research methods, team alignment methods, creativity methods and design management and review methods selected to help your team work together efficiently. They combine analytical and creative thinking approaches for the complex and rapidly evolving global consumer behaviors and markets that designers now work in.

I have kept the descriptions simple to give readers the essential information to adapt, combine and apply the methods in their own way. I hope that you will gradually build a personal toolkit of favored methods that you have tried and found effective. Different design practitioners can select different methods for their toolkit and apply them in different ways. There is no best combination.

Space permits me to include about 150 methods in this section. If you would like to see some more methods please see my books Design Methods, Design Methods 2, Design Research Methods Mapping Methds for Design and Brainstorming Methods which include hundreds of additional methods. Details of these books can be found at the back of this book.

Photo: photocase.com – Alexalex

these books by the same author contain additional methods to those described in this chapter.

Design Methods 1
200 ways to apply design thinking
Author: Curedale, Robert A
Publisher: Design Community College.
Edition 1 November 2013
ISBN-10:0988236206
ISBN-13:978-0-9882362-0-2

Design Methods 2
200 more ways to apply design thinking
Author: Curedale, Robert A Publisher: Design
Community College.
Edition 1 January 2013
ISBN-13: 978-0988236240
ISBN-10: 0988236249

Design Research Methods
150 ways to inform design
Author: Curedale, Robert A
Publisher: Design Community College.
Edition 1 January 2013
ISBN-10: 0988236257
ISBN-13: 978-0-988-2362-5-7

50 Brainstorming Methods
for team and individual ideation
Author: Curedale, Robert A
Publisher: Design Community College.
Edition 1 January 2013
ISBN-10: 0988236230
ISBN-13: 978-0-9882362-3-3

50 Selected Design Methods
to inform your design
Author: Curedale, Robert A
Publisher: Design Community College.
Edition 1 January 2013
ISBN-10:0988236265
ISBN-13:978-0-9882362-6-4

Mapping Methods
for design and strategy
Curedale, Robert A
Publisher: Design Community College.
Edition 1 April 2013
ISBN-10: 0989246817
ISBN-13: 978-0-9892468-1-1

THE EMERGING LANDSCAPE OF DESIGN RESEARCH

PARTICIPATORY MINDSET
users seen as participants

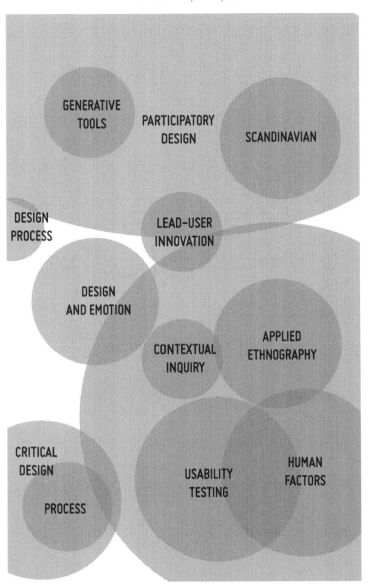

GENERATIVE TOOLS

PARTICIPATORY DESIGN

SCANDINAVIAN

DESIGN PROCESS

LEAD-USER INNOVATION

DESIGN LED

RESEARCH LED

DESIGN AND EMOTION

CONTEXTUAL INQUIRY

APPLIED ETHNOGRAPHY

CRITICAL DESIGN

USABILITY TESTING

HUMAN FACTORS

PROCESS

EXPERT MINDSET
users seen as subjects

Source: adapted from Liz Sanders

tool: a device used to carry out a particular function

technique: a way to carry out a particular task

method: a particular procedure for accomplishing something in a systematic way

methodology: a system of methods used in a particular area of activity

mindset: an established set of attitudes, or frame of reference

culture: the customs, designs, social institutions of a particular nation, people or group. A set of learned beliefs values and behaviors shared by a group of people.

Source: adapted from Liz Sanders

WARMING UP EXERCISES

What is it?

An icebreaker is a short exercise at the beginning of a design project that helps the design team work productively together as quickly as possible. The duration of an icebreaker is usually less than 30 minutes.

They are an important component of collaborative or team based design. The Design Thinking approach recognizes the value of designers working productively as members of a diverse cross-disciplinary teams with managers, engineers, marketers and other professionals.

References

1. Fergueson, S., & Aimone, L. (2002). Making people feel valued. Communication: Journalism Education Today, 36(1), 5-11
2. Sisco, B. R. (1991). Setting the climate for effective teaching and learning. New Directions for Adult and Continuing Education, (50), 41-50.

Why use this method?

When a designer works with others in a new team it is important that the group works as quickly as possible in a creative constructive dialogue. An icebreaker is a way for team members to quickly start working effectively;y together. It is a worthwhile investment of half an hour at the beginning of a project and can be fun. Ice breakers help start people thinking creatively, exchanging ideas and help make a team work effectively. For meetings in a business setting in which contribute.

When use this method

1. When team members do not know each other
2. When team members come from different cultures
3. When team needs to bond quickly
4. When team needs to work to a common gaol quickly.
5. When the discussion is new or unfamiliar.
6. When the moderator needs to know the participants.

COMMON GROUND

What is it?
An ice-breaker is an exercise that is used at the beginning of a design project or workshop to help to stimulate constructive interaction. It helps everyone to engage in the dialogue and contribute effectively,

Why use this method?
1. Helps create a comfortable and productive environment.
2. Helps people get to know each other.
3. Helps participants engage the group and tasks.
4. Helps participants contribute effectively.
5. Creates a sense of community.

Challenges
1. Be aware of time constraints.
2. Should limit the time to 15 to 30 minutes
3. Make it simple
4. It should be fun
5. You should be creative
6. Be enthusiastic
7. If something isn't working move on.
8. Consider your audience
9. Keep in mind technology requirements such as a microphone or projector.
10. Chairs can be arranged in a circle to help participants read body language.
11. Select exercises appropriate for your group.

When to use this method
1. Define intent

How to use this method
1. The moderator ask the group to divide into pairs of participants
2. Each participant should select a group member that they do not know if possible.
3. Each person should interview the other person that they are paired with and make a list of 5 to ten things that they have in common.
4. One person from each pair should then present the list to the larger group.

Resources
1. White board
2. Dry erase markers
3. A comfortable space

References
1. Fergueson, S., & Aimone, L. (2002). Making people feel valued. Communication: Journalism Education Today, 36(1), 5-11
2. Sisco, B. R. (1991). Setting the climate for effective teaching and learning. New Directions for Adult and Continuing Education, (50), 41-50.

DESERT ISLAND

What is it?
An ice-breaker is an exercise that is used at the beginning of a design project or workshop to help to stimulate constructive interaction. It helps everyone to engage in the dialogue and contribute effectively,

Why use this method?
1. Helps create a comfortable and productive environment.
2. Helps people get to know each other.
3. Helps participants engage the group and tasks.
4. Helps participants contribute effectively.
5. Creates a sense of community.

Challenges
1. Be aware of time constraints. Should limit the time to 15 to 30 minutes
2. Make it simple
3. It should be fun
4. You should be creative
5. Consider your audience
6. Keep in mind technology requirements such as a microphone or projector.
7. Chairs can be arranged in a circle to help participants read body language.

When to use this method
1. Define intent
2. Explore Concepts

How to use this method
1. Moderator introduces the warming up exercise.
2. Each person has 30 second to list all of the things that they should take. Each person should list at least 3 things.
3. Each person should defend why their 3 items should be one of the chosen items selected by their team.
4. Each team can vote for three items preferred by their team.
5. Each of the teams presents the 3 items that they have agreed upon to the larger group.

Resources
1. A comfortable space.
2. A moderator

References
1. Fergueson, S., & Aimone, L. (2002). Making people feel valued. Communication: Journalism Education Today, 36(1), 5-11
2. Sisco, B. R. (1991). Setting the climate for effective teaching and learning. New Directions for Adult and Continuing Education, (50), 41-50.

EXPECTATIONS

What is it?

An ice-breaker is an exercise that is used at the beginning of a design project or workshop to help to stimulate constructive interaction. It helps everyone to engage in the dialogue and contribute effectively,

Why use this method?

1. Helps create a comfortable and productive environment.
2. Helps people get to know each other.
3. Helps participants engage the group and tasks.
4. Helps participants contribute effectively.
5. Creates a sense of community.

Challenges

1. Be aware of time constraints. Should limit the time to 15 to 30 minutes
2. Make it simple
3. It should be fun
4. You should be creative
5. Be enthusiastic
6. If something isn't working move on.
7. Consider your audience
8. Keep in mind technology requirements such as a microphone or projector.
9. Chairs can be arranged in a circle to help participants read body language.
10. Select exercises appropriate for your group.

When to use this method

1. Define intent

How to use this method

1. Each team member introduces themselves
2. Each team member outlines what is their expectations of the project.
3. Each team member shares their vision of the best possible outcome for the project.
4. Allow about 2 minutes per person

Resources

1. White board
2. Dry erase markers
3. A comfortable space

References

1. Fergueson, S., & Aimone, L. (2002). Making people feel valued. Communication: Journalism Education Today, 36(1), 5-11
2. Sisco, B. R. (1991). Setting the climate for effective teaching and learning. New Directions for Adult and Continuing Education, (50), 41-50.

DIVERSITY

What is it?
An ice-breaker is an exercise that is used at the beginning of a design project or workshop to help to stimulate constructive interaction. It helps everyone to engage in the dialogue and contribute effectively,

Why use this method?
1. Helps create a comfortable and productive environment.
2. Helps people get to know each other.
3. Helps participants engage the group and tasks.
4. Helps participants contribute effectively.
5. Creates a sense of community.

Challenges
1. Be aware of time constraints.
2. Should limit the time to 15 to 30 minutes
3. Make it simple
4. It should be fun
5. You should be creative
6. Be enthusiastic
7. If something isn't working move on.
8. Consider your audience
9. Keep in mind technology requirements such as a microphone or projector.
10. Chairs can be arranged in a circle to help participants read body language.
11. Select exercises appropriate for your group.

When to use this method
1. Define intent

How to use this method
2. The moderator introduces the exercise.
3. Place a number of objects or cards on the floor that represent the relative positions of the continents on a map of the earth.
4. The moderator asks each person to move to the spot where they were born.
5. When the group is in position the moderator asks each person to tell the group one thing about the place they were born.
6. Allow one or two minutes per person.
7. When this is complete the moderator asks the group to move to the place where they have spent the most of their adult life and tell the group one thing about that place.

Resources
1. White board
2. Dry erase markers
3. A large comfortable space

References
1. Fergueson, S., & Aimone, L. (2002). Making people feel valued. Communication: Journalism Education Today, 36(1), 5-11
2. Sisco, B. R. (1991). Setting the climate for effective teaching and learning. New Directions for Adult and Continuing Education, (50), 41-50.

HOPES AND HURDLES

What is it?

Hopes and hurdles is a brainstorm that identifies factors that may help or hinder the success of success of a project:

1. Business drivers and hurdles
2. User and employee drivers and hurdles
3. Technology drivers and hurdles
4. Environmental drivers and hurdles.
5. Vendors
6. Competitive benchmarking.

Why use this method?

1. This method helps identify where Resources should be focused for most return on investment.
2. Enables stakeholders to understand other stakeholders expectations.

Challenges

1. It provides a tangible focus for discussion.
2. It draws out tacit knowledge from your team.
3. It helps build team consensus.
4. It drives insights
5. Do not get too detailed
6. Some information may be sensitive.

When to use this method

1. Define intent
2. Know Context
3. Know User
4. Frame insights

How to use this method

1. Define the problem.
2. Find a moderator
3. Brainstorm hopes and hurdles
   - Which are our own advantages?
   - What are we able to do quite well?
   - What strategic Resources can we rely upon?
   - What could we enhance?
   - What should we avoid to do?
   - What are we doing poorly?
4. Collect the ideas on a white board or wall with post-it-notes.
5. Organize the contributions into two lists.
6. Prioritize each element
7. Use the lists to create strategic options.

Resources

1. White board
2. Marker pens
3. Post-it notes
4. Flip chart
5. Video Camera
6. Camera

THE INTERVIEW

What is it?

An ice-breaker is an exercise that is used at the beginning of a design project or workshop to help to stimulate constructive interaction. It helps everyone to engage in the dialogue and contribute effectively,

Why use this method?

1. Helps create a comfortable and productive environment.
2. Helps people get to know each other.
3. Helps participants engage the group and tasks.
4. Helps participants contribute effectively.
5. Creates a sense of community.

Challenges

1. Be aware of time constraints. Should limit the time to 15 to 30 minutes
2. Make it simple
3. It should be fun
4. You should be creative
5. Consider your audience
6. Keep in mind technology requirements such as a microphone or projector.
7. Chairs can be arranged in a circle to help participants read body language.

When to use this method

1. Define intent
2. Explore Concepts

How to use this method

1. Moderator introduces the warming up exercise.
2. The group is paired into groups of two people who do not know each other.
3. The paired groups spend five minutes interviewing each other.
4. The interviewer introduces the interviewee to the group.
5. 3 minutes per person.

Resources

1. A comfortable space.
2. A moderator

References

1. Fergueson, S., & Aimone, L. (2002). Making people feel valued. Communication: Journalism Education Today, 36(1), 5-11
2. Sisco, B. R. (1991). Setting the climate for effective teaching and learning. New Directions for Adult and Continuing Education, (50), 41-50.

JUMPSTART STORYTELLING

What is it?
An ice-breaker is an exercise that is used at the beginning of a design project or workshop to help to stimulate constructive interaction. It helps everyone to engage in the dialogue and contribute effectively,

Why use this method?
1. Stories reveal what is happening.
2. Stories inspire us to take action.
3. Stories are remembered.
4. Stories share and imbed values.
5. Stories connect people.

WHO INVENTED IT?
Seth Kahan

When to use this method
1. Helps create a comfortable and productive environment.
2. Helps people get to know each other.
3. Helps participants engage the group and tasks.
4. Helps participants contribute effectively.
5. Creates a sense of community narrative in the first 5 minutes of the project.

Resources
1. Paper
2. Pens
3. White board
4. Dry-erase markers
5. Post-it-notes.

Challenges
1. Be aware of time constraints. Should limit the time to 15 to 30 minutes
2. Make it simple
3. It should be fun
4. You should be creative
5. Consider your audience
6. Keep in mind technology requirements such as a microphone or projector.

Chairs can be arranged in a circle to help participants read body language.

How to use this method
1. Divide the participants into groups of 5
2. Ask everyone to provide a story that is related to the objective of the workshop.
3. Each person gets 90 seconds.
4. Ask the participants to remember the story that resonated the most with them;
5. Reform the groups of 5 with different people.
6. Ask everyone to retell their story.
7. Note how the story improves with each retelling.
8. 90 seconds per story.
9. Ask each participant to reassess which story resonates with them the most.
10. Ask everyone to remember the person who told the most powerful, relevant, engaging story.
11. When clusters appear invite the people the group favored to retell their story to the whole group.

MILESTONES

What is it?

An ice-breaker is an exercise that is used at the beginning of a design project or workshop to help to stimulate constructive interaction. It helps everyone to engage in the dialogue and contribute effectively,

WHO INVENTED IT?

Ava S, Butler 1996

Why use this method?

1. Helps create a comfortable and productive environment.
2. Helps people get to know each other.
3. Helps participants engage the group and tasks.
4. Helps participants contribute effectively.
5. Creates a sense of community.

Challenges

1. Be aware of time constraints.
2. Should limit the time to 15 to 30 minutes
3. Make it simple
4. It should be fun
5. You should be creative
6. Be enthusiastic
7. If something isn't working move on.
8. Consider your audience
9. Keep in mind technology requirements such as a microphone or projector.
10. Chairs can be arranged in a circle to help participants read body language.
11. Select exercises appropriate for your group.

When to use this method

1. Define intent

How to use this method

1. The moderator creates a milestone chart on a white board
2. The moderator estimates the age of the oldest members of the group and on a horizontal line write years from the approximate birth year of the older members to the present at 5 year intervals.
1960 1965 1970 1975 .
3. Using post-it notes each participant adds three personal milestones to the chart. One milestone per post-it-note under the year that the milestone occurred.
4. During the break participants read the milestones.

Resources

5. Whiteboard
6. Dry erase markers
7. Post-it-notes
8. A comfortable space

References

1. Butler, Ava S. (1996) Teamthink Publisher: Mcgraw Hill ISBN 0070094330

ASSUMPTION SURFACING

What is it?
This is a method of analyzing your assumptions, considering alternative assumptions and prioritizing solutions.

Who invented it?
Richard O. Mason, Ian Mitroff 1981

Why use this method?
1. The purpose of this method is to analyze assumptions to understand which are most plausible and may have the highest impact.
2. A method for approaching ill-structured or "wicked" problems
3. To compare and to evaluate systematically the assumptions of different people.
4. To examine the relationship between underlying assumption

Resources
1. Pen
2. Paper
3. White board
4. Dry Erase markers

When to use this method
1. Define intent

How to use this method
1. List the decisions that you have made.
2. For each decision list the assumptions that you made
3. Under each assumption list an alternative counter assumption.
4. Delete from your list choices where it makes little difference whether the original assumption or the counter assumption are correct.
5. Analyze the remaining assumptions on a 2x2 matrix high low impact on one axis and high low plausibility on the other axis.
6. High impact and plausibility assumptions should be given high priority.

References
1. Mason, R.O., and Mitroff, I.I., 1981; "Challenging Strategic Planning Assumptions: Theory, Cases and Techniques", NY, Wiley, ISBN 0-471-08219-8

BOUNDARY EXAMINATION

What is it?
Boundary examination is a way of refining the definition of a problem.

Who invented it?
Edward De bono 1982

Why use this method?
1. The boundary setting may be part of the problem.
2. The boundary may reflect biases.

Resources
1. Pen
2. Paper
3. White board
4. Dry erase markers

When to use this method
1. Define intent

How to use this method
1. Define the problem with a written statement.
1. Underline the key words
1. Analyze each key word for underlying assumptions.
2. Consider how the meaning of the problem statement changes as the keywords are replaced by synonyms.
1. Redefine the problem boundary by substituting new keywords.

References
1. Learn-To-Think: Coursebook and Instructors Manual with Michael Hewitt-Gleeson de Saint-Arnaud (1982), ISBN 0-88496-199-0
2. De Bono's Course in Thinking (1982)

BHAG

What is it?
BHAG stands for Big Hairy Audacious Goal.
It is a type of goal that is bigger than a usual mission statement.

Some examples of BHAGs are:
1. Google bhag is to make all digital information in the world accessible to people everywhere
2. Nokia bhag is to connect one billion people to the internet. For the first time.

Who invented it?
J Collins and J Porras,1996

Why use this method?
1. Bold visions stimulate bold steps
2. BHAGs encourage you to set your sights high and long term.

When to use this method
Define intent

Resources
1. Pen
2. Paper
3. White board
4. Dry erase markers

How to use this method
1. It needs to motivate people and get them excited.
2. It shouldn't be in your comfort zone
3. It should take a herculean effort to achieve.
4. It should not be possible to achieve with incremental change.
5. BHAGs have time frames of 10-30 years.
6. The BHAG should be aligned to the organization's core values.

References
1. Collins, J and Porras, J. Built to Last: Successful Habits of Visionary Companies. Harper Business; 1 edition (November 2, 2004) ISBN-10: 0060566108 ISBN-13: 978-0060566104

CHECKLIST: ENVIRONMENTALLY RESPONSIBLE DESIGN

Some of the ways in which we can work to improve the environmental performance of the products that we design:

1. Use environmentally responsible strategies appropriate to the product;
2. Reduce overall material content and increase the percentage of recycled material in products;
3. Reduce energy consumption of products that use energy;
4. Specify sustainability grown materials when using wood or agricultural materials;
5. Design disposable products or products that wear out to be more durable and precious;
6. Eliminate unused or unnecessary product features;
7. Design continuously transported products for minimal weight;
8. Design for fast, economical disassembly of major components prior to recycling;
9. Design products so that toxic components are easily removed prior to recycling;
10. Perform comprehensive environmental assessment;
11. Consider all of the ecological impacts from all of the components in the products over its entire life cycle, including extraction of materials from nature, conversion of materials into products, product use, disposal or recycling and transport between these phases;
12. Consider all ecological impacts including global warming, acid rain, smog, habitat damage, human toxicity, water pollution, cancer causing potential, ozone layer depletion and resource depletion;
13. Strive to reduce the largest ecological impacts,
14. Conduct life cycle impact assessment to comprehensively identify opportunities for improving ecological performance
15. Encourage new business models and effective communication
16. Support product 'take back' systems that enable product up-grading and material recycling;
17. Lease the product or sell the service of the product to improve long-term performance and end-of-life product collection;
18. Communicate the sound business value of being ecologically responsible to clients and commissioners
19. Discuss market opportunities for meeting basic needs and reducing consumption,

Source: adapted from design-sustainability.com

FUTURE WHEEL

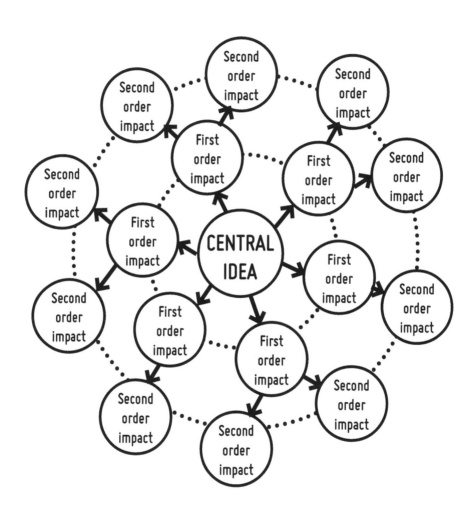

FUTURE WHEEL

What is it?
The future wheel is a method to graphically represent and analyze the direct and indirect outcomes of a proposed change.

Who invented it?
Jerome Glenn 1972

Why use this method?
1. A method of envisioning outcomes of decisions.
2. Can be used to study possible outcomes of trends.
3. Helps create a consciousness of the future.

Challenges
1. Can be subjective

When to use this method
1. Define intent

How to use this method
1. Define the proposed change
2. Identify and graph the first level of outcomes
3. Identify and graph the subsequent level of outcomes
4. Link the dependencies
5. Identify insights
6. Identify the actions
7. Implement the actions

Resources
1. Pen
2. Paper
3. White board
4. Dry erase markers

References
1. Futures Wheel, Futures Research Methodology Version 3.0, The Millennium Project, Washington, DC 2009

GOAL GRID

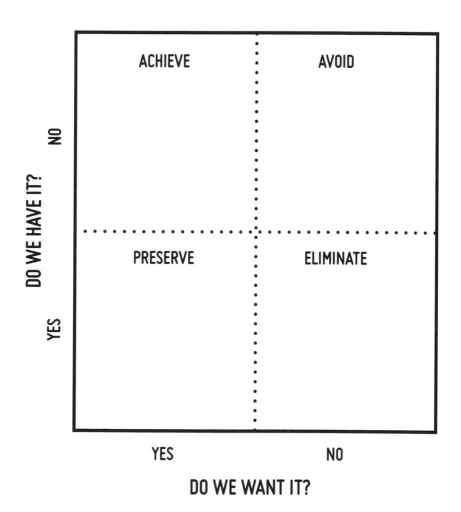

GOAL GRID

What is it?

A goal grid is a method for clarifying goals.

"The Goals Grid also provides a structure for analyzing patterns in goals and objectives and for detecting potential conflict with the goals and objectives of others." *Fred Nickols*

Who invented it?

Ray Forbes, John Arnold and Fred Nickols 1992

Why use this method?

1. A goal grid is a method for clarifying goals.

Resources

1. Pen
2. Paper
3. White board
4. Dry erase markers
5. Post-it notes.

When to use this method

1. Define intent

How to use this method

1. The team brainstorms a list of goals.
2. The moderator asks the team these questions:
   ° "Do we have it?"
   ° "Do we want it?"
   ° "What are we trying to achieve?"
   ° "What are we trying to preserve?"
   ° "What are we trying to avoid?"
   ° "What are we trying to eliminate?"

References

1. Arnold, John D. (1980). The Art of Decision Making. AMACOM, New York.
2. Barnard, Chester A (1938). The Functions of the Executive. Harvard University Press, Cambridge
3. Nickols, Fred (2003) The Goals Grid: A Tool for Clarifying Goals & Objectives

REFRAMING THE PROBLEM

What is it?
This method helps develop innovative solutions with a number of questions.

Who invented it?
Tudor Rickards 1974 Manchester Business School

Why use this method?
1. To create different perspectives and new ideas.

Resources
1. Pen
2. Paper
3. White board
4. Dry Erase markers

References
1. Rickards, Tudor (1974). Problem Solving Through Creativity. Wiley. pp. 198. ISBN 0-470-72045-X.
2. Rickards, Tudor; Runco, Mark A., Moger, Susan (2008). 978-0-415-77317-1 The Routledge Companion To Creativity. Routledge. pp. 400. ISBN 978-0-415-77317-1.

When to use this method
1. Define intent

How to use this method
1. Define the problem that you would like to address.

Complete these sentences while considering your problem.
1. There is more than one way of looking at a problem. You could also define this problem in another way as."
2. "The underlying reason for the problem is."
3. "I think that the best solution is."
4. "If I could break all laws of reality I would try to solve it by."
5. "You could compare this problem to the problem of."
6. "Another, different way of thinking about it is"

PREMORTEM

What is it?
The premortem is a risk-mitigation planning tool that attempts to identify project threats at the outset.

Who invented it?
Gary Klein, 1998

Why use this method?
1. The Premortem technique is low cost and high value

When to use this method
1. Define intent

References
2. Klein., Gary. Sources of Power: How People Make Decisions. 1998. MIT Press.

Resources
1. Evaluation forms can be printed or online.

How to use this method
1. Determine a period after completion of the project when it should be known whether the project was successful. It could be one or five years.
2. Imagine the project was a complete failure.
3. What could have been the cause?
4. Ask each team member to suggest ten reasons for the failure.
5. Think about the internal and external context and the stakeholders relationships.
6. Ask each team meber to select one of the reasons for failure they have listed and describe it to the group.
7. Each person should present one reason.
8. Collect and review the full list of reasons from each participant.
9. Review the session and strengthen the strategy based on the premortem.

REFRAMING MATRIX

PRODUCT PERSPECTIVE

1. Is there something wrong with the product or service?
2. Is it priced correctly?
3. How well does it serve the market?
4. Is it reliable?

PLANNING PERSPECTIVE

1. Are our business plans, marketing plans, or strategy at fault?
2. Could we improve these?

POTENTIAL PERSPECTIVE

1. How would we increase sales?
2. If we were to seriously increase our targets or our production volumes, what would happen with this problem?

PEOPLE PERSPECTIVE

1. What are the people impacts and people implications of the problem?
2. What do people involved with the problem think?
3. Why are customers not using or buying the product?

DESIGN PROBLEM ....

....

REFRAMING MATRIX

What is it?
The reframing matrix is a method of approaching a problem by imagining the perspectives of a number of different people and exploring the possible solutions that they might suggest.

Who invented it?
Michael Morgan 1993

Why use this method?
1. This is a method for assisting in empathy which is an important factor in gaining acceptance and creating successful design.

Challenges
1. The reframing is not done with stakeholders present or in context so may be subjective

Resources
1. Pens
2. Paper
3. Post it notes
4. White board
5. Dry erase markers

When to use this method
1. Define intent

How to use this method
1. Define a problem.
2. On a white board or paper draw a large square and divide it into four quadrants.
3. Select 4 different perspectives to approach the problem. They could be four professions or four people or four other perspectives that are important for your problem.
4. With your team brainstorm a number of questions that you believe are important from the perspectives that you have selected.
5. The moderator writes the questions in the relevant quadrants of the matrix.
6. The group discusses each of these questions.
7. The answers are recorded and the perspectives are incorporated into the considerations for design solutions.

References
1. Morgan, M. Creating Workforce Innovation: Turning Individual Creativity into Organizational Innovation. Publisher: Business & Professional Pub (October 1993) ISBN-10: 1875680020 ISBN-13: 978-1875680023

WWWWWH

What is it?

'Who, What, Where, When, Why, and How'? is a method for getting a thorough understanding of the problem, It is used to obtain basic information in police investigations. A well known golden rule of journalism (and many other fields too) is that if you want to know the full story about something you have to answer all the five W's. Journalists argue your story isn't complete until you answer all six questions.

1. Who is involved?
2. What occurred?
3. When did it happen?
4. Where did it happen?
5. Why did it occur?

"I keep six honest serving-men, They taught me all I knew; Their names are What and Why and When, And How and Where and Who"
Rudyard Kipling

Who invented it?

Hermagoras of Temnos, Greece 1st century BC.

Why use this method?

This method helps create a story that communicates clearly the nature of an activity or event to stakeholders.

When to use this method

1. Define intent
2. Know Context
3. Know User
4. Frame insights

How to use this method

1. Ask the questions starting with the 5 w's and 1 h question words.
2. Identify the people involved
3. Identify the activities and make a list of them.
4. Identify all the places and make a list of them.
5. Identify all the time factors and make a list of them.
6. Identify causes for events of actions and make a list of them.
7. Identify the way events took place and make a list of them.
8. Study the relationships between the information.

Challenges

1. The answers may be subjective.

Resources

1. Pen
2. Paper

some sample WWWWWH questions

Who

1. Is affected?
2. Who believes that the problem affects them?
3. Needs the problem solved?
4. Does not want the problem to be solved?
5. Could stand in the way of a solution?

When

1. Does it happen
2. Doesn't it happen?
3. Did it start?
4. Will it end?
5. Is the solution needed?
6. Might it happen in the future?
7. Will it be a bigger problem?
8. Will it improve?

Where

1. Does it happen?
2. Doesn't it happen
3. Else does it happen?
4. Is the best place to solve the problem

Why

1. Is this situation a problem?
2. Do you want to solve it?
3. Do you not want to solve it?
4. Does it not go away?
5. Would someone else want to solve it?
6. Can it be solved?
7. Is it difficult to solve?

What

1. May be different in the future
2. Are its weaknesses?
3. Do you like?
4. Makes you unhappy about it?
5. Is flexible?
6. Is not flexible?
7. Do you know?
8. Do you not understand?
9. How have you solved similar problems?
10. Are the underlying ideas?
11. Are the values involved?
12. Are the elements of the problem and how are they related?
13. What can you assume to be correct
14. Is most important
15. Is least important
16. Are your goals?
17. Do you need to discover?

AEIOU

What is it?
One of a number of ethnographic frameworks have been developed to give structure to observations and to ensure that the researcher doesn't miss important data.

Activities: Goal directed sets of actions which people want to accomplish.
Environments: where activities take place
Objects: located in an environment. Their use, function, meaning and context.
Users: The people and their behaviors, preferences and needs.

Source Recording ethnographic observations: palojono

Who invented it?
The Doblin Group Elab 1997

Why use this method?
1. To give structure to research
2. In order to collect most important information.
3. To provide some certainty in the uncertain environment of fieldwork

When to use this method
1. Know Context
2. Know User
3. Frame insights

Resources
1. Computer
2. Notebook
3. Pens
4. Video camera
5. Digital camera
6. Digital voice recorder
7. Release forms
8. Interview plan or structure
9. Questions, tasks and discussion items

NINE DIMENSIONS

What is it?

One of a number of ethnographic frameworks have been developed to give structure to observations and to ensure that the researcher doesn't miss important data.

Space: Layout of the physical setting, rooms outdoor spaces etc.
Actors: The names and details of the people involved
Activities: the various activities of the actors
Objects: Physical elements: furniture etc
Acts: Specific Individual actions
Events: Particular occasions Eg meetings
Time: The sequence of events
Goals: What actors are attempting to accomplish
Feelings: Emotions in particular contexts

Source Recording ethnographic observations: palojono

Who invented it?

Spradley, J. P. 1980

Why use this method?

1. To give structure to research
2. In order to collect most important information.
3. To provide some certainty in the uncertain environment of fieldwork

When to use this method

1. Know Context
2. Know User
3. Frame insights

Resources

1. Computer
2. Notebook
3. Pens
4. Video camera
5. Digital camera
6. Digital voice recorder
7. Release forms
8. Interview plan or structure
9. Questions, tasks and discussion items

References

1. Spradley, J. P. (1980). Participant Observation. New York: Holt, Rinehart & Winston.

POSTA

What is it?

One of a number of ethnographic frameworks have been developed to give structure to observations and to ensure that the researcher doesn't miss important data.

1. People
2. Objects
3. Settings
4. Time
5. Activities

Who invented it?

May have been invented by Pat Sachs Social Solutions and Gitte Jordan Institute for Research on Learning

Why use this method?

6. To give structure to research
7. In order to collect most important information
8. To provide some certainty in the uncertain environment of fieldwork

When to use this method

1. Know Context
2. Know User
3. Frame insights

How to use this method

Observe participant in the work setting around, observing what they do and how they interact with other people and tools in their environment. Or they may focus on key objects or artifacts in the environment, with special attention to the various roles that they play (functional, psychological and social). During another observation, the team may take notes and photo-graphs of the work setting and try to understand how the configuration of space mediates the work. Finally, they chart activities, including both formal workflow and informal work practices.

Resources

1. Computer
2. Notebook
3. Pens
4. Video camera
5. Digital camera
6. Digital voice recorder
7. Release forms
8. Interview plan or structure
9. Questions, tasks and discussion items

LATCH

What is it?
One of a number of ethnographic frameworks have been developed to give structure to observations and to ensure that the researcher doesn't miss important data.

1. **Location**
   Compare information sources.
2. **Alphabet**
   Used for very large volume of data.
3. **Time**
   Used for events that occur over a measurable duration of time.
4. **Category**
   Grouped by similarity of characteristics.
5. **Hierarchy**
   Information is organized on a scale

Who invented it?
Richard Saul Wurman, 1996

Why use this method?
6. To give structure to research
7. In order to collect most important information.
8. To provide some certainty in the uncertain environment of fieldwork

When to use this method
1. Know Context
2. Know User
3. Frame insights

Resources
1. Notebook
2. Pens
3. Video camera
4. Digital camera
5. Digital voice recorder
6. Release forms

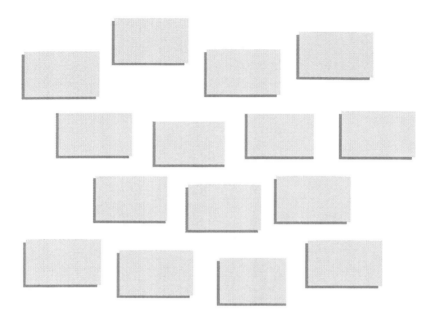

Put individual answers or ideas on post-it-notes Spread post-it-notes or cards on a wall or large table.

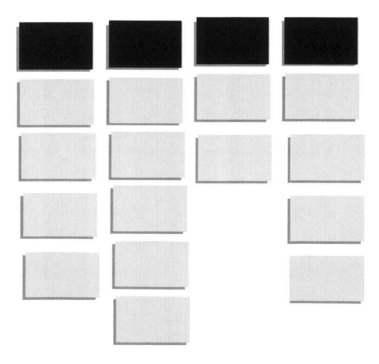

Group similar items and name each group with a different colored card or Post-it-note above the group.

AFFINITY DIAGRAM

What is it?

Affinity diagrams are a tool for analyzing large amounts of data and discovering relationships which allow a design direction to be established based on the affinities. This method may uncover important hidden relationships.

Affinity diagrams are created through consensus of the design team on how the information should be grouped in logical ways.

Who invented it?

Jiro Kawaita, Japan, 1960

Why use this method?

Traditional design methods are less useful when dealing with complex or chaotic problems with large amounts of data. This method helps to establish relationships of affinities between pieces of information. From these relationships insights and relationships can be determined which are the starting point of design solutions. It is possible using this method to reach consensus faster than many other methods.

Resources

1. White board
2. Large wall spaces or tables
3. Dry-erase markers
4. Sharpies
5. Post-it notes
6. Digital camera

When to use this method

1. Know Context
2. Know User
3. Frame insights

How to use this method

1. Select your team
2. Place individual opinions or answers to interview questions or design concepts on post-it-notes or cards.
3. Spread post-it-notes or cards on a wall or large table.
4. Group similar items.
5. This can be done silently by your design team moving them around as they each see affinities. Work until your team has consensus.
6. Name each group with a different colored card or Post-it-note above the group.
7. Repeat by grouping groups.
8. Rank the most important groups.
9. Photograph results
10. Analyze affinities and create insights.
11. 5 to 20 participants

References

1. Brassard, M. (1989). The Memory Jogger Plus+, pp. 17 - 39. Methuen, MA: Goal/QPC.
2. King, R. (1989). Hoshin Planning, The Developmental Approach, pp. 4-2 - 4-5. Methuen, MA: Goal/QPC.

ANTHROPUMP

What is it?
This method involves the research videotaping one or more participant's activities. The videos are replayed to the participants and they are asked to explain their behavior.

Who invented it?
Rick Robinson, John Cain, E- Lab Inc.,

Why use this method?
1. Used for collecting data before concept and for evaluating prototypes after concept phases of projects,

Challenges
1. Best conducted by someone who has practice observing human interactions in a space.

Resources
1. Video camera
2. Video projector
3. Note pad
4. White board
5. Dry erase markers

When to use this method
1. Know Context
2. Know User
3. Frame insights

How to use this method
1. People are first captured on video while interacting with products.
2. The participants are then asked to watch the tapes while researchers question them about what they see, how they felt, etc. In effect, research subjects analyses their own actions and experiences.
3. The company invites people who have been captured on video to watch their tapes as researchers pose questions about what's happening.
4. E Lab videotapes and dissects these follow-up sessions, analyzing research subjects analyzing themselves.

Source: [1]

References
1. http://www.fastcompany.com/magazine/05/october-november-96

AUTOETHNOGRAPHY

What is it?
This is research where the researcher studies their own activities and behavior rather than others. May also refer to research of the cultural group that the researcher is part of.

Who invented it?
Duncan 1993

Why use this method?
1. Easy access to self
2. Inexpensive

Challenges
1. Some quantitative researchers consider this method unscientific and unreliable.
2. The study may be too personal
3. May be difficult for the researcher to be objective when studying self.

When to use this method
1. Know Context
2. Know User
3. Frame insights

Resources
1. Camera
2. Video camera
3. Note pad

How to use this method
1. Be objective
2. Record data while the activity is being undertaken or soon after
3. Analyze and summarize data "
4. Create Reflexive journal summary

References
1. Chang, Heewon. (2008). Autoethnography as method. Walnut Creek, CA: Left Coast Press.
2. Duncan, M., Autoethnography: Critical appreciation of an emerging art. International Journal of Qualitative Methods, 3, 4, (2004), Article 3,
3. Ellis, Carolyn. (2004). The Ethnographic I: A methodological novel about autoethnography. Walnut Creek: AltaMira Press.
4. Maréchal, Garance. (2010). Autoethnography. In Albert J. Mills, Gabrielle Durepos & Elden Wiebe (Eds.), Encyclopedia of case study research (Vol. 2, pp. 43–45). Thousand Oaks, CA: Sage Publications.

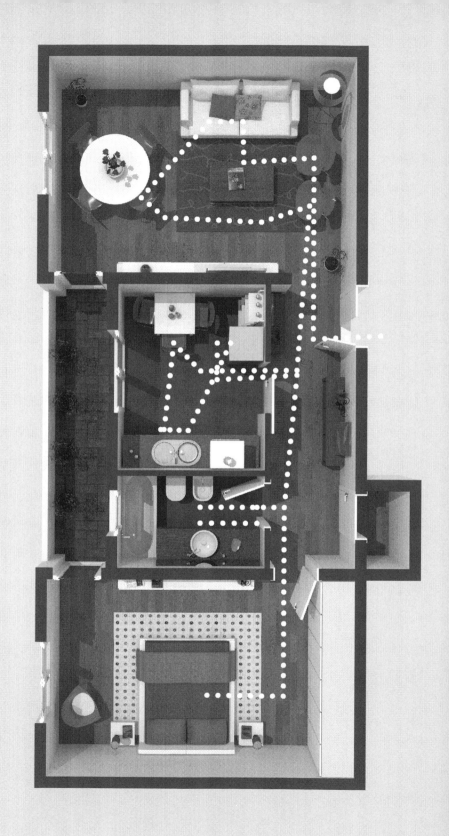

BEHAVIORAL MAP

What is it?
Behavioral mapping is a method used to record and analyze human activities in a location. This method is used to document what participants are doing and time spent at locations and travelling. Behavioral maps can be created based on a person or a space

Who invented it?
Ernest Becker 1962

Why use this method?
1. This method helps develop an understanding of space layouts, interactions and experiences and behaviors.
2. Helps understand way finding.
3. Helps optimize use of space.
4. A limitation of this method is that motivations remain unknown.
5. Use when you want to develop more efficient or effective use of space in retail environments, exhibits, architecture and interior design.

When to use this method
1. Define intent
2. Know Context
3. Know User
4. Frame insights
5. Explore Concepts

Image: Copyright Memendesig...Dreamstime.com

How to use this method
1. Decide who are the users.
2. Ask what is the purpose of the space?
3. Consider what behaviors are meaningful.
4. Consider different personas.
5. Participants can be asked to map their use of a space on a floor plan and can be asked to reveal their motivations.
6. Can use shadowing or video ethnographic techniques.
7. Create behavioral map.
8. Analyze behavioral map
9. Reorganize space based on insights.

Resources
1. A map of the space.
2. Video camera
3. Digital still camera
4. Notebook
5. Pens

References
1. Nickerson 1993: Bnet. Understanding your consumers through behavioral mapping.
2. A Practical Guide to Behavioral Research Tools and Techniques. Fifth Edition Robert Sommer and Barbara Sommer ISBN13: 9780195142099ISBN10: 0195142098 Aug 2001

206

CRITERIA	A	B	C	D	E	F	G	H	I
USABILITY	1	2	3	1	4	1	1	2	3
SPEED TO MARKET	2	1	1	2	2	4	2	1	4
BRAND COMPATIBILITY	3	3	4	1	3	0	3	1	2
RETURN ON INVESTMENT	3	3	5	3	0	3	2	1	3
FITS STRATEGY	2	3	1	1	4	1	1	3	3
AESTHETIC APPEAL	1	1	1	4	0	3	1	2	2
DIFFERENTIATION	2	4	0	2	2	4	0	4	4
TOOLING COST	2	2	2	0	1	1	3	3	0
FITS DISTRIBUTION	2	2	1	1	1	2	0	4	3
USES OUR FACTORY	2	2	3	1	2	1	4	0	3
FITS TRENDS	1	3	2	2	1	3	4	3	2
TOTAL	21	26	23	18	20	23	21	24	29

Sample benchmarking matrix for products

BENCHMARKING

What is it?
Benchmarking is a method for organizations to compare their products, services or customer experiences with other industry products, services and experiences in order to identify the best practices.

Who invented it?
Robert Camp Xerox, 1989
Benchmarking: the search for industry best practices that lead to superior performance.

Why use this method?
1. A tool to identify, establish, and achieve standards of excellence.
2. A structured process of continually searching for the best methods, practices, and processes and either adopting them
3. The practice of measuring your performance against world-class organizations.

When to use this method
1. Define intent
2. Know Context
3. Know User
4. Frame insights

Challenges
1. Can be expensive
2. Organizations often think their companies were above the average for the industry when they are not.

How to use this method
1. Identify what you would like to be bench marked,
2. Define the process,
3. Identify potential partners
4. Identify similar industries and organizations.
5. Identify organizations that are leaders.
6. Identify data sources
7. Identify the products or organizations to be bench marked
8. Select the benchmarking factors to measure.
9. Undertake benchmarking
10. Visit the "best practice" companies to identify leading edge practices
11. Analyze the outcomes
12. Target future performance
13. Adjust goal
14. Modify your own product or service to conform with best practices identified in benchmarking process.

Resources
1. Post-it-notes
2. Pens
3. Dry-erase markers
4. White board
5. Paper

References
1. Benchmarking for Competitive Advantage. Robert J Boxwell Jr, New York: McGraw-Hill. 1994. pp. 225. ISBN 0-07-006899-2.
2. Beating the competition: a practical guide to Benchmarking. Washington, DC: Kaiser Associates. 1988. pp. 176. ISBN 978-1-56365-018-5.

	ACTIVITY PHASE	ACTIVITY PHASE	ACTIVITY PHASE	ACTIVITY PHASE	ACTIVITY PHASE	ACTIVITY PHASE
CUSTOMER ACTIONS	What does user do?					
TOUCHPOINTS	moments places customer contact					
LINE OF INTERACTION						
DIRECT CONTACT	What your Staff do					
LINE OF VISIBILITY						
BACK OFFICE	What your Staff do					
EMOTIONAL EXPERIENCE						

BLUEPRINT

What is it?

A blueprint is a process map often used to describe the delivery of services information is presented as a number of parallel rows of activities. These are sometimes called swim lanes. They may document activities over time such as:

1. Customer Actions
2. Touch points
3. Direct Contact visible to customers
4. Invisible back office actions
5. Support Processes
6. Physical Evidence
7. Emotional Experience for customer.

Who invented it?

Lynn Shostack 1983

When to use this method

1. Know Context
2. Know User
3. Frame insights

WHY TO USE THIS METHOD

1. Can be used for design or improvement of existing services or experiences.
2. Is more tangible than intuition.
3. Makes the process of service development more efficient.
4. A common point of reference for stakeholders for planning and discussion.
5. Tool to assess the impact of change.

How to use this method

1. Define the service or experience to focus on.
2. A blueprint can be created in a brainstorming session with stakeholders.
3. Define the customer demographic.
4. See though the customer's eyes.
5. Define the activities and phases of activity under each heading.
6. Link the contact or customer touchpoints to the needed support functions
7. Use post-it-notes on a white board for initial descriptions and rearrange as necessary drawing lines to show the links.
8. Create the blueprint then refine iteratively.

Resources

1. Paper
2. Pens
3. White board
4. Dry-erase markers
5. Camera
6. Blueprint templates
7. Post-it-notes

References

1. (1991) G. Hollins, W. Hollins, Total Design: Managing the design process in the service sector, Trans Atlantic Publications
2. (2004) R. Kalakota, M.Robinson, Services Blueprint: Roadmap for Execution, Addison-Wesley, Boston.

CULTURAL INVENTORY

What is it?
It is a survey focused on the cultural assets of a location or organization.

Who invented it? Julian Haynes Steward may have been the first to use the term in 1947.

Why use this method?
1. Can be used in strategic planning
2. Can be used to solve problems.

Challenges
1. Requires time and resources

When to use this method
1. Know Context
2. Know User
3. Frame insights
4. Explore Concepts

How to use this method
1. Create your team
2. Collect existing research
3. Review existing research and identify gaps
4. Host a meeting of stakeholders
5. Promote the meeting
6. Ask open-ended questions about the culture and heritage
7. Set a time limit of 2 hours for the meeting.
8. Plan the collection phase
9. Compile inventory. This can be in the form of a web site
10. Distribute the inventory and obtain feedback.

Resources
1. Diary
2. Notebooks
3. Pens
4. Post-it notes
5. Voice recorder
6. Post cards
7. Digital Camera

References
1. Spradley, James P. Participant Observation. Holt, Rinehart and Winston, 1980.

CULTURAL PROBES

What is it?
A cultural probe is a method of collecting information about people, their context and their culture. The aim of this method is to record events, behaviors and interactions in their context. This method involves the participants to record and collect the data themselves.

Who invented it?
Bill Gaver Royal College of Art London 1969

Why use this method?
1. This is a useful method when the participants that are being studied are hard to reach for example if they are travelling.
2. It is a useful technique if the activities being studied take place over an extended period or at irregular intervals.
3. The information collected can be used to build personas.

Challenges?
4. It is important with this method to select the participants carefully and give them support during the study.

When to use this method
1. Define intent
2. Know Context
3. Know User
4. Frame insights

How to use this method
1. Define the objective of your study.
2. Recruit your participants.
3. Brief the participants
4. Supply participants with kit. The items in the kit are selected to collect the type of information you want to gather and can include items such as notebooks, diary, camera, voice recorder or post cards.
5. You can use an affinity diagram to analyze the data collected

Resources
1. Diary
2. Notebooks
3. Pens
4. Post-it notes
5. Voice recorder
6. Post cards
7. Digital Camera

References
1. Bailey, Kathleen M. (1990) The use of diary studies in teacher education programs In Richards, J. C. & Nunan, D. (org.). Second Language Teacher Education (pp. 215-226). Cambridge: Cambridge University Press.

ANTICIPATE ENTER ENGAGE EXIT REVIEW

CUSTOMER MORE POSITIVE EXPERIENCES

CUSTOMER POSITIVE EXPERIENCES

BASELINE

CUSTOMER NEGATIVE EXPERIENCES

CUSTOMER MORE NEGATIVE EXPERIENCES

EMOTIONAL EXPERIENCE

CUSTOMER EXPERIENCE MAP

What is it?
Customer experience also called customer journey mapping is a method of documenting and visualizing the experiences that customers have as they use a product or service and their responses to their experiences.
It allows your team to access and analyze the interacting factors that form a customer experience.

Why use this method?
1. Helps develop a consistent, predictable customer experience,
2. Presents an overview of your customer's experience from their point of view.
3. Helps reduce the number of dissatisfied customers
4. Can be used with different personas.

When to use this method
1. Know Context
2. Know User
3. Frame insights

How to use this method
1. Identify your team.
2. Identify the customer experience to be analyzed. Identify the context. Identify personas.
3. Define the experience as a time line with stages such as anticipation, entry, engagement, exit, and reflection.
4. Use post-it notes to add positive and negative experiences to the relevant parts of the time line.
5. Order the experiences around a baseline by how positive or negative the experience were.
6. Analyze the parts of the time line and activities that have the most negative experiences. These are opportunities for design.

Resources
1. Post-it-notes
2. Printed or projected template
3. White board
4. Markers

References
1. Joshi, Hetal. "Customer Journey Mapping: The Road to Success." Cognizant. (2009) Web. 26 Jul. 2013.
2. World Class Skills Programme. "Customer Journey Mapping." Developing Responsive Provision. (2006): n. page. Web. 27 Jul. 2013.

CAMERA JOURNAL

What is it?
The research subjects record their activities with a camera and notes. The researcher reviews the images and discusses them with the participants.

Why use this method?
1. Helps develop empathy for the participants.
2. Participants are involved in the research process.
3. Helps establish rapport with participants.
4. May reveal aspects of life that are seldom seen by outsiders.

Challenges
1. Should obtain informed consent.
2. May not be ideal for research among particularly vulnerable people.
3. May be a relatively expensive research method.
4. May be time consuming.
5. Best used with other methods.
6. Technology may be unreliable.
7. Method may be unpredictable'.
8. Has to be carefully analyzed

When to use this method
1. Know Context
2. Know User
3. Frame insights

How to use this method
1. Define subject of study
2. Define participants
3. Gather data images and insight statements.
4. Analyze data.
5. Identify insights
6. Rank insights
7. Produce criteria for concept generation from insights.
8. Generate concepts to meet needs of users.

Resources
1. Cameras
2. Voice recorder
3. Video camera
4. Note pad
5. Pens

References
1. Latham, A. (2003). Researching and Writing Everyday Accounts ofthe City: An Introduction to the Diary-Photo Diary-interview Method in Knowles, C and Sweetmen, P (eds) Picturing the Social Landscape: Visual Methods and the Sociological Imagination. London, Routledge.
2. Latham,A.R.(2003)'Research, performance, and doing human geography: some reflections on the diary-photo diary-interview method', Environment and Planning A,35(11),1993-2017

DIARY STUDY

What is it?
This method involves participants recording specific events, feelings or interactions, in a diary supplied by the researcher. User Diaries help provide insight into behavior. Participants record their behavior and thoughts. Diaries can uncover behavior that may not be articulated in an interview or easily visible to outsiders.

Who invented it?
Gordon Allport, may have been the first to describe diary studies in 1942.

Why use this method?
1. Can capture data that is difficult to capture using other methods.
2. Useful when you wish to gather information and minimize your influence on research subjects.
3. When the process or event you're exploring takes place intermittently or
4. When the process or event you're exploring takes place over a long period.

Challenges
1. Process can be expensive and time consuming.
2. Needs participant monitoring.
3. Diary can fit into users' pocket.
4. It is difficult to get materials back.

When to use this method
1. Know Context
2. Know User
3. Frame insights

How to use this method
1. A diary can be kept over a period of one week or longer.
2. Define focus for the study.
3. Recruit participants carefully.
4. Decide method: preprinted, diary notebook or online.
5. Prepare diary packs. Can be preprinted sheets or blank 20 page notebooks with prepared questions or online web based diary.
6. Brief participants.
7. Distribute diaries directly or by mail.
8. Conduct study. Keep in touch with participants.
9. Conduct debrief interview.
10. Look for insights.

Resources
1. Diary
2. Preprinted diary sheets
3. Online diary
4. Pens
5. Disposable cameras
6. Digital camera
7. Self addressed envelopes

References
1. Bailey, Kathleen M. (1990) The use of diary studies in teacher education programs In Richards, J. C. & Nunan, D. (org.). Second Language Teacher Education (pp. 215-226). Cambridge: Cambridge University Press.

DESIGN WORKSHOP

What is it?

A design workshop is a strategic design method that involves bringing the design team together with stakeholders to explore issue related to explore issues related to the people who are being designed for or to create design solutions.

Why use this method?

1. Fast and inexpensive.
2. Increased probability of implementation.
3. Stakeholders can share information.
4. Promotes trust.

Challenges

1. Managing workflow can be challenging.
2. Stakeholders may have conflicting visions.

When to use this method

1. Know Context
2. Know User
3. Frame insights
4. Explore Concepts

How to use this method

1. See charettes and creative toolkits.

Resources

1. Paper flip chart
2. White board
3. Colored markers
4. Cards
5. Masking tape
6. Rolls of butcher paper
7. Post-it notes
8. Adhesive dots
9. Glue
10. Pins
11. Pens
12. Scissors
13. Spray adhesive
14. Screen
15. Laptop
16. Projector
17. Extension leads
18. Video Camera
19. Digital Camera
20. Chairs
21. Tables

DESIGN CHARETTE

What is it?
A design charette is a collaborative design workshop usually held over one day or several days. Charettes are a fast way of generating ideas while involving diverse stakeholders in your decision process. Charettes have many different structures and often involve multiple sessions. The group divides into smaller groups. The smaller groups present to the larger group.

Who invented it?
The French word, "charrette" spelt with two r's means "cart" This use of the term is said to originate from the École des Beaux Arts in Paris during the 19th century, where a cart, collected final drawings while students finished their work.

Why use this method?
1. Fast and inexpensive.
2. Increased probability of implementation.
3. Stakeholders can share information.
4. Promotes trust.

Challenges
1. Managing workflow can be challenging.
2. Stakeholders may have conflicting visions.

When to use this method
1. Define intent
2. Know context and user
3. Frame insights
4. Explore concepts
5. Make Plans

Resources
1. Large space
2. Tables
3. Chairs
4. White boards
5. Dry-erase markers
6. Camera
7. Post-it-notes

References
1. Day, C. (2003). Consensus Design: Socially Inclusive Process. Oxford, UK, and Burlington, MA: Elsevier Science, Architectural Press.

CREATIVE TOOLKITS

What is it?
Collections of modular objects that can be used for participatory modeling and prototyping to inform and inspire design teams. Often used in creative codesign workshops. It is a generative design method which facilitates creative play. The elements can be reused in a number of research sessions in different geographic locations.

Who invented it?
Pioneered by Liz Sanders and Lego
Johan Roos and Bart Victor 1990s.

Why use this method?
Helps develop:
1. Problem solving
2. Change management
3. Strategic thinking
4. Decision making
5. Services, product and experience redesign
6. Can be fun
7. Identify opportunities
8. Re frame challenges
9. Leverages creative thinking of the team

When to use this method
1. Know Context
2. Know User
3. Frame insights
4. Explore Concepts

How to use this method
1. Form cross-disciplinary team 5 to 20 members. It's best to have teams of not more than 8
2. Identify design problem. Create agenda.
3. Start with a warming up exercise.
4. Write design problem in visible location such as white board.
5. Workshop participants first build individual prototypes exploring the problem.
6. Divide larger group into smaller work groups of 3 to 5 participants.
7. Ask each participant to develop between 1 and design solutions. Can use post-it notes or cards.
8. Through internal discussion each group should select their preferred group design solution.
9. The group builds a collective model incorporating the individual contributions.
10. Each group build a physical model of preferred solution and presents it to larger group.
11. Larger group selects their preferred design solutions by discussion and voting.
12. Capture process and ideas with video or photographs.
13. Debriefing and harvest of ideas.

References
1. Statler, M., Roos, J., and B. Victor, 2009, 'Ain't Misbehavin': Taking Play Seriously in Organizations,' Journal of Change Management, 9(1): 87-107.

DRAMATURGY

What is it?
Dramaturgy is a method that uses drama techniques to help understand user behaviors and needs. It a form of prototyping.

Who invented it?
Robert, Benford D., and Scott A. Hunt

Why use this method?
1. Created to make personas more dynamic.

Challenges
1. Some team members may be uncomfortable with drama based activity.
2. The method is not in context
3. The method may be subjective as it does not involve the people being designed for,

When to use this method
4. Know Context
5. Know User
6. Frame insights
7. Explore Concepts

How to use this method
1. Choose a character
2. Create groups of 2 or 3 members of your design team
3. Ask your teams to write monologues for the characters based on public, private and intimate levels.
4. Ask your team to discuss the rituals of the character's lives
5. Ask your team to create maps of the stakeholders
6. Create scenes exploring crucial moments in your character's experiences or interactions.
7. Present these scenarios with groups of actors.
8. Explore the problems and challenges of the character's experiences and interactions.

References
1. Robert, Benford D., and Scott A. Hunt. "Dramaturgy and Social Movements: The Social Construction and Communication of Power." Social Inquiry 62.1 (2007): 36–55. Wiley Online Library.

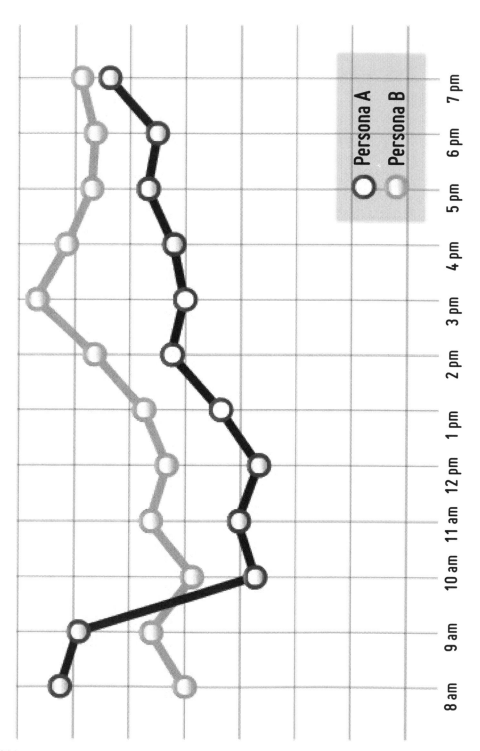

EMOTIONAL JOURNEY MAP

What is it?
An emotional journey map is a map that visually illustrates people's emotional experience throughout an interaction with an organization or brand.

Why use this method?
1. It provides a focus for discussion
2. It focusses on what may make your customers unhappy
3. Provides a visually compelling story of customer experience.
4. Customer experience is more than interaction with a product.
5. By understanding the journey that your customers are making, you will be in a position to make informed improvements.

Challenges
1. Customers often do not take the route in an interaction that the designer expects.
2. Failure to manage experiences can lead to lost customers.

When to use this method
1. Know Context
2. Know User
3. Frame insights
4. Explore Concepts
5. Make Plans

How to use this method
1. Define the activity of your map. For example it could be a ride on the underground train.
2. Collect internal insights
3. Research customer perceptions
4. Analyze research
5. Map journey.
6. Across the top of the page do a time line Break the journey into stages using your customer's point of view
7. Capture each persona's unique experience
8. Use a scale from 0 to 10. The higher the number, the better the experience.
9. Plot the emotional journey.
10. Analyze the lease pleasant emotional periods and create ideas for improving the experience during those periods.
11. Create a map for each persona.

Resources
1. Paper
2. Pens
3. White board
4. Post-it-notes

References
1. Joshi, Hetal. "Customer Journey Mapping: The Road to Success." Cognizant. (2009) Web. 26 Jul. 2013.
2. World Class Skills Programme. "Customer Journey Mapping." Developing Responsive Provision. (2006): n. page. Web. 27 Jul. 2013.

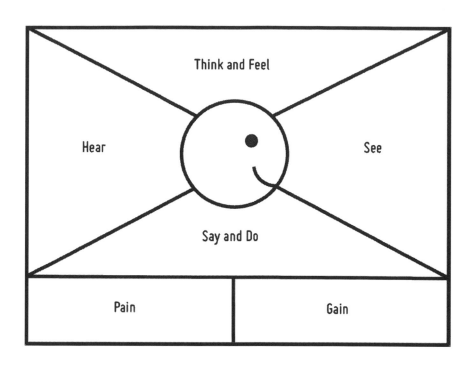

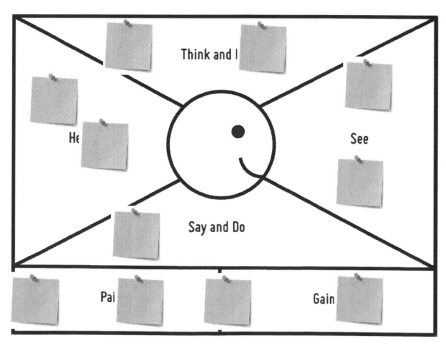

EMPATHY MAP

What is it?
Empathy Map is a tool that helps the design team empathize with people they are designing for, You can create an empathy map for a group of customers or a persona.

Who invented it?
Scott Matthews and Dave Gray at PLANE now Dachis Group.

Why use this method?
This tool helps a design team understand the customers and their context.

Challenges
1. Emotions must be inferred by observing clues.
2. This method does not provide the same level of rigor as traditional personas but requires less investment.

When to use this method
1. Know Context
2. Know User
3. Frame insights

Resources
1. Empathy map template
2. White board
3. Dry-erase markers
4. Post-it-notes
5. Pens
6. Video Camera

How to use this method
1. A team of 3 to 10 people is a good number for this method.
2. This method can be used with personas.
3. Draw a cirle to represent your target persona.
4. Divide the circle into sections that represent aspects of that person's sensory experience.
5. Ask your team to describe from the persona's point of view their experience.
6. What are the persona's needs and desires?
7. Populate the map by taking note of the following traits of your user as you review your notes, audio, and video from your fieldwork: What are they thinking, feeling, saying, doing, hearing, seeing?
8. Fill in the diagram with real, tangible, sensory experiences.
9. 20 minutes to one hour is a good duration for this exercise.
10. Ask another group of people to look at your map and suggest improvements or refinements.

References
1. Gray, Dave; Brown, Sunni; Macanufo, James (2010). Gamestorming: A Playbook for Innovators, Rulebreakers, and Changemakers. O'Reilly Media, Inc

EMPATHY PROBES

What is it?
This method involves participants recording specific events, feelings or interactions, in a diary supplied by the researcher. User Diaries help provide insight into behavior. Participants record their behavior and thoughts. Diaries can uncover behavior that may not be articulated in an interview or easily visible to outsiders.

Who invented it?
Gordon Allport, may have been the first to describe diary studies in 1942.

Why use this method?
Can capture data that is difficult to capture using other methods.
1. Cultural probes are appropriate when you need to gather information from users with minimal influence on their actions,
2. When the process or event you're exploring takes place intermittently or
3. When the process or event you're exploring takes place over a long period.

Challenges
1. Process can be expensive and time consuming.
2. Needs participant monitoring.
3. Diary can fit into users' pocket.
4. It is difficult to get materials back.

When to use this method
1. Know Context
2. Know User
3. Frame insights

How to use this method
1. A diary can be kept over a period of one week or longer.
2. Define focus for the study.
3. Recruit participants carefully.
4. Decide method: preprinted, diary notebook or online.
5. Prepare diary packs. Can be preprinted sheets or blank 20 page notebooks with prepared questions or online web based diary.
6. Brief participants.
7. Distribute diaries directly or by mail.
8. Conduct study. Keep in touch with participants.
9. Conduct debrief interview.
10. Look for insights.

Resources
1. Diary
2. Preprinted diary sheets
3. Online diary
4. Pens
5. Disposable cameras
6. Digital camera
7. Self addressed envelopes

References
1. Bailey, Kathleen M. (1990) The use of diary studies in teacher education programs In Richards, J. C. & Nunan, D. (org.). Second Language Teacher Education (pp. 215–226). Cambridge: Cambridge University Press.

EMPATHY TOOLS

What is it?
Empathy tools are aids or tools that help designers empathize with the people they are designing for. They can be used to test a prototype design or in activities such as role playing or body storming.

Who invented it?
Brandt, E. and Grunnet, C 2000

Why use this method?
1. To help a designer understand the experiences of people that they are designing for.

Challenges
1. Empathy tools are imperfect approximations of user experiences.

When to use this method
1. Know Context
2. Know User
3. Frame insights
4. Explore Concept

How to use this method
1. Wear heavy gloves to experience less sensitivity in your hands
2. Wear fogged glasses to experience less acute vision
3. Wear black glasses to eat to experience issues locating food and utensils.
4. Spend a day in a wheelchair.
5. Wear earplugs to experience diminished hearing

Resources
1. Wheelchair
2. Fogged glasses
3. Blackened glasses
4. Gloves
5. Earplugs
6. Crutches
7. Walking stick

References
1. Brandt, E. and Grunnet, C., "Evoking the Future: Drama and Props in User-centered Design", PDC 2000

EYETRACKING

What is it?
Eye tracking is a group of methods of studying and recording a person's eye movements over time. The most widely used current designs are video-based eye trackers. One of the most prominent fields of commercial eye tracking research is web usability but this method is also used widely for evaluating retail interiors and products.

Who invented it?
Louis Émile Javal 1879
Alfred L. Yarbus 1950s

Why use this method?
1. Examine which details attract attention.
2. To record where a participant's attention is focussed for example on a supermarket shelf which products and parts of products attract the most attention from shoppers.

Challenges
1. Each method of eye tracking has advantages and disadvantages, and the choice of an eye tracking system depends on considerations of cost and application.
2. A poorly adjusted system can produce unreliable information.

When to use this method
1. Know Context
2. Know User
3. Explore Concepts

Types of systems
1. Measures eye movement with a device attached to the eye. For example a contact lens with a magnetic field sensor.
2. Non contact measurement of eye movement. For example infrared, is reflected from the eye and sensed by a video camera.
3. Measures eye movement with electrodes placed around the eyes.

Types of outputs
1. Heat maps
2. Gaze plots
3. Gaze replays

Resources
1. Eye tracking device
2. Software
3. Laptop computer

References
1. Bojko, A. (2006). Using Eye Tracking to Compare Web Page Designs: A Case Study. Journal of Usability Studies, Vol.1, No. 3.
2. Chandon, Pierre, J. Wesley Hutchinson, and Scott H. Young (2001), Measuring Value of Point-of-Purchase Marketing with Commercial Eye-Tracking Data.
3. Wedel, M. & Pieters, R. (2000). Eye fixations on advertisements and memory for brands: a model and findings. Marketing Science, 19 (4), 2000, 297–312.

FLY-ON-THE-WALL

What is it?
Observation method where the observer remains as unobtrusive as possible and observes and collects data relevant to a research study in context with no interaction with the participants being observed. The name derived from the documentary film technique of the same name.

Who invented it?
ALex Bavelas 1944
Lucy Vernile, Robert A. Monteiro 1991

Why use this method?
1. Low cost
2. No setup necessary
3. Can observe a large number of participants.
4. Objective observations
5. Compared to other methods such as focus groups, setup, data collection, and processing are much faster.

Challenges
1. No interaction by the observer.
2. Observer cannot delve deeper during a session.
3. No interruption allowed
4. Observer cannot obtain details on customer comments during a session

When to use this method
1. Know Context
2. Know User
3. Frame insights

How to use this method
1. Define activity to study
2. Select participants thoughtfully
3. Choose a context for the observation
4. Carefully observe the interaction or experience. This is best done by members of your design team.
5. It is important to influence the participants as little as possible by your presence.
6. Observe but do not interact with participants while observing them in context.
7. Capture Data
8. Identify issues
9. Identify needs
10. Create design solutions based on observed and experienced human needs.

Resources
1. Digital camera
2. Video camera
3. Notebook
4. Pens
5. Voice recorder

References
1. McDonald, Seonaidh. "Studying Actions in Context: A Qualitative Shadowing Method for Organizational Research." Qualitative Research. The Robert Gordon University. SAGE Publications. London. 2005. p455-473.

INNOVATION DIAGNOSTIC

What is it?
An innovation diagnostic is an evaluation of an organization's innovation capabilities. It reviews practices by stakeholders which may help or hinder innovation. An innovation diagnostic is the first step in preparing an implementing a strategy to create an organizational culture that supports innovation.

Why use this method?
1. It helps organizations develop sustainable competitive advantage.
2. Helps identify innovation opportunities
3. Helps develop innovation strategy.

When to use this method
4. Know Context
5. Know User
6. Frame insights
7. Explore Concepts
8. Make Plans

How to use this method
An innovation diagnostic reviews organizational and stakeholder practices using both qualitative and quantitative methods including
1. The design and development process
2. Strategic practices and planning.
3. The ability of an organization to monitor and respond to relevant trends.
4. Technologies
5. Organizational flexibility
6. Ability to innovate repeatedly and consistently

References
1. It Byrd, Jacqueline and Paul Lockwood Brown. The Innovation Equation: Building Creativity and Risk-Taking in Your Organization. Chapter One: Perspectives on Innovation. September 2002
2. Chesbrough, Henry William. Open Innovation: The New Imperative for Creating and Profiting from Technology. 2003.
3. Kandybin, Alexander and Martin Kihn. "Raising Your Return on Innovation Investment. strategy+business . May 11, 2004
4. Christensen, Clayton M.and Michael E. Raynor. The Innovator's Solution: Creating and Sustaining Successful Growth.2003
5. Akgun, A. E., Lynn, G.S., & Byrne, J.C. (2004). "Taking the Guess Work out of New ProductDevelopment: How successful high-tech companies get that way."Journal of Business Strategy 25(4): 41-46
6. Branzei, O. & Vertinsky, I. (2006) "Strategic pathways to product innovation capabilities inSMEs"Journal of Business Venturing 21 : 71-105

DAY IN THE LIFE

What is it?
A study in which the designer observes the participant in the location and context of their usual activities, observing and recording events to understand the activities from the participant's point of view. This is sometimes repeated. Mapping a 'Day in the Life' as a storyboard can provide a focus for discussion.

Who invented it?
ALex Bavelas 1944

Why use this method?
1. This method informs the design process by observation of real activities and behaviors.
2. This method provides insights with relatively little cost and time.

Challenges
1. Choose the participants carefully *
2. Document everything. Something that seems insignificant may become significant later.

When to use this method
1. Know Context
2. Know User
3. Frame insights

How to use this method
1. Define activities to study
2. Recruit participants
3. Prepare
4. Observe subjects in context.
5. Capture data,
6. Create storyboard with text and timeline.
7. Analyze data
8. Create insights.
9. Identify issues
10. Identify needs
11. Add new/more requirements to concept development

Resources
1. Camera
2. Notebook
3. Video camera
4. Voice recorder
5. Pens

References
1. Shadowing: And Other Techniques for Doing Fieldwork in Modern Societies [Paperback] Barbara Czarniawska. Publisher: Copenhagen Business School Pr (December 2007) ISBN-10: 8763002159 ISBN-13: 978-8763002158

INTERVIEW METHODS

What is it?
An interview is a conversation where questions are asked to obtain information.

Why use this method?
Contextual interviews uncover tacit knowledge about people's context that the people may not be consciously aware of. The information gathered can be detailed.

Challenges
1. Keep control
2. Be prepared
3. Be aware of bias
4. Be neutral
5. Select location carefully

Resources
6. Note pad
7. Confidentiality agreement
8. Digital voice recorder
9. Video camera
10. Digital still camera

When to use this method
1. Know Context
2. Know User
3. Frame insights

How to use this method
1. Contextual inquiry may be structured as 2 hour one on one interviews.
2. The researcher does not usually impose tasks on the user.
3. Go to the user's context. Talk, watch listen and observe.
4. Understand likes and dislikes.
5. Collect stories and insights.
6. See the world from the user's point of view.
7. Take permission to conduct interviews.
8. Do one-on-one interviews.
9. The researcher listens to the user.
10. 2 to 3 researchers conduct an interview.
11. Understand relationship between people, product and context.
12. Document with video, audio and notes.

Resources
1. Computer
2. Notebook
3. Pens
4. Video camera
5. Release forms
6. Interview plan or structure
7. Questions, tasks and discussion items
8. Confidentiality agreement

References
1. Kvale, Steinar. Interviews: An Introduction to Qualitative Research Interviewing, Sage Publications, 1996
2. Foddy, William. Constructing Questions for Interviews, Cambridge University Press, 1993

INTERVIEW: CONTEXTUAL INQUIRY

What is it?

Contextual inquiry involves one-on-one observations and interviews of activities in the context. Contextual inquiry has four guiding principles:

1. Context
2. Partnership with users.
3. Interpretation
4. Focus on particular goals.

Who invented it?

Whiteside, Bennet, and Holtzblatt 1988

Why use this method

1. Contextual interviews uncover tacit knowledge about people's context.
2. The information gathered can be detailed.
3. The information produced by contextual inquiry is relatively reliable

Challenges

1. End users may not have the answers
2. Contextual inquiry may be difficult to challenge even if it is misleading.

When to use this method

1. Know Context
2. Know User
3. Frame insights

How to use this method

1. Contextual inquiry may be structured as 2 hour one on one interviews.
2. The researcher does not usually impose tasks on the user.
3. Go to the user's context. Talk, watch listen and observe.
4. Understand likes and dislikes.
5. Collect stories and insights.
6. See the world from the user's point of view.
7. Take permission to conduct interviews.
8. Do one-on-one interviews.
9. The researcher listens to the user.
10. 2 to 3 researchers conduct an interview.
11. Understand relationship between people, product and context.
12. Document with video, audio and notes.

References

1. Beyer, H. and Holtzblatt, K., Contextual Design: Defining Customer-Centered Systems, Morgan Kaufmann Publishers Inc., San Francisco (1997).
2. Wixon and J. Ramey (Eds.), Field Methods Case Book for Product Design. John Wiley & Sons, Inc., NY, NY, 1996.

INTERVIEW: CONTEXTUAL LADDERING

What is it?
Contextual laddering is a one-on-one interviewing technique done in context. Answers are further explored by the researcher to uncover root causes or core values.

Who invented it?
Gutman 1982, Olsen and Reynolds 2001.

Why use this method?
1. Laddering can uncover underlying reasons for particular behaviors.
2. Laddering may uncover information not revealed by other methods.
3. Complement other methods
4. Link features and product attributes with user/customer values

Challenges
1. Analysis of data is sometimes difficult.
2. Requires a skilled interviewer who can keep the participants engaged.
3. Laddering may be repetitive
4. Sometimes information may not be represented hierarchically.

When to use this method
1. Know Context
2. Know User
3. Explore Concepts

Image Copyright 2013 iofoto
rom Shutterstock.com

How to use this method
1. Interviews typically take 60 to 90 minutes.
2. The introduction. The researcher gives information about the length of the interview, content, confidentiality and method of recording.
3. The body of the interview. The researcher investigates the user in context and documents the information gathered.
4. Ask participants to describe what kinds of features would be useful in or distinguish different products.
5. Ask why.
6. If this answer doesn't describe the root motivation ask why again.
7. Repeat step 3. until you have reached the root motivation.
8. Wrap up. Verification and clarification

Resources
1. Note pad
2. Confidentiality agreement
3. Digital voice recorder
4. Video camera
5. Digital still camera
6. Interview plan or structure
7. Questions, tasks and discussion items

References
1. Reynolds TJ, Gutman J (2001) Laddering theory, method, analysis, and interpretation. In: Reynolds TJ et al (eds) Understanding consumer decision making. The means-end approach to marketing and advertising strategy. Lawrence Erlbaum associates, New Jersey, pp 25—62

234

INTERVIEW: CONVERSATION CARDS

What is it?
Cards used for initiating conversation in a contextual interview and to help subjects explore.

Who invented it?
Originator unknown. Google Ngram indicates the term first appeared around 1801 in England for a collection of "Moral and Religious Anecdotes particularly adapted for the entertainment and instruction of young persons, and to support instead of destroying serious conversation"

Why use this method?
1. Questions are the springboard for conversations.
2. Can be used to initiate sensitive conversations.

Challenges
1. How will data from the cards be used?
2. How will cards be evaluated?
3. How many cards are necessary to be representative?
4. What are potential problems relating card engagement
5. Use one unit of information per question.

When to use this method
1. Know Context
2. Know User
3. Frame insights

How to use this method
1. Decide on goal for research.
2. Formulate about 10 questions related to topic
3. Create the cards.
4. Recruit the subjects.
5. Undertake pre interview with sample subject to test.
6. Use release form if required.
7. Carry light equipment.
8. Record answers verbatim.
9. Communicate the purpose and length of the interview.
10. Select location. It should not be too noisy or have other distracting influences
11. Work through the cards.
12. Video or record the sessions for later review.
13. Analyze
14. Create Insights

Resources
1. Conversation Cards.
2. Notebook
3. Video Camera
4. Pens
5. Interview plan or structure
6. Questions, tasks and discussion items

References
1. Rubin, Herbert and Irene Rubin. Qualitative Interviewing: The Art of Hearing Data. 2nd edition. Thousand Oaks, CA: Sage Publications, 2004. Print.
2. Kvale, Steinar. Interviews: An Introduction to Qualitative Research Interviewing, Sage Publications, 1996

INTERVIEW: EMOTION CARDS

What is it?
Emotion cards are a field method of analyzing and quantifying peoples emotional response to a design. The method classifies emotions into sets of emotions which each can be associated with a specific recognizable facial expression.

The emotion card tool consists of sixteen cartoon-like faces, half male and half female, each representing distinct emotions. Each face represents a combination of two emotion dimensions,Pleasure and Arousal. Based on these dimensions, the emotion cards can be divided into four quadrants: Calm-Pleasant, Calm-Unpleasant, Excited-Pleasant, and Excited-Unpleasant.

Who invented it?
Bradley 1994
Pieter Desmet 2001

Why use this method?
1. It is an inexpensive method.
2. The results are easy to analyze.
3. Emotional responses are subtle and difficult to measure.
4. Emotion cards is a cross-cultural tool.
5. Facial emotions are typically universally recognized

Challenges
1. Emotions of male and female faces are interpreted differently.
2. Sometimes users want to mark more than one picture to express a more complex

emotional response.

When to use this method
1. Know Context
2. Know User
3. Frame insights
4. Explore Concepts

How to use this method
1. Decide the goal of the study.
2. Recruit the participants.
3. Brief the participants.
4. When each interaction is complete the researcher asks the participant to select one of a number of cards that shows facial expressions that they associate with the interaction.

Resources
1. Emotion cards
2. Notebook
3. Pens
4. Video camera
5. Release forms
6. Interview plan or structure
7. Questions, tasks and discussion items

References
1. Desmet, P.M.A. Emotion through expression;designing mobile telephones with an emotional fit. Report of Modeling the Evaluation Structure of KANSEI, 3 (2000), 103-110.

INTERVIEW: E-MAIL

What is it?
With this method an interview is conducted via an e-mail exchange.

Why use this method?
1. Extended access to people.
2. Background noises are not recorded.
3. Interviewee can answer the questions at his or her own convenience
4. It is not necessary to take notes
5. It is possible to use online translators.
6. Interviewees do not have to identify a convenient time to talk.

Challenges
1. Interviewer may have to wait for answers.
2. Interviewer is disconnected from context.
3. Lack of communication of body language.

When to use this method
1. Know Context
2. Know User
3. Frame insight

How to use this method
1. Choose a topic
2. Identify a subject.
3. Contact subject and obtain approval.
4. Prepare interview questions.
5. Conduct interview
6. Analyze data.

Resources
1. Computer
2. Internet connection
3. Notebook
4. Pens
5. Interview plan or structure
6. Questions, tasks and discussion items
7. Confidentiality agreement

References
1. Foddy, William. Constructing Questions for Interviews, Cambridge University Press, 1993

INTERVIEW: EXTREME USER

What is it?
Interview experienced or inexperienced users of a product or service. in order to discover useful insights that can be applied to the general users.

Why use this method?
Extreme user's solutions to problems can inspire solutions for general users. Their behavior can be more exaggerated than general users so it is sometimes easier to develop useful insights from these groups.

Challenges
1. Keep control
2. Be prepared
3. Be aware of bias
4. Be neutral
5. Select location carefully

When to use this method
1. Know Context
2. Know User
3. Frame insights
4. Explore Concepts

How to use this method
1. Do a timeline of your activity and break it into main activities
2. Identify very experienced or very inexperienced users of a product or service in an activity area.
3. Explore their experiences through interview.
4. Discover insights that can inspire design.
5. Refine design based on insights.

Resources
1. Computer
2. Notebook
3. Pens
4. Video camera
5. Release forms
6. Interview plan or structure
7. Questions, tasks and discussion items
8. Confidentiality agreement

References
1. Rubin, Herbert and Irene Rubin. Qualitative Interviewing: The Art of Hearing Data. 2nd edition. Thousand Oaks, CA: Sage Publications, 2004. Print.
2. Kvale, Steinar. Interviews: An Introduction to Qualitative Research Interviewing, Sage Publications, 1996
3. Foddy, William. Constructing Questions for Interviews, Cambridge University Press, 1993

INTERVIEW: GROUP

What is it?
This method involves interviewing a group of people.

Why use this method?
People will often give different answers to questions if interviewed on=on=-one and in groups. If resources are available it is useful to interview people in both situations.

Challenges
1. Group interview process is longer than an individual interview

When to use this method
1. Know Context
2. Know User
3. Frame insight

Resources
1. Computer
2. Notebook
3. Pens
4. Video camera
5. Release forms
6. Interview plan or structure
7. Questions, tasks and discussion items
8. Confidentiality agreement

How to use this method
1. Welcome everyone and introduce yourself
2. Describe the process.
3. Ask everyone to introduce themselves.
4. Conduct a group activity or warming-up exercise.
5. Break the larger group into smaller groups of 4 or 5 people and give them a question to answer. Ask each participant to present their response to the larger group.
6. Allow about 25 minutes.
7. Ask each interviewee to write a summary
8. Collect the summaries.
9. Ask if have any further comments.
10. Thank everyone and explain the next steps.
11. Give them your contact details.

References
12. Kvale, Steinar. Interviews: An Introduction to Qualitative Research Interviewing, Sage Publications, 1996
13. Foddy, William. Constructing Questions for Interviews, Cambridge University Press, 1993

INTERVIEW:
GUIDED STORYTELLING

What is it?
Guided storytelling is interview technique, where the designer asks a participant to walk you through a scenario of use for a concept. Directed story telling guides participants to describe their experiences and thoughts on a specific topic.

Who invented it?
Whiteside, Bennet, and Holtzblatt 1988

Why use this method?
1. Guided storytelling uncovers tacit knowledge.

Challenges
1. Keep control
2. Be prepared
3. Be aware of bias
4. Be neutral
5. Select location carefully

When to use this method
1. Know Context
2. Know User
3. Frame insight

Resources
1. Computer
2. Notebook
3. Pens
4. Video camera

5. Release forms
6. Interview plan or structure
7. Questions, tasks and discussion items
8. Confidentiality agreement

How to use this method
1. Contextual inquiry may be structured as 2 hour one on one interviews.
2. The researcher does not usually impose tasks on the user.
3. Go to the user's context. Talk, watch listen and observe.
4. Understand likes and dislikes.
5. Collect stories and insights.
6. See the world from the user's point of view.
7. Take permission to conduct interviews.
8. Do one-on-one interviews.
9. The researcher listens to the user.
10. 2 to 3 researchers conduct an interview.
11. Understand relationship between people, product and context.

References
1. Rubin, Herbert and Irene Rubin. Qualitative Interviewing: The Art of Hearing Data. 2nd edition. Thousand Oaks, CA: Sage Publications, 2004. Print.
2. Kvale, Steinar. Interviews: An Introduction to Qualitative Research Interviewing, Sage Publications, 1996
3. Foddy, William. Constructing Questions for Interviews, Cambridge University Press, 1993

INTERVIEW: MAN IN THE STREET

What is it?
Man in the street interviews are impromptu interviews usually recorded on video. They are usually conducted by two people, a researcher and a cameraman.

Why use this method?
1. Contextual interviews uncover tacit knowledge.
2. The information gathered can be detailed.

Challenges
1. Keep control
2. Be prepared
3. Be aware of bias
4. Be neutral
5. Ask appropriate questions
6. Select location carefully
7. Create a friendly atmosphere, interviewee to feel relaxed.
8. Clearly convey the purpose of the interview.
9. This method results in accidental sampling which may not be representative of larger groups.

When to use this method
1. Know Context
2. Know User
3. Frame insights

How to use this method
1. Decide on goal for research.
2. Formulate about 10 questions related to topic
3. Use release form if required.
4. Conduct a preliminary interview.
5. Select location. It should not be too noisy or have other distracting influences
6. Approach people, be polite. Say, "Excuse me, I work for [your organization] and I was wondering if you could share your opinion about [your topic]."
7. If someone does not wish to respond, select another subject to interview.
8. Limit your time. Each interview should be no be longer than about 10 minutes.
9. Conduct 6 to 10 interviews

Resources
1. Video camera
2. release forms

References
1. Rubin, Herbert and Irene Rubin. Qualitative Interviewing: The Art of Hearing Data. 2nd edition. Thousand Oaks, CA: Sage Publications, 2004. Print.
2. Kvale, Steinar. Interviews: An Introduction to Qualitative Research Interviewing, Sage Publications, 1996
3. Foddy, William. Constructing Questions for Interviews, Cambridge University Press, 1993

INTERVIEW: NATURALISTIC GROUP

What is it?

Naturalistic group interview is an interview method where the participants know each other prior to the interview and so have conversations that are more natural than participants who do not know each other.

Why use this method?

1. This method has been applied in research in Asia where beliefs are informed by group interaction.
2. Can help gain useful data in cultures where people are less willing to share their feelings.

Challenges

1. Familiarity of participants can lead to groupthink.

When to use this method

2. Know Context
3. Know User

How to use this method

1. The interview context should support natural conversation.
2. Select participants who have existing social relationships.
3. Group the participants in natural ways so that the conversation is as close as possible to the type of discussion they would have in their everyday life.
4. Groups should be no larger than four people for best results.

Resources

1. Video camera
2. Note pad
3. Pens
4. Use local moderator

References

1. Bengtsson, Anders, and Giana M. Eckhardt. "Naturalistic Group Interviewing in China." Qualitative Market Research: An International Journal. 12:1 (2010): 36-44.

INTERVIEW: ONE-ON-ONE

What is it?
The one-on-one interview is an interview that is between a researcher and one participant in a face-to-face situation.

Why use this method?
1. The best method for personal information
2. Works well with other methods in obtaining information to inform design.
3. Can be used to exchange ideas or to gather information to inform design

Challenges
1. Keep control
2. Be prepared
3. Be aware of bias
4. Be neutral
5. Select location carefully
6. Record everything
7. Combine one on one interviews with group interviews.

When to use this method
1. Know Context
2. Know User
3. Frame insights

Resources
4. Notebook
5. Pens
6. Video camera
7. Release forms
8. Interview plan
9. Questions, and tasks

How to use this method
1. May be structured as 2 hour one on one interviews.
2. Select the questions and the subjects carefully.
3. Create interview guide,
4. Conduct a preinterview to refine the guide.
5. The researcher does not usually impose tasks on the user.
6. Go to the user's context. Talk, watch listen and observe.
7. Understand likes and dislikes.
8. Collect stories and insights.
9. See the world from the user's point of view.
10. Take permission to conduct interviews.
11. Understand relationship between person, product and context.
12. Document with video, audio and notes.

References
1. Rubin, Herbert and Irene Rubin. Qualitative Interviewing: The Art of Hearing Data. 2nd edition. Thousand Oaks, CA: Sage Publications, 2004. Print.
2. Kvale, Steinar. Interviews: An Introduction to Qualitative Research Interviewing, Sage Publications, 1996
3. Foddy, William. Constructing Questions for Interviews, Cambridge University Press, 1993

INTERVIEWS: PHOTO ELICITATION

What is it?
Photos are used by a researcher as a focus to discuss the experiences, thoughts and feelings of participants.

Why use this method?
1. A method sometimes used to interview children.
2. Photos can make staring a conversation with a participant easier.
3. Photos can uncover meaning which is not uncovered in a face to face interview.

Challenges
1. Photos can create ethical questions for the researcher.
2. A researcher may show bias in selecting subject of photos.

Resources
1. Note pad
2. Pens
3. Camera
4. Video camera
5. Digital voice recorder

When to use this method
1. Know Context
2. Know User

How to use this method
1. Define the context.
2. Select the participants
3. Either researcher or participant may take the photos.
4. Researcher analyses photos and plans the interview process
5. Researcher shows the photos to the participant and discusses their thoughts in relation to the photographs.
6. The interview is analyzed by the researcher.
7. The researcher creates a list of insights.

References
1. M. Clark-Ibáñez. Framing the social world with photo-elicitation interviews. American Behavioral Scientist,47(12):1507--1527, 2004.

INTERVIEW: STRUCTURED

What is it?
In a structured interview the researcher prepares a list of questions, script or an interview guide that they follow during the interview. Most interviews use a structured method.

Why use this method?
1. A structured interview is often used for for phone interviews.
2. It is easy to analyze the results.
3. Structured interviews are often used by quantitative researchers.

Challenges
1. Respondents may be less likely to discuss sensitive experiences.

When to use this method
1. Know Context
2. Know User
3. Frame insight

How to use this method
1. The researcher should follow the script exactly.
2. The interviewer is required to show consistency in behavior across all interviews

Resources
1. Computer
2. Notebook
3. Pens
4. Video camera
5. Release forms
6. Interview plan
7. Questions, and tasks
8. Confidentiality agreement

References
1. Rubin, Herbert and Irene Rubin. Qualitative Interviewing: The Art of Hearing Data. 2nd edition. Thousand Oaks, CA: Sage Publications, 2004. Print.
2. Kvale, Steinar. Interviews: An Introduction to Qualitative Research Interviewing, Sage Publications, 1996
3. Foddy, William. Constructing Questions for Interviews, Cambridge University Press, 1993

INTERVIEW: UNSTRUCTURED

What is it?
Unstructured interviews are interviews where questions can be modified as needed by the researcher during the interview.

Why use this method?
1. A useful technique for understanding how a subject may perform under pressure.
2. Unstructured interviews are used in ethnographies and case studies
3. Respondents may be more likely to discuss sensitive experiences.

Challenges
1. Interviewer bias is unavoidable

When to use this method
1. Know Context
2. Know User
3. Frame insight

How to use this method
1. Researchers need a list of topics to be covered during the interview

Resources
1. Computer
2. Notebook
3. Pens
4. Video camera
5. Release forms
6. Interview plan
7. Questions, and tasks
8. Confidentiality agreement

References
1. Rubin, Herbert and Irene Rubin. Qualitative Interviewing: The Art of Hearing Data. 2nd edition. Thousand Oaks, CA: Sage Publications, 2004. Print.
2. Kvale, Steinar. Interviews: An Introduction to Qualitative Research Interviewing, Sage Publications, 1996
3. Foddy, William. Constructing Questions for Interviews, Cambridge University Press, 1993

INTERVIEW: TELEPHONE

What is it?
With this method an interview is conducted via telephone.

Who invented it?

Why use this method?
Wide geographical access
1. Allows researcher to reach hard to reach people.
2. Allows researcher to access closed locations.
3. Access to dangerous or politically sensitive sites

Challenges
1. Lack of communication of body language.
2. Interviewer is disconnected from context.

When to use this method
1. Know Context
2. Know User
3. Frame insight

How to use this method
1. Choose a topic
2. Identify a subject.
3. Contact subject and obtain approval.
4. Prepare interview questions.
5. Conduct interview
6. Analyze data.

Resources
7. Computer
8. Notebook
9. Pens

References
1. Rubin, Herbert and Irene Rubin. Qualitative Interviewing: The Art of Hearing Data. 2nd edition. Thousand Oaks, CA: Sage Publications, 2004. Print.
2. Kvale, Steinar. Interviews: An Introduction to Qualitative Research Interviewing, Sage Publications, 1996
3. Foddy, William. Constructing Questions for Interviews, Cambridge University Press, 1993

MAGIC THING

What is it?

A Magic Thing is a prop that is a focus for ideas in the context where an proposed design will be used. It can be a material such as wood or hard foam without surface detail. Participants carry a "magic thing" with them as they undertake their activities in context to imagine how a portable device could function.

Who invented it?

Jeff Hawkins. Howard 2002. Jeff Hawkins, one of the inventors of the Palm Pilot PDA, carried a small block of wood to help him brainstorm interaction in various environments.

Why use this method?

1. It is a form of physical prototype that simulates interaction when little information is available.

Challenges

1. The researcher can put some imaginary constraints on the device so that it's technological capabilities are not too far from reality.

When to use this method

1. Know Context
2. Know User
3. Frame insights
4. Generate Concepts
5. Create Solutions

How to use this method

1. The researcher briefs the participants on a design scenario.
2. The participants are given a prop, their magic thing.
3. The participants are briefed on the technological capabilities of the magic thing.
4. The participants and design team then act out scenarios in context.
5. The role playing is recorded by video or user diaries.
6. The material is analyzed and insights identified.

Resources

1. A magic thing such as a block of wood about the size of a proposed device.
2. Video camera

References

1. Lacucci, G., Mäkelä A., Ranta, M., Mäntylä, M., Visualizing Context, Mobility and Group Interaction: Role Games to Design Product Concepts for Mobile Communication, In: the Proceeding of COOP'2000, Designing Cooperative Systems Conference, 23–26 May 2000, IOS Press, 2000.

METHOD BANK

What is it?
A Method Bank is a central bank where design methods are documented by an organization's employees and can be accessed and applied by other employees.

Who invented it?
1. Lego have compiled a Design Practice and emerging methods bank. Microsoft have a methods bank in their Online User Experience best practice intranet.
2. Starbucks have a methods bank in their online workflow management tool

Why use this method?
1. This approaches helps document tacit knowledge within an organization.

When to use this method
1. Define intent
2. Know Context
3. Know User
4. Frame insights
5. Explore Concepts
6. Make Plans
7. Deliver Offering

How to use this method
1. Methods are uploaded to the intranet bank.
2. The bank may include descriptions, video, images charts or sketches.

Resources
1. Intranet
2. Camera
3. Video camera
4. Templates
5. Data base.
6. Computers

MOBILE DIARY STUDY

What is it?
A mobile diary studies is a method that uses portable devices to capture a person's experiences in context when and where they happen such as their work place or home. Participants can create diary entries from their location on mobile phones or tablets.

Why use this method?
1. Most people carry a mobile phone.
2. It is a convenient method of recording diary entries.
3. It is easier to collect the data than collecting written diaries.
4. Collection of data happens in real time.
5. Mobile devices have camera, voice and written capability.

Challenges
1. Can miss non verbal feedback.
2. Technology may be unreliable

When to use this method
1. Know Context
2. Know User
3. Frame insights

How to use this method
1. Define intent
2. Define audience
3. Define context
4. Define technology
5. Automated text messages are sent to participants to prompt an entry.
6. Analyze data

Resources
1. Smart phones,
2. Cameras,
3. Laptops and
4. Tablets

References
1. Coover, R. (2004) 'Using Digital Media Tools and Cross-Cultural Research,Analysis and Representation', Visual Studies19(1): 6—25.
2. Dicks, B., B. Mason, A. Coffey and P. Atkinson (2005) Qualitative Research and Hypermedia: Ethnography for the Digital Age. London: SAGE.
3. Kozinets R.V. (2010a), Netnography. Doing Ethnographic Research Online, Sage, London.

OBSERVATION

What is it?

This method involves observing people in their natural activities and usual context such as work environment. With direct observation the researcher is present and indirect observation the activities may be recorded by means such as video or digital voice recording.

Why use this method?

1. Allows the observer to view what users actually do in context.
2. Indirect observation uncovers activity that may have previously gone unnoticed

Challenges

1. Observation does not explain the cause of behavior.
2. Obtrusive observation may cause participants to alter their behavior.
3. Analysis can be time consuming.
4. Observer bias can cause the researcher to look only where they think they will see useful information.

When to use this method

1. Know Context
2. Know User
3. Frame insights

How to use this method

1. Define objectives
2. Define participants and obtain their cooperation.
3. Define The context of the observation: time and place.
4. In some countries the law requires that you obtain written consent to video people.
5. Define the method of observation and the method of recording information. Common methods are taking written notes, video or audio recording.
6. Run a test session.
7. Hypothesize an explanation for the phenomenon
8. Predict a logical consequence of the hypothesis
9. Test your hypothesis by observation
10. Analyze the data gathered and create a list of insights derived from the observations.

Resources

1. Note pad
2. Pens
3. Camera
4. Video camera
5. Digital voice recorder

References

1. Kosso, Peter (2011). A Summary of Scientific Method. Springer. pp. 9. ISBN 9400716133,

OBSERVATION: COVERT

What is it?

Covert observation is to observe people without them knowing. The identity of the researcher and the purpose of the research are hidden from the people being observed.

Why use this method?

1. This method may be used to reduce the effect of the observer's presence on the behavior of the subjects.
2. To capture behavior as it happens.
3. Researcher is more likely to observe natural behavior

Challenges

1. The method raises serious ethical questions.
2. Observation does not explain the cause of behavior.
3. Can be difficult to gain access and maintain cover
4. Analysis can be time consuming.
5. Observer bias can cause the researcher to look only where they think they will see useful information.

Resources

1. Camera
2. Video Camera
3. Digital voice recorder

When to use this method

1. Know Context
2. Know User

How to use this method

1. Define objectives.
2. Define participants and obtain their cooperation.
3. Define The context of the observation: time and place.
4. In some countries the law requires that you obtain written consent to video people.
5. Define the method of observation and the method of recording information. Common methods are taking written notes, video or audio recording.
6. Run a test session.
7. Hypothesize an explanation for the phenomenon.
8. Predict a logical consequence of the hypothesis.
9. Test your hypothesis by observation
10. Analyze the data gathered and create a list of insights derived from the observations.

References

1. Ethical Challenges in Participant Observation: A Reflection on Ethnographic Fieldwork By Li, Jun Academic journal article from The Qualitative Report, Vol. 13, No. 1

OBSERVATION: DIRECT

What is it?
Direct Observation is a method in which a re-searcher observes and records behavior events, activities or tasks while something is happening recording observations as they are made.

Who invented it?
Radcliff-Brown 1910
Bronisław Malinowski 1922
Margaret Mead 1928

Why use this method?
1. To capture behavior as it happens.

Challenges
1. Observation does not explain the cause of behavior.
2. Analysis can be time consuming.
3. Observer bias can cause the researcher to look only where they think they will see useful information.
4. Obtain a proper sample for generalization.
5. Observe average workers during average conditions.
6. The participant may change their behavior because they are being watched.

Resources
1. Note pad
2. Pens
3. Camera
4. Video Camera
5. Digital voice recorder

When to use this method
6. Know Context
7. Know User

How to use this method
1. Define objectives.
2. Make direct observation plan
3. Define participants and obtain their cooperation.
4. Define The context of the observation: time and place.
5. In some countries the law requires that you obtain written consent to video people.
6. Define the method of observation and the method of recording information. Common methods are taking written notes, video or audio recording.
7. Run a test session.
8. Hypothesize an explanation for the phenomenon.
9. Predict a logical consequence of the hypothesis.
10. Test your hypothesis by observation
11. Analyze the data gathered and create a list of insights derived from the observations.

References
1. Zechmeister, John J. Shaughnessy, Eugene B. Zechmeister, Jeanne S. (2009). Research methods in psychology (8th ed. ed.). Boston [etc.]: McGraw-Hill. ISBN 9780071283519.

OBSERVATION: INDIRECT

What is it?
This is a method where the observer is unobtrusive and is sometimes used for sensitive research subjects.

Why use this method?
1. To capture behavior as it happens in it's natural setting.
2. Indirect observation uncovers activity that may have previously gone unnoticed
3. May be inexpensive
4. Can collect a wide range of data

Challenges
1. Observation does not explain the cause of behavior.
2. Analysis can be time consuming.
3. Observer bias can cause the researcher to look only where they think they will see useful information.
4. Obtain a proper sample for generalization.
5. Observe average workers during average conditions.
6. The participant may change their behavior because they are being watched.

When to use this method
1. Know Context
2. Know User

How to use this method
3. Determine research goals.

Resources
1. Note pad
2. Pens
3. Camera
4. Video Camera
5. Digital voice recorder

References
1. Friedman, M. P., & Wilson, R. W. (1975). Application of unobtrusive measures to the study of textbook usage by college students. Journal of Applied Psychology, 60, 659 - 662.
2. Zechmeister, John J. Shaughnessy, Eugene B. Zechmeister, Jeanne S. (2009). Research methods in psychology (8th ed. ed.). Boston [etc.]: McGraw-Hill. ISBN 9780071283519.

OBSERVATION: NON PARTICIPANT

What is it?
The observer does not become part of the situation being observed or intervene in the behavior of the subjects. Used when a researcher wants the participants to behave normally. Usually this type of observation occurs in places where people normally work or live

Why use this method?
1. To capture behavior as it happens.

Challenges
1. Observation does not explain the cause of behavior.
2. Analysis can be time consuming.
3. Observer bias can cause the researcher to look only where they think they will see useful information.
4. Obtain a proper sample for generalization.
5. Observe average workers during average conditions.
6. The participant may change their behavior because they are being watched.

When to use this method
1. Know Context
2. Know User

How to use this method
1. Determine research goals.
2. Select a research context
3. The site should allow clear observation and be accessible.
4. Select participants
5. Seek permission.
6. Gain access
7. Gather research data.
8. Analyze data
9. Find common themes
10. Create insights

Resources
1. Note pad
2. Pens
3. Camera
4. Video Camera
5. Digital voice recorder

References
1. Zechmeister, John J. Shaughnessy, Eugene B. Zechmeister, Jeanne S. (2009). Research methods in psychology (8th ed. ed.). Boston [etc.]: McGraw-Hill. ISBN 9780071283519.

OBSERVATION: PARTICIPANT

What is it?
Participant observation is an observation method where the researcher participates. The researcher becomes part of the situation being studied. The researcher may live or work in the context of the participant and may become an accepted member of the participant's community. This method was used extensively by the pioneers of field research.

Who invented it?
Radcliff-Brown 1910
Bronisław Malinowski 1922
Margaret Mead 1928

Why use this method?
1. The goal of this method is to become close and familiar with the behavior of the participants.
2. To capture behavior as it happens.

Challenges?
1. My be time consuming
2. May be costly
3. The researcher may influence the behavior of the participants.
4. The participants may not show the same behavior if the observer was not present.
5. May be language barriers
6. May be cultural barriers
7. May be risks for the researcher.
8. Be sensitive to privacy, and confidentiality.

When to use this method
1. Know Context
2. Know User

How to use this method
1. Determine research goals.
2. Select a research context
3. The site should allow clear observation and be accessible.
4. Select participants
5. Seek permission.
6. Gain access
7. Gather research data.
8. Analyze data
9. Find common themes
10. Create insights

Resources
1. Note pad
2. Pens
3. Camera
4. Video Camera
5. Digital voice recorder

References
1. Malinowski, Bronisław (1929) The sexual life of savages in north-western Melanesia: an ethnographic account of courtship, marriage and family life among the natives of the Trobriand Islands, British New Guinea. New York: Halcyon House.
2. Marek M. Kaminski. 2004. Games Prisoners Play. Princeton University Press. ISBN 0-691-11721-7

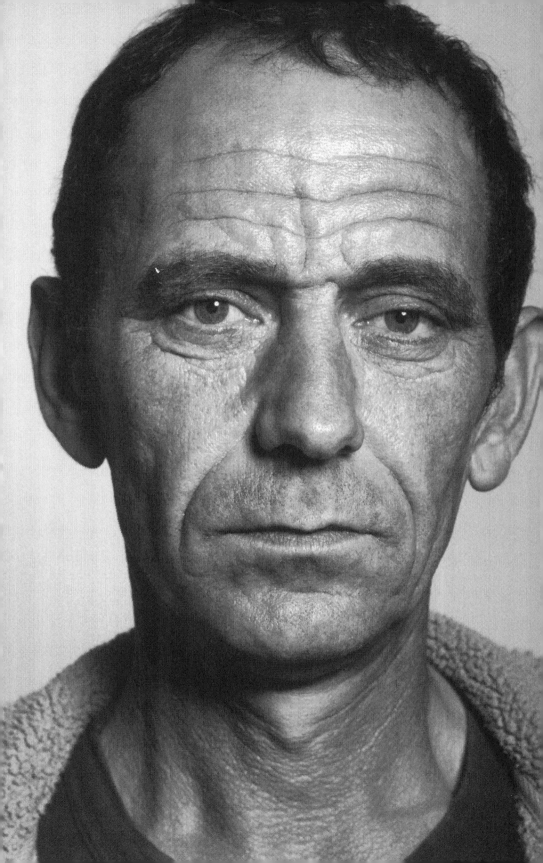

OBSERVATION: OVERT

What is it?
A method of observation where the subjects are aware that they are being observed

Who invented it?
Radcliff-Brown 1910
Bronisław Malinowski 1922
Margaret Mead 1928

Why use this method?
1. To capture behavior as it happens.

Challenges
1. Observation does not explain the cause of behavior.
2. Analysis can be time consuming.
3. Observer bias can cause the researcher to look only where they think they will see useful information.

Resources
1. Note pad
2. Pens
3. Camera
4. Video Camera
5. Digital voice recorder

References
1. Zechmeister, John J. Shaughnessy, Eugene B. Zechmeister, Jeanne S. (2009). Research methods in psychology (8th ed. ed.). Boston [etc.]: McGraw-Hill. ISBN 9780071283519.

When to use this method
1. Know Context
2. Know User

How to use this method
1. Define objectives.
2. Define participants and obtain their cooperation.
3. Define The context of the observation: time and place.
4. In some countries the law requires that you obtain written consent to video people.
5. Define the method of observation and the method of recording information. Common methods are taking written notes, video or audio recording.
6. Run a test session.
7. Hypothesize an explanation for the phenomenon.
8. Predict a logical consequence of the hypothesis.
9. Test your hypothesis by observation
10. Analyze the data gathered and create a list of insights derived from the observations.

OBSERVATION: STRUCTURED

What is it?
Particular types of behavior are observed and counted like a survey. The observer may create an event so that the behavior can be more easily studied. This approach is systematically planned and executed.

Why use this method?
1. Allows stronger generalizations than unstructured observation.
2. May allow an observer to study behavior that may be difficult to study in unstructured observation.
3. To capture behavior as it happens.
4. A procedure is used which can be replicated.

Challenges
1. Observation does not explain the cause of behavior.
2. Analysis can be time consuming.
3. Observer bias can cause the researcher to look only where they think they will see useful information.

Resources
1. Note pad
2. Pens
3. Camera
4. Video Camera
5. Digital voice recorder

When to use this method
1. Know Context
2. Know User

How to use this method
1. Define objectives.
2. Define participants and obtain their cooperation.
3. Define The context of the observation: time and place.
4. In some countries the law requires that you obtain written consent to video people.
5. Define the method of observation and the method of recording information. Common methods are taking written notes, video or audio recording.
6. Run a test session.
7. Hypothesize an explanation for the phenomenon.
8. Predict a logical consequence of the hypothesis.
9. Test your hypothesis by observation
10. Analyze the data gathered and create a list of insights derived from the observations.

References
1. Zechmeister, John J. Shaughnessy, Eugene B. Zechmeister, Jeanne S. (2009). Research methods in psychology (8th ed. ed.). Boston [etc.]: McGraw-Hill. ISBN 9780071283519.

OBSERVATION: UNSTRUCTURED

What is it?
This method is used when a researcher wants to see what is naturally occurring without predetermined ideas. We use have an open-ended approach to observation and record all that we observe

Why use this method?
1. To capture behavior as it happens.
2. This form of observation is appropriate when the problem has yet to be formulated precisely and flexibility is needed in observation to identify key components of the problem and to develop hypotheses
3. Observation is the most direct measure of behavior

Challenges
1. Replication may be difficult.
2. Observation does not explain the cause of behavior.
3. Analysis can be time consuming.
4. Observer bias can cause the researcher to look only where they think they will see useful information.
5. Data cannot be quantified
6. In this form of observation there is a higher probability of observer's bias.

When to use this method
1. Know Context
2. Know User

How to use this method
1. Select a context to explore
2. Take a camera, note pad and pen
3. Record things and questions that you find interesting
4. Record ideas as you form them
5. Do not reach conclusions.
6. Ask people questions and try to understand the meaning in their replies.

Resources
1. Note pad
2. Pens
3. Camera
4. Video Camera
5. Digital voice recorder

References
1. Zechmeister, John J. Shaughnessy, Eugene B. Zechmeister, Jeanne S. (2009). Research methods in psychology (8th ed. ed.). Boston [etc.]: McGraw-Hill. ISBN 9780071283519.

PERSONA

PERSONA NAME
....

DEMOGRAPHICS
....
....
....
....

CHARACTERISTIC STATEMENT
....
....
....
....
....

GOALS
....
....
....
....

AMBITIONS
....
....
....
....

INFLUENCERS AND ACTIVITIES
....
....
....
....

SCENARIOS
....
....
....
....

OTHER CHARACTERISTICS

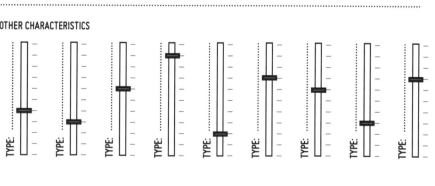

TYPE: TYPE: TYPE: TYPE: TYPE: TYPE: TYPE: TYPE: TYPE:

PERSONAS

What is it?
"A persona is a archetypal character that is meant to represent a group of users in a role who share common goals, attitudes and behaviors when interacting with a particular product or service Personas are user models that are presented as specific individual humans. They are not actual people, but are synthesized directly from observations of real people."(Cooper)

Who invented it?
Alan Cooper 1998

Why use this method?
1. Helps create empathy for users and reduces self reference.
2. Use as tool to analyze and gain insight into users.
3. Help in gaining buy-in from stake holders.

Challenges
Portigal (2008) has claimed that personas give a "cloak of smug customer-centricity" while actually distancing a team from engagement with real users and their needs

References
1. Pruitt, John & Adlin, Tamara. The Persona Lifecycle : Keeping People in Mind Throughout Product Design. Morgan Kaufmann, 2006. ISBN 0-12-566251-3

When to use this method
1. Know Context
2. Know User
3. Frame insights
4. Explore Concept

How to use this method
1. Inaccurate personas can lead to a false understandings of the end users. Personas need to be created using data from real users.
2. Collect data through observation, interviews, ethnography.
3. Segment the users or customers
4. Create the Personas
5. Avoid Stereotypes
6. Each persona should be different. Avoid fringe characteristics. Personas should each have three to four life goals which are personal aspirations,
7. Personas are given a name, and photograph.
8. Design personas can be followed by building customer journeys

Resources
1. Raw data on users from interviews or other research
2. Images of people similar to segmented customers.
3. Computer
4. Graphics software

PERSONAL INVENTORY

What is it?
This method involves studying the contents of
a research subject's purse, or wallet. Study the
things that they carry everyday.

Who invented it?
Rachel Strickland and Doreen Nelson 1998

Why use this method?
1. To provide insights into the user's
    lifestyle, activities, perceptions, and
    values.
2. to understand the needs priorities and
    interests

When to use this method
1. Know Context
2. Know User
3. Frame insights

How to use this method
1. Formulate aims of research
2. Recruit participants carefully.
3. "the participant is asked to bring their
    'most often carried bag' and lay the
    objects they carry on a flat surface,
    talking through the purpose and last-use
    of each item. Things to look out for where
    the bag is kept in the home and what
    is clustered around it, what is packed/
    repacked on arrival/departure, and
    the use of different bags for different
    activities." *Jan Chipchase*
4. Document the contents with photographs
    and notes
5. ask your research subject to talk about
    the objects and their meaning.
6. Analyze the data.

Resources
1. Camera
2. Note pad

SHADOWING

What is it?

Shadowing is observing people in context. The researcher accompanies the user and observes user experiences and activities. It allows the researcher and designer to develop design insights through observation and shared experiences with users.

Who invented it?

Alex Bavelas 1944

Lucy Vernile, Robert A. Monteiro 1991

Why use this method?

1. This method can help determine the difference between what subjects say they do and what they really do.
2. It helps in understanding the point of view of people. Successful design results from knowing the users.
3. Define intent
4. Can be used to evaluate concepts.

Challenges

1. Selecting the wrong people to shadow.
2. Hawthorne Effect, The observer can influence the daily activities under being studied.

When to use this method

1. Know Context
2. Know User
3. Frame insights
4. Generate Concepts

How to use this method

1. Prepare
2. Select carefully who to shadow.
3. Observe people in context by members of your design team.
4. Capture behaviors that relate to product function.
5. Identify issues and user needs.
6. Create design solutions based on observed and experienced user needs.
7. Typical periods can be one day to one week.

Resources

1. Video camera
2. Digital still camera
3. Note pad
4. Laptop Computer

References

1. McDonald, Seonaidh. "Studying Actions in Context: A Qualitative Shadowing Method for Organizational Research." Qualitative Research. The Robert Gordon University. SAGE Publications. London. 2005. p455–473.
2. Alan Bryman, Emma Bell. Business Research Methods. Oxford University Press 2007 ISBN 978-0-19-928498-6

PATIENT STAKEHOLDER MAP

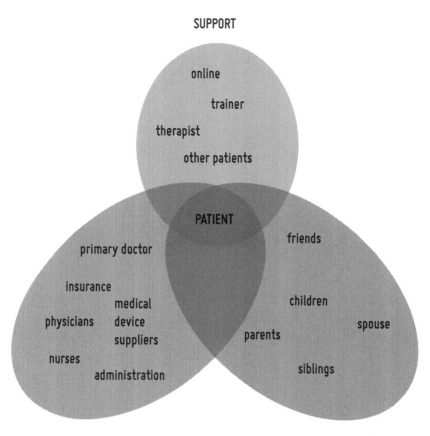

SUPPORT

online

trainer

therapist

other patients

PATIENT

primary doctor

friends

insurance

children

medical

physicians   device

spouse

suppliers   parents

nurses

administration

siblings

HEALTH CARE

FAMILY & FRIENDS

STAKEHOLDER MAP

What is it?
Stakeholders maps are used to document the key stake holders and their relationship. They can include end users, those who will benefit, those who may be adversely affected, those who hold power and those who may sabotage design outcomes. At the beginning of a design project it is important to identify the key stake holders and their relationships. The map serves as a reference for the design team.

Who invented it?
Mitchell 1997

Why use this method?
1. Stakeholder mapping helps discover ways to influence other stakeholders.
2. Stakeholder mapping helps discover risks.
3. Stakeholder mapping helps discover positive stakeholders to involve in the design process.

Challenges?
1. Stakeholder mapping helps discover negative stakeholders and their associated risks.

Resources
1. White board
2. Post-it-notes
3. Pens
4. Dry-erase markers
5. Interview data

When to use this method
1. Define intent
2. Know Context
3. Know User
4. Frame insights

How to use this method
1. Develop a categorized list of the members of the stakeholder community.
2. Assign priorities
3. Map the 'highest priority' stakeholders.
4. Can initially be documented on a white board, cards, post-it-notes and consolidated as a diagram through several iterations showing hierarchy and relationships.

Some of the commonly used 'dimensions' include:
1. Power (three levels)
2. Support (three levels)
3. Influence (three levels)
4. Need (three levels)

References
1. Mitchell, R. K., B. R. Agle, and D.J. Wood. (1997). "Toward a Theory of Stakeholder Identification and Salience: Defining the Principle of Who and What really Counts." in: Academy of Management Review 22(4): 853 – 888
2. Savage, G. T., T. W. Nix, Whitehead and Blair. (1991). "Strategies for assessing and managing organizational stakeholders." In: Academy of Management Executive 5(2): 61 – 75.

STORYBOARD

PROJECT

NAME

DATE

PAGE

DIALOGUE

ACTION

DIALOGUE

ACTION

DIALOGUE

ACTION

267

STORYBOARDS

What is it?

The storyboard is a narrative tool derived from cinema. A storyboard is a form of prototyping which communicates each step of an activity, experience or interaction. Used in films and multimedia as well as product and UX design. Storyboards consists of a number of 'frames' that communicate a sequence of events in context.

Who invented it?

Invented by Walt Disney in 1927. Disney credited animator Webb Smith with creating the first storyboard. By 1937–38 all studios were using storyboards.

Why use this method?

1. Can help gain insightful user feedback.
2. Conveys an experience.
3. Can use a storyboard to communicate a complex task as a series of steps.
4. Allows the proposed activities to be discussed and refined.
5. Storyboards can be used to help designers identify opportunities or use problems.

Challenges?

1. Interaction between the storyboard and a user is limited (Landay & Myers, 1996).
2. Participants may not be able to draw well.
3. There haven't been conclusive studies about the effectiveness of storyboards
4. Storyboarding is linear.

When to use this method

1. Generate Concepts
2. Create Solutions

How to use this method

1. Decide what story you want to describe.
2. Choose a story and a message: what do you want the storyboard to express?
3. Create your characters
4. Think about the whole story first rather than one panel at a time.
5. Create the drafts and refine them through an iterative process. Refine.
6. Illustrations can be sketches or photographs.
7. Consider: Visual elements, level of detail, text, experiences and emotions, number of frames, and flow of time.
8. Keep text short and informative.
9. 6 to 12 frames.
10. Tell your story efficiently and effectively.
11. Brainstorm your ideas.

Resources

1. Pens
2. Digital camera
3. Storyboard templates
4. Comic books for inspiration

References

1. Giuseppe Cristiano Storyboard Design Course: Principles, Practice, and Technique Barron's Educational Series (October 1, 2007) ISBN-10: 0764137328

THROUGH OTHER EYES

What is it?
At several times during a design project it is useful to invite an outside group to review the state of the design and to tell your design team if they think that your design direction is real and good.

Why use this method?
A design team can follow design directions that seem unworkable or unrealistic to end users because they may be remote from the end users of a product or service.

When to use this method
1. Explore concepts

Resources
1. Pen
2. Paper
3. White board
4. Dry erase markers

How to use this method
1. Define your design problem clearly
2. Select a group of outside people who are representative of the end users of a product or service.
3. Prepare a presentation that may include prototypes or images and statements that clearly communicate the favored concept direction.
4. Prepare a question guide to help your design team obtain useful feedback
5. Review your design with the outside group.
6. Refine your design based on the feedback
7. Provide feedback to the outside reviewers to let them know how their input has been useful.
8. It may be necessary to ask the external participants to sign a non disclosure agreement before to the design review.

WIZARD OF OZ

What is it?

Wizard of Oz method is a research method in which research participants interact with a computer interface that subjects believe to be responding to their input, but which is being operated by an unseen person. The unseen operator is sometimes called the "wizard"

Who invented it?

John F. Kelley
Johns Hopkins University. 1980 USA
Nigel Cross

Why use this method?

1. Wizard of Oz is good for the testing of preliminary interface prototypes.
2. A relatively inexpensive type of simulation
3. Identify problems with an interface concept
4. Investigate visual affordance of an interface.

Challenges

1. Requires training for the wizard.
2. It is difficult for wizards to provide consistent responses across sessions.
3. Computers respond differently than humans
4. It is difficult to evaluate systems with a complex interface using this method.

When to use this method

1. Know Context
2. Know User
3. Frame insights
4. Explore Concepts

How to use this method

1. The wizard sits in a place not visible to the research participant.
2. The wizard observes the user's actions, and initiates the system's responses.
3. The "wizard" watches live video from a camera focused on the participant's hands and simulate the effects of the participant's actions.
4. Users are unaware that the actions of the system are being produced by the wizard.

Resources

1. Video camera
2. Software interface prototype
3. Computers

References

1. Höysniemi, J., Hämäläinen, P., and Turkki, L. 2004. Wizard of Oz prototyping of computer vision based action games for children. In Proceeding of the 2004 Conference on interaction Design and Children: Building A Community (Maryland, June 1—03, 2004). IDC '04. ACM Press, New York, NY, 27–34

BACKCASTING

What is it?

Backcasting is a method for planning the actions necessary to reach desired future goals. This method is often applied in a workshop format with stakeholders participating. The future scenarios are developed for periods of between 1 and 20 years in the future. The participants first identify their goals and then work backwards to identify the necessary actions to reach those goals.

Who invented it?

AT&T 1950s, Shell 1970s

Why use this method?

1. It is inexpensive and fast
2. Backcasting is a tool for identifying, planning and reaching future goals.
3. Backcasting provides a strategy to reach future goals.

Challenges

1. Need a good moderator
2. Needs good preparation

Resources

1. Post-it-notes
2. White board
3. Pens
4. Dry-erase markers
5. Cameras

When to use this method

1. Define intent
2. Know Context
3. Know User
4. Frame insights
5. Explore Concepts
6. Make Plans
7. Deliver Offering

How to use this method

A typical backcasting question is"How would you define success for yourself in 2015?
1. Define a framework
2. Analyze the present situation in relation to the framework
3. Prepare a vision and a number of desirable future scenarios.
4. Back-casting: Identify the steps to achieve this goal.
5. Further elaboration, detailing
6. Step by step strategies towards achieving the outcomes desired.
7. Ask do the strategies move us in the right direction? Are they flexible strategies?. Do the strategies represent a good return on investment?
8. Implementation, policy, organization embedding, follow-up

References

1. Quist, J., & Vergragt, P. 2006. Past and future of backcasting: The shift to stakeholder participation and a proposal for a methodological framework. Futures Volume 38, Issue 9, November 2006, 1027-1045

BANNED

What is it?
Banned is a method involving creating future scenarios based on imagining a world if a product, service system or experience did not exist and how people would possibly adapt.

Who invented it?
Herman Kahn, Rand Corporation 1950, US

Why use this method?
1. May uncover new design directions and possibilities not dependent on existing products services and systems.
2. Expose problems and opportunities.
3. Banned Scenarios become a focus for discussion related to a user experience. which helps evaluate and refine concepts. They can be used to challenge concepts through prototyping user interactions.

References
1. "Scenarios," IDEO Method Cards. ISBN 0-9544132-1-0
2. Carroll, John M. Making Use: Scenario-based design of human-computer interactions. MIT Press, 2000.
3. Carroll J. M. Five Reasons for Scenario Based Design. Elsevier Science B. V. 2000.
4. Carroll, John M. Scenario-Based Design: Envisioning Work and Technology in System Development.

When to use this method
1. Know Context
2. Know User
3. Frame insights
4. Generate Concepts

How to use this method
This exercise can be done individually or in group.
1. Decide the question to investigate.
2. Decide time and scope for the scenario process.
3. Identify stake holders.
4. Identify uncertainties.
5. Define the scenarios.
6. Can use with personas. Who is the persona? What is the experience? What is the outcome?
7. Create storyboards.
8. Analyze the scenarios through discussion.
9. Iterate as necessary.
10. Summarize insights

Resources
1. Storyboard templates
2. Post-it-notes
3. Pens
4. Dry-erase markers
5. Video cameras
6. Empathy tools
7. Props

BENEFITS MAP

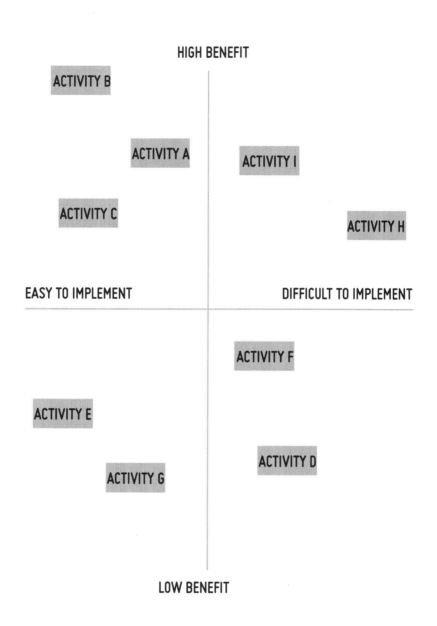

BENEFITS MAP

What is it?
The benefits map is a simple tool that helps your team decide what will give you the best return on investment for time invested

Why use this method?
1. Aids communication and discussion within the organization.
2. It is human nature to do tasks which are not most urgent first.
3. To gain competitive advantage,
4. Helps build competitive strategy
5. Helps build communication strategy
6. Helps manage time effectively

Challenges
1. Can be subjective

When to use this method
1. Know Context
2. Know User
3. Frame insights
4. Explore Concepts

How to use this method
1. Moderator draws axes on whiteboard or flip chart.
2. Worthwhile activity at the start of a project.
3. Map individual tasks.
4. Interpret the map.
5. Create strategy.
6. Tasks which have high benefit with low investment may be given priority.

Resources
1. Pen
2. Paper
3. White board
4. Dry erase markers

THINK OUT LOUD PROTOCOL

What is it?
Think aloud or thinking out loud protocols involve participants verbalizing their thoughts while performing a set of tasks. Users are asked to say whatever they are looking at, thinking, doing, and feeling.

A related but method is the talk-aloud protocol. where participants describe their activities but do not give explanations. This method is thought to be more objective

Who invented it?
Clayton Lewis IBM 1993

Why use this method?
1. Helps a researcher understand interaction with a product or service,.
2. Enables observers to see first-hand the process of task completion
3. The terminology the user uses to express an idea or function the design or and documentation.
4. Allows testers to understand how the user approaches the system.

Challenges
1. The design team needs to be composed of persons with a variety of skills.
2. Pick a diverse, cross disciplinary team.

When to use this method
1. Know Context
2. Know User
3. Frame insights
4. Explore Concepts

How to use this method
1. Identify users.
2. Choose Representative Tasks.
3. Create a Mock-Up or Prototype.
4. Select Participants.
5. Provide the test users with the system or prototype to be tested and tasks.
6. Brief participants.
7. Take notes of everything that users say, without attempting to interpret their actions and words.
8. Iterate
9. Videotape the tests, then analyze the videotapes.

Resources
1. Computer
2. Video camera
3. Note pad
4. Pens

References
1. Lewis, C. H. (1982). Using the "Thinking Aloud" Method In Cognitive Interface Design (Technical report). RC-9265.

BLUE OCEAN STRATEGY

What is it?

Blue Ocean Strategy is a business strategy proposed by W. Chan Kim and Renée Mauborgne. The authors propose that companies can experience high growth and profits by exploiting "blue ocean" or uncontested, differentiated market spaces.

Blue Ocean strategy:

1. Create uncontested market space
2. Make competition irrelevant.
3. Create and capture new demand.
4. Break the value-cost trade off.
5. Align the whole system of a company's activities in pursuit of differentiation and low cost.

Red Ocean Strategy

6. Compete in existing market place.
7. Beat the competition.
8. Exploit existing demand.
9. Make the value-cost trade off.
10. Align the whole system of a company's activities with it's strategic choice of differentiation or low cost.

Who invented it?

W. Chan Kim and Renée Mauborgne 2004

Why use this method?

1. BOS contains a road map for assessing a company and its business and strategy.
2. Useful for mature companies that need new strategy.
3. A number of methods that help an an organization understand what value they are delivering.

Challenges

1. Blue Ocean Strategy does not define where or how to find Blue Oceans.
2. Some critics of the Blue Ocean approach suggest that the strategy is a new way of packaging old ideas.

When to use this method

1. Define intent
2. Know Context
3. Know User
4. Frame insights
5. Explore Concepts
6. Make Plans
7. Deliver Offering

References

1. Kim and Mauborgne. Blue Ocean Strategy. Harvard Business School Press. 2005.
2. Kim, Chan (2005). Blue Ocean Strategy. Boston: Harvard Business School Press. p. 210. ISBN 1-59139-619-0.

TRENDS	POLITICAL	ECONOMIC	USER NEEDS	TECHNOLOGY	UNCERTAINTIES	TRENDS

CONTEXT MAP

What is it?

A context map is a tool for representing complex factors affecting an organization or design visually. Context maps are sometimes used by directors or organizations as a tool to enable discussion of the effects of change and related interacting business, cultural and environmental factors in order to create a strategic vision for an organization. A context map can be used to analyze trends

Who invented it?

Joseph D. Novak Cornell University 1970s.

Why use this method?

Uses include:
1. New knowledge creation
2. Documenting the knowledge existing informally within an organization.
3. Creating a shared strategic vision

When to use this method

1. Define intent
2. Know Context
3. Know User
4. Frame insights

Resources

1. Template
2. White board
3. Paper flip chart
4. Pens
5. Dry-erase markers
6. Post-it-notes

How to use this method

1. Put together a team of between 4 and 20 participants with diverse backgrounds and outlooks.
2. Appoint a good moderator
3. Prepare a space. Use a private room with a white board or large wall.
4. Distribute post-it notes to each participant.
5. Brainstorm the list of factors one at a time.
6. These can include Trends, technology, trends, political factors, economic climate customer needs, uncertainties.
7. Each participant can contribute.
8. All contributions are recorded on the white board or on the wall with the post-it-notes.
9. When all factors have been discussed prioritize each group of contributions to identify the most critical.
10. This can be done by rearranging the post-it-notes or white board notes.
11. Video the session and photograph the notes after the session.
12. Analyze the map and create strategy.

References

1. Context Map: A Method to Represent the Interactions Between Students' Learning and Multiple Context Factors written by Gyoungho Lee and Lei Bao Physics Education Research Conference 2002

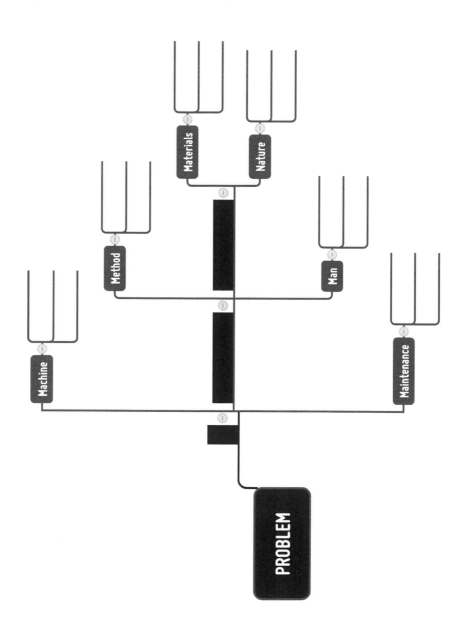

279

FISHBONE DIAGRAM

What is it?

Fishbone diagrams also called Ishikawa diagrams, are diagrams that show the causes of a specific event.

Mazda Motors used an Ishikawa diagram to design the Miata sports car, The goal was was "Jinba Ittai" Horse and Rider as One. Every factor identified in the diagram was included in the final design. Ishikawa described the process as fishboning your problem and letting it cook overnight.

Who invented it?

Kaoru Ishikawa University of Tokyo 1968

Why use this method?

1. People tend to fix a problem by responding to an immediately visible cause while ignoring the deeper issues. This approach may lead to a problem reoccurring.
2. Use in the predesign phase to understand the root causes of a problem to serve as the basis for design.
3. Identifies the relationship between cause and effect.

When to use this method

1. Define intent
2. Know Context
3. Know User
4. Frame insights

How to use this method

1. Prepare the six arms of the Ishikawa Diagram on a white board.
2. Define the problem clearly as a short statement in the head of the diagram.
3. Describe the causes of each bone and write them at the end of each branch. Use the 4 M's as categories; Machine, Man Methods, Materials.
4. Conduct the brainstorming session using brainstorming guidelines Ask each team member to define the cause of the problem. You may list as many causes as necessary. Typically 3 to 6 are listed.
5. Minor causes are then listed around the major causes.
6. Interpret the Ishikawa Diagram once it's finished.

Resources

1. White board
2. Dry-erase markers
3. Room with privacy
4. Paper
5. Pens

References

1. Ishikawa, Kaoru, Guide to Quality Control, Asian Productivity Organization, UNIPUB, 1976, ISBN 92-833-1036-5
2. Ishikawa, Kaoru (1990); (Translator: J. H. Loftus); Introduction to Quality Control; 448 p; ISBN 4-906224-61-X OCLC 41428

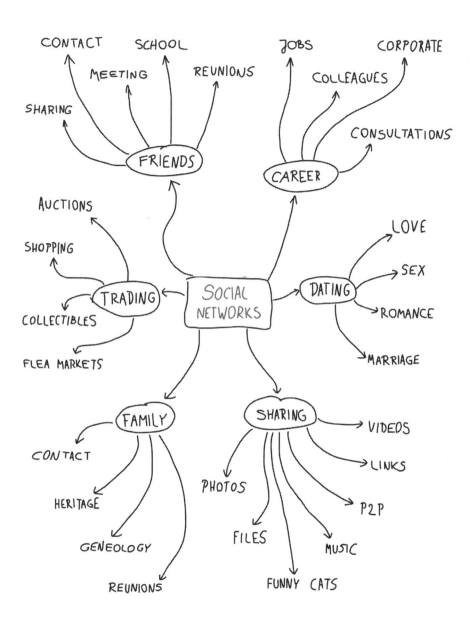

CONTACT SCHOOL JOBS CORPORATE

MEETING REUNIONS COLLEAGUES

SHARING CONSULTATIONS

FRIENDS CAREER

AUCTIONS LOVE

SHOPPING SEX

TRADING SOCIAL NETWORKS DATING ROMANCE

COLLECTIBLES MARRIAGE

FLEA MARKETS

FAMILY SHARING VIDEOS

CONTACT LINKS

HERITAGE PHOTOS P2P

GENEOLOGY FILES MUSIC

REUNIONS FUNNY CATS

MIND MAP

What is it?

A mind map is a diagram used to represent the affinities or connections between a number of ideas or things. Understanding connections is the starting point for design. Mind maps are a method of analyzing information and relationships.

Who invented it?

Porphry of Tyros 3rd century BC.
Allan Collins, Northwestern University 1960, USA

Why use this method?

1. The method helps identify relationships.
2. There is no right or wrong with mind maps. They help with they help with memory and organization.
3. Problem solving and brainstorming
4. Relationship discovery
5. Summarizing information
6. Memorizing information

Challenges

Print words clearly, use color and images for visual impact.

When to use this method

7. Know Context
8. Know User
9. Frame insights
10. Explore Concepts
11. Make Plans

How to use this method

1. Start in the center with a key word or idea. Put box around this node.
2. Use images, symbols, or words for nodes.
3. Select key words.
4. Keep the key word names of nodes s simple and short as possible.
5. Associated nodes should be connected with lines to show affinities.
6. Make the lines the same length as the word/image they support.
7. Use emphasis such as thicker lines to show the strength of associations in your mind map.
8. Use radial arrangement of nodes.

Resources

1. Paper
2. Pens
3. White board
4. Dry-erase markers

References

1. Mind maps as active learning tools', by Willis, CL. Journal of computing sciences in colleges. ISSN: 1937-4771. 2006. Volume: 21 Issue: 4
2. Mind Maps as Classroom Exercises John W. Budd The Journal of Economic Education, Vol. 35, No. 1 (Winter, 2004), pp. 35-46 Published by: Taylor & Francis, Ltd.

LINKING DIAGRAM

Objectives	Weighting	Responsibility
Reduce SKUs by 25%	10	Industrial Design
		Engineering
Establish new factory in China	8	Transportation
Decrease returns by 25%	6	Human Resources
		Manufacturing
Increase sales by 25%	7	Quality
Establish distribution Network in China	7	Marketing
Increase speed to market by 30%	4	Sales
		Sourcing
Reduce manufacturing costs by25%	9	Management

LINKING DIAGRAM

What is it?
A linking diagram is a graphical method of displaying relationships between factors in data sets.

Why use this method?
1. To analyze relationships of complex data

Resources
1. Pen
2. Paper
3. White board
4. Dry erase markers

When to use this method
1. Know Context
2. Know User
3. Frame insights

How to use this method
1. Select a problem to analyze.
2. Team brainstorms two lists of factors that relate to the problem such as outcomes and actions.
3. Team rates the items by importance. 1–10, 10 being most important.
4. Draw lines between related items in each list.
5. Review and refine
6. List insights
7. Take actions based on the insights.

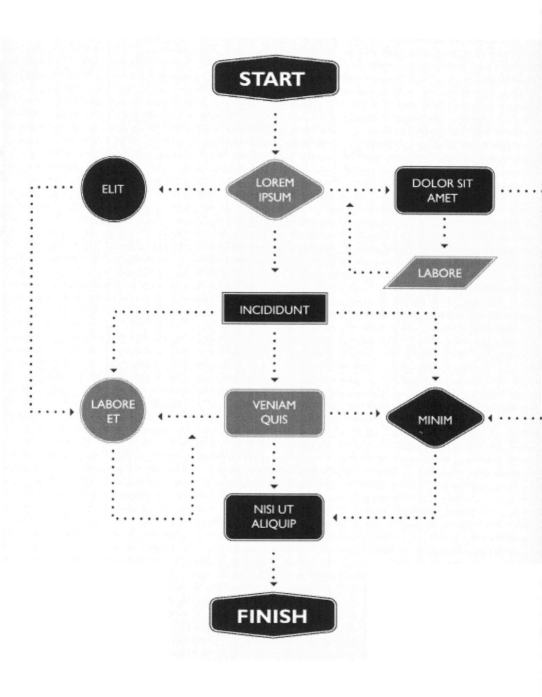

PROCESS FLOW DIAGRAM

What is it?
A process flowchart is a type of diagram that represents a process, showing the steps as boxes

Who invented it?
Frank Gilbreth, American Society of Mechanical Engineers,1921

Why use this method?
1. To represent a flow of process or decisions or both.

Challenges
1. Use standard symbols.
2. Arrows should show the direction of flow.
3. A junction is indicated by two incoming and one outgoing line.
4. The two most common types of boxes are for a process step and for a decisions.

Resources
1. Pen
2. Paper
3. White board
4. Dry erase markers.

When to use this method
1. Know Context
2. Frame insights

How to use this method
1. Define the process boundaries
2. Complete the big picture first.
3. Draw a start box.
4. Draw the first box below the start box. Ask, 'What happens first?'.
5. Add further boxes below the previous box, Ask 'What happens next?'.
6. Connect the boxes with arrows
7. Describe the process to be charted
8. Review.

References
1. Frank Bunker Gilbreth, Lillian Moller Gilbreth (1921) Process Charts. American Society of Mechanical Engineers.
2. Bohl, Rynn: "Tools for Structured and Object-Oriented Design", Prentice Hall, 2007.

ACTION PLAN

ACTION PLAN:						
OBJECTIVE:						
No.	ITEM	PERSON	RESOURCE	DATE	ACTUAL	STATUS
1						
2						
3						
4						
5						
6						
7						
8						
9						
10						
11						
12						
13						

ACTION PLAN

What is it?

An action plan is a document that summarizes action items, due dates and other related information.

Why use this method?

1. To focus team effort.
2. To monitor progress towards a goal.

Challenges

1. Start with the final delivery date required and work backwards to assign delivery dates for individual actions.
2. The action plan should be displayed where it can be accessed by all team members.

When to use this method

1. Define intent

How to use this method

1. Team brainstorms actions needed to reach a goal and the times when each action should be completed.
2. The moderator draws the action plan on a white board.
3. Team members are assigned responsibility for individual actions.
4. The plan is reviewed by the team to ensure that there are no conflicts.
5. The plan is signed off on by the team.
6. The plan is posted in the project room for future reference.

APPRECIATIVE INQUIRY

What is it?

Appreciative Inquiry is an organizational method which focuses on developing what an organization does well. It involves an inquiry which uncovers and appreciates the positive aspects all levels of an organization including customers and suppliers.

Who invented it?

Geoffrey Vickers 1968
Stowell and West,1991
West, 1992;
West and Thomas, 2005;
West and Braganca, 2011

When to use this method

1. Define intent

Why use this method?

1. Applicable to organizations facing rapid change or growth
2. Appreciating, valuing the Best of What Is
3. Envisioning what might be
4. Engaging in dialogue about what should be
5. Innovating, what will be
6. Build a common vision.
7. Uncover and amplify the positive factors in organizations.
8. Create openness and positive communication between individuals and groups where a negative work environment exists
9. Provide an alternative approach to team building.
10. Show the power and value of teamwork.
11. Illuminating the core values, and practices that support successful teams.
12. Develop communities.

How to use this method

There are a number of approaches to implementing appreciative Inquiry. These include mass interviews and a large, gathering called an appreciative inquiry Summit.

Appreciative inquiry is usually worked out by using a 4-D Cycle

1. "Discovery: People talk to one another, often via structured interviews, to discover the times when their organization is at its best. These stories are told as richly as possible.
2. Dream: The dream phase is commonly run as a large group conference with the help of facilitators. People are encouraged to envision the organization as though the peak moments identified in the discovery phase were the norm rather than the exception.
3. Design: A team is empowered to go away and design ways to create the organization dreamed in the large group conference.
4. Delivery: The final phase delivers the dream and the new design. It is one of experimentation and improvisation. Teams are formed to follow up on the design elements and to continue the appreciative process. This phase may itself contain more small-scale appreciative inquiries into specific aspects of organizational life."

Source: Asian Development Bank

Sample questionnaire

1. "Think of a peak experience or high point in your work or experience in your organization.
2. In that experience, think about the things you valued most about yourself, the nature of your work, and your organization itself.
3. Think about the core factors that give life to your organization, The really positive values it can build upon.
4. What three wishes would you like to have that would heighten the vitality and health of your organization?"

Source: Asian Development Bank

References

1. David Cooperrider, Diana Whitney, and Jacqueline Stavros. 2007. Appreciative Inquiry Handbook. San Francisco: Berrett-Koehler.
2. Appreciative Inquiry Commons. 2008. Available: http://appreciativeinquiry.case.edu
3. Theodore Kinni, "The Art of Appreciative Inquiry", The Harvard Business School Working Knowledge for Business Leaders Newsletter, September 22, 2003.

DECISION RINGS

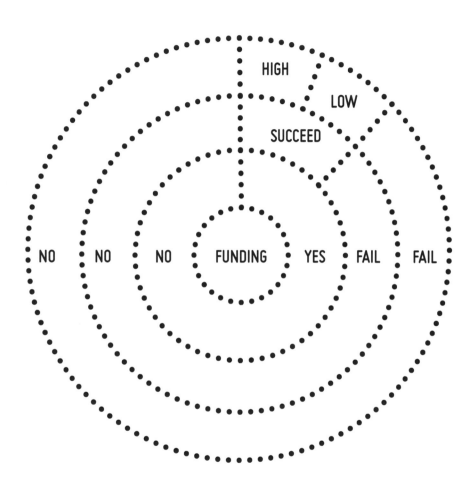

DECISION RINGS

What is it?
Decision rings are a graphical way of visualizing the likelihood or benefit of the outcome of decisions.

Why use this method?
1. A visual way of representing a problem.

Resources
1. Pen
2. Paper
3. Computer
4. Software

References
1. Tufte, E. (1992), The Visual Display of Quantitative Information, Graphics Press.
2. Baron, J. & R. Brown (1991), Teaching Decisionmaking to Adolescents, Erlbaum.

When to use this method
1. Define intent
2. Frame insights
3. Explore Concepts
4. Make Plans

How to use this method
1. Draw a number of concentric circles.
2. If your problem decision involves n stages, draw n+1 concentric circles.
3. Split the first ring into segments equal to the number of choices for the first decision.
4. Divide the next stage into segments based on the segments of the previous stage
5. Divide each subsequent segment into the number of boxes equal to the alternative solutions.
6. Divide each subsequent box into boxes proportional to the probability of the associated outcome
7. Repeat for each decision stage.

FORCE FIELD DIAGRAM

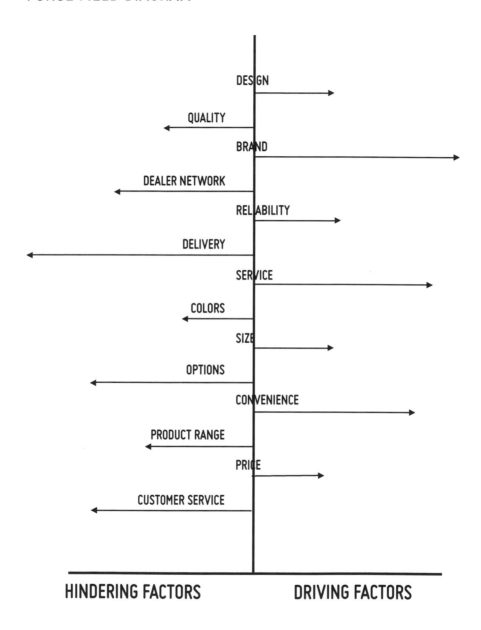

HINDERING FACTORS   DRIVING FACTORS

FORCE FIELD ANALYSIS

What is it?
Force field analysis is a method of mapping and analyzing factors which assist or work against desired goals.

Who invented it?
Kurt Lewin 1940s
John R. P. French 1947

Why use this method?
1. Allows visual comparison of factors affecting the success of a project for discussion of solutions.

Challenges
1. It is best to focus on barriers.
2. Assign a strategy to each barrier

Resources
1. Pen
2. Paper
3. White board
4. Dry erase markers
5. Post-it notes.

References
1. Cartwright, D. (1951). Foreword to the 1951 Edition. Field Theory in Social Science and Selected Theoretical Papers—Kurt Lewin. Washington, D.C.: American Psychological Association, 1997. Originally published by Harper & Row.

When to use this method
1. Define intent
2. Know Context
3. Know User

How to use this method
1. Select a moderator and a team of stakeholders.
2. The moderator describes the problem being focused on to the team
3. The moderator draws the letter T on a white board
4. The moderator writes the problem above the cross stroke on the T
5. The team brainstorms a list of forces working against the goal and the moderator lists them on the right hand of the upstroke on the letter T.
6. The team brainstorms a list or forces working towards the goal and the moderator writes them on the right hand of the upstroke on the letter T.
7. Forces listed can be internal and external.
8. They can be associated with the environment, the organization, people strategy, culture, values, competitors, conflicts or other factors.
9. Prioritize and quantify both lists of forces
10. The moderator draws a horizontal letter T and above the horizontal line draws arrows for each factor indicating their relative significance in the opinion of the team.
11. The moderator draws arrows for each negative factor below the line showing their relative significance.

294

RADAR CHART

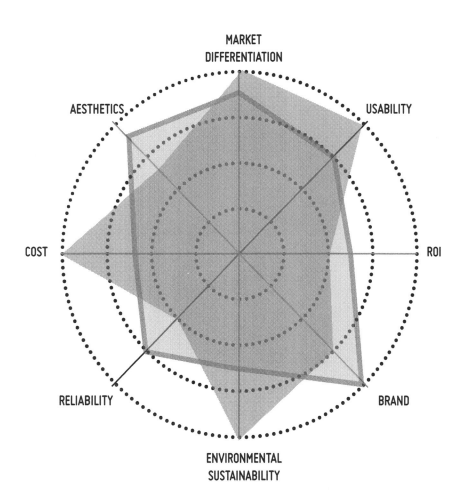

MARKET
DIFFERENTIATION

USABILITY

AESTHETICS

COST

ROI

RELIABILITY

BRAND

ENVIRONMENTAL
SUSTAINABILITY

RADAR CHART

What is it?

The radar chart is a star shape chart that allows information to be logged radially for a number of variables. The radar chart is also known as a web chart, spider chart, star chart, star plot, cobweb chart, irregular polygon, polar chart, or kiviat diagram.

Who invented it?

Georg von Mayr 1877

Challenges

1. Radar charts may not provide information for trade off decisions.

Why use this method?

1. A spider diagram is a way of displaying a great deal of information in a condensed form,

When to use this method

1. Know Context
2. Know User
3. Frame insights

How to use this method

1. Draw a circle on a flipchart paper
2. For each item to evaluate draw a line from the center to the circle.
3. Write the item on the intersection between the line and the circle.
4. Draw spider lines from the inside to the outside of the circle (see photo).
5. Gather the participants around the flipchart.
6. Ask them to put one dot for each item: If highly ranked the dot should be close top the center; if poorly ranked the dot should be close to the circle.
7. Present and discuss the result with the group.

Resources

1. Paper
2. Pens
3. Computer
4. Graphic software

References

1. Chambers, John, William Cleveland, Beat Kleiner, and Paul Tukey, (1983). Graphical Methods for Data Analysis. Wadsworth. pp. 158–162

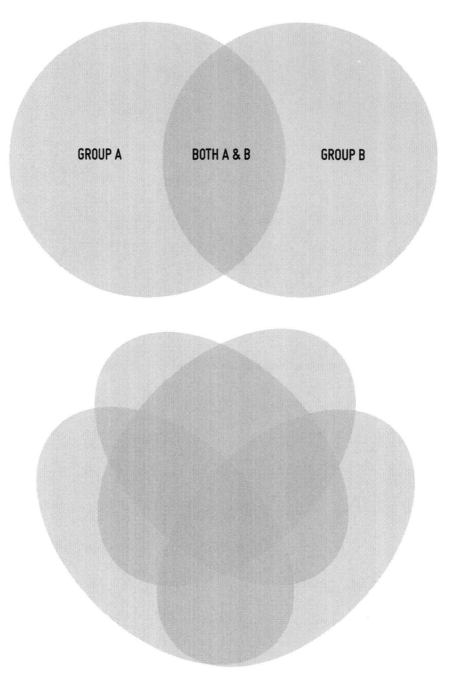

Venn's four-set diagram using ellipses

VENN DIAGRAM

What is it?
Venn diagrams normally are constructed from overlapping circles. The interior of the circle and the areas of overlap symbolically represents the elements of discreet sets.

Who invented it?
John Venn 1880

Why use this method?
1. A useful tool for simplifying and communicating data related to user populations and design features

When to use this method
1. Know Context
2. Know User
3. Frame insights

Resources
1. Paper
2. Pens
3. Software

References
1. Grimaldi, Ralph P. (2004). Discrete and combinatorial mathematics. Boston: Addison-Wesley. p. 143. ISBN 0-201-72634-3.
2. Edwards, A.W.F. (2004). Cogwheels of the mind: the story of Venn diagrams. JHU Press. ISBN 978-0-8018-7434-5.

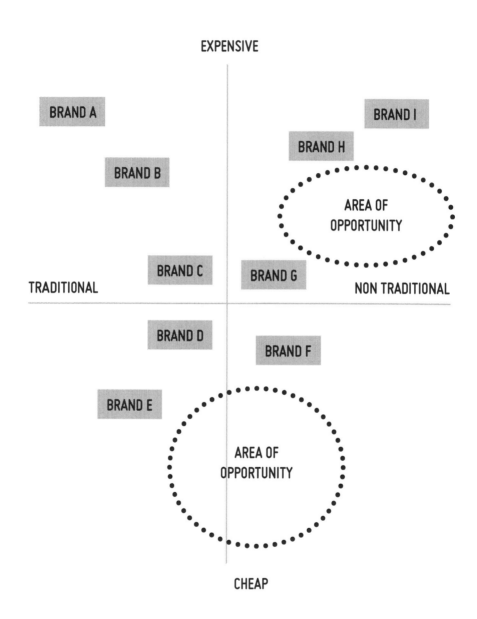

PERCEPTUAL MAP

What is it?
Perceptual mapping is a method that creates a map of the perceptions of people of competing alternatives to be compared.

Who invented it?
Unknown

Why use this method?
1. Aids communication and discussion within the organization
2. To gain competitive advantage,
3. Helps build competitive strategy
4. Helps build communication strategy
5. Helps identify potential new products
6. Helps build brand strategy

Challenges
1. Because the position of a product or service on the map is subjective, you can ask several people to locate the position through group discussion.
2. Works well for clearly defined functional attributes such as price, product features

When to use this method
1. Know Context
2. Know User
3. Frame insights
4. Explore Concepts

How to use this method
1. Define characteristics of product or service to map.
2. Identify competing brands, services or products to map.
3. Map individual items.
4. Interpret the map.
5. Create strategy.

Resources
1. Pen
2. Paper
3. White board
4. Dry erase markers

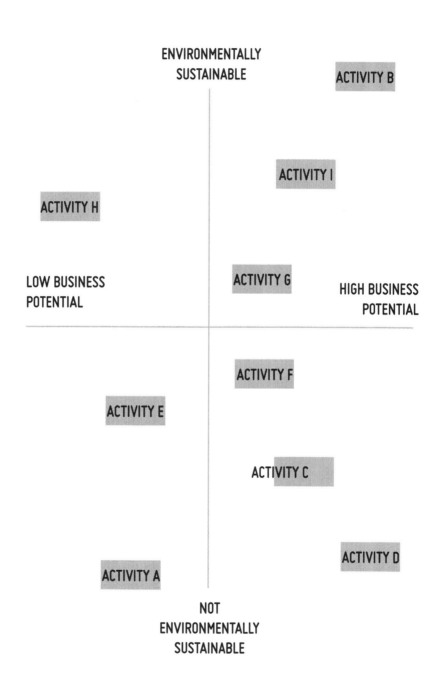

SUSTAINABILITY MAP

What is it?
This method allows the team to assess the relative business potential and environmental impact of products and services.

Why use this method?
1. Aids communication and discussion within the organization.
2. To gain competitive advantage with environmental sustainability,
3. Helps build competitive strategy
4. Helps build team alignment

Challenges
1. Can be subjective

When to use this method
1. Know Context
2. Know User
3. Frame insights
4. Explore Concepts

How to use this method
1. Moderator draws grid on whiteboard or flip chart.
2. Team brainstorms
3. Interpret the map.
4. Create strategy.
5. Products and services which have both high environmental sustainability and good business proposition are given priority.

Resources
1. Pen
2. Paper
3. White board
4. Dry erase markers

SWOT ANALYSIS

What is it?

SWOT Analysis is a useful technique for understanding your strengths and weaknesses, and for identifying both the opportunities open to you and the threats you face.

Who invented it?

Albert Humphrey 1965 Stanford University

Why use this method?

1. SWOT analysis can help you uncover opportunities that you can exploit.
2. You can analysis both your own organization, product or service as well as those of competitors.
3. Helps develop a strategy of differentiation.
4. It is inexpensive

Challenges

1. Use only verifiable information.
2. Have system for implementation.

When to use this method

1. Define intent
2. Know Context
3. Know User
4. Frame insights

Resources

1. Post-it-notes
2. SWOT template
3. Pens
4. White board
5. Video camera
6. Dry-erase markers

How to use this method

1. Explain basic rules of brainstorming.
2. Ask questions related to the SWOT categories.
3. Record answers on a white board or video
4. Categorize ideas into groups
5. Consider when evaluating "What will the institution gain or lose?"

References

1. Armstrong. M. A handbook of Human Resource Management Practice (10th edition) 2006, Kogan Page, London ISBN 0-7494-4631-5

Some sample SWOT questions

Strengths

1. Advantages of proposition
2. Capabilities
3. Competitive advantages
4. Marketing – reach, distribution
5. Innovative aspects
6. Location and geographical
7. Price, value, quality?
8. Accreditation, certifications
9. Unique selling proposition
10. Human resources
11. Experience,
12. Assets
13. Return on investment
14. Processes, IT, communications
15. Cultural, attitudinal, behavioral
16. Management cover, succession

Weaknesses

1. Value of proposition
2. Things we cannot do.
3. Things we are not good at
4. Perceptions of brand
5. Financial
6. Own known vulnerabilities
7. Time scales, deadlines and pressures
8. Reliability of data, plan predictability
9. Morale, commitment, leadership
10. Accreditation,
11. Cash flow, start-up cash-drain
12. Continuity, supply chain robustness
13. Effects on core activities, distraction
14. Processes and systems
15. Management cover, succession

Opportunities

1. Market developments
2. Competitors' vulnerabilities
3. New USP's
4. Tactics – surprise, major contracts
5. Business and product development
6. Information and research
7. Partnerships, agencies, distribution
8. Industrial trends
9. Technologies
10. Innovations
11. Global changes
12. Market opportunities
13. Specialized market niches
14. New exports or imports
15. Volumes, production, economies
16. Seasonal, weather, fashion influences

Threats

1. Political effects
2. Legislative effects
3. Obstacles faced
4. Insurmountable weaknesses
5. Environmental effects
6. IT developments
7. Competitor intentions
8. Loss of key staff
9. Sustainable financial backing
10. Market demand
11. New technologies, services, ideas
12. Vital contracts and partners
13. Sustaining internal capabilities
14. Economy – home, abroad
15. Seasonality, weather effects

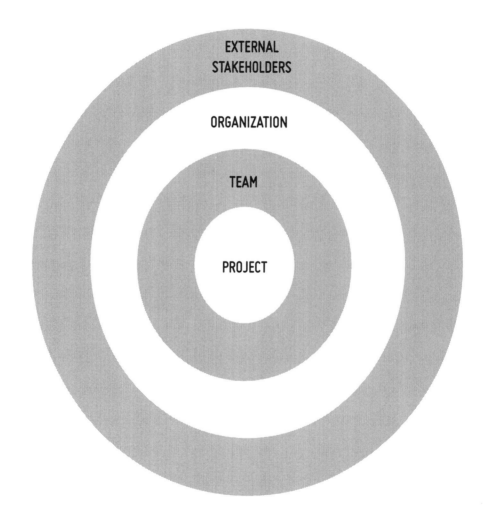

EXTERNAL
STAKEHOLDERS

ORGANIZATION

TEAM

PROJECT

ONION MAP

What is it?
An onion map is a chart that shows dependencies of a system. The items in each circle depend on the items in the smaller circle.

Who invented it?
Onion models have been used for centuries to indicate hierarchical levels of dependency. Peter Apian's 1539 Cosmographia used an onion model to illustrate the pre-Copernican model of the universe.

Why use this method?
1. It is an effective way of describing complex relationships
2. It provides a focus for team discussion and alignment
3. It is fast
4. It is inexpensive.

When to use this method
1. Know Context
2. Know User
3. Frame insights

How to use this method
1. Define the system to be represented by the onion diagram.
2. Create a circle to define the innermost level of dependency
3. Create concentric circles around the inner circle to represent progressively higher levels of dependency
4. Name the levels.

Resources
1. Pen
2. Paper
3. Software
4. Computer
5. White board
6. Dry-erase markers

References
1. Hofstede, G. (1992). Culture and Organisations: Software of the Mind. McGraw Hill, Maidenhead

MIRROR

What is it?

This method allows teams to review each other and analyze another teams performance and share information.

Why use this method?

1. Improves effectiveness of teams
2. Allows sharing of information

When to use this method

1. Define intent
2. Know Context
3. Know User
4. Frame insights
5. Explore Concepts
6. Make Plans
7. Deliver Offering

How to use this method

1. Moderator presents a number of questions to two teams.
2. Each team moves into a separate private space to discuss the questions.
3. The teams create a list of conclusions
4. Teams return to shared space
5. Teams present their conclusions.
6. Group discussion with moderator where both teams discuss other teams observations and reach agreement on changes to improve team effectiveness.

Resources

1. Two private spaces
2. White boards
3. Dry erase markers
4. Post-it-notes
5. Pens
6. Paper.

OCTAGON

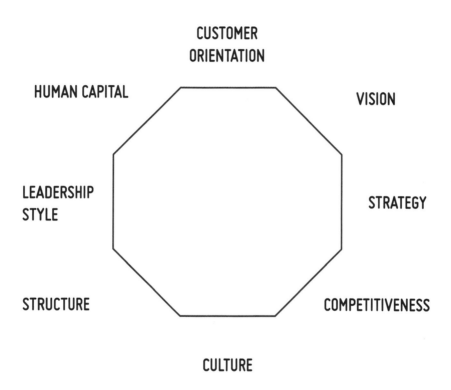

CUSTOMER
ORIENTATION

HUMAN CAPITAL

VISION

LEADERSHIP
STYLE

STRATEGY

STRUCTURE

COMPETITIVENESS

CULTURE

OCTAGAON

What is it?
The Octagon is a method that can be used in interviews with organizational stakeholders to help understand the intangible factors of an organization's culture and leadership style.

Who invented it?
Bossard Consulting

Why use this method?
1. To gain an understanding of stakeholders in an organization.

Challenges
1. Obtain authorization to use statements.

When to use this method
1. Know Context
2. Know User
3. Frame insights

How to use this method
1. Select a group of managers or stakeholders in an organization.
2. Conduct interviews with each stakeholder and ask each to supply a short single sentence comment on each of the Octagon headings.
3. Analyze the statements.
4. Create a list of insights.

Resources
1. Pen
2. Paper
3. Note pad
4. Prepared forms with questions.

BAR CHART

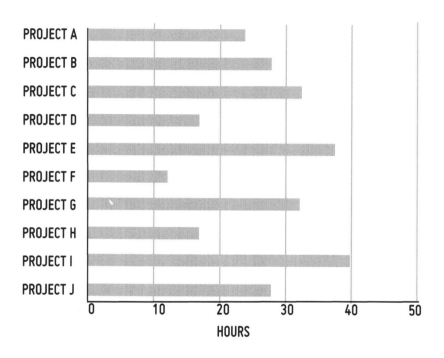

BAR CHART

What is it?
A simple bar chart is useful to present information for a quick problem or opportunity analysis. It provides a comparison of quantities of items or frequencies of events within a particular time period.

Who invented it?
The first bar graph appeared in the 1786 book The Commercial and Political Atlas, by William Playfair (1759–1823)

Why use this method?
1. To display a "snapshot" comparison of categories.
2. To depict the relationship between variations over time.
3. To illustrate process variability or trends.
4. To indicate a potential problem area (high or low frequencies).

Challenges
1. Care should be taken not to insert more than five bars or cover more than five time periods. This would make the Bar Chart cluttered and difficult to interpret.

When to use this method
1. Frame insights

How to use this method
1. Collect data from sources
2. Draw the vertical and horizontal axes.
3. Decide on the scale
4. Draw a bar for each item.
5. Label the axes

Resources
1. Pen
2. Paper
3. Graph paper
4. Computer
5. Graphics software

References
1.   Kelley, W. M.; Donnelly, R. A. (2009) The Humongous Book of Statistics Problems. New York, NY: Alpha Books ISBN 1592578659

BRAINSTORMING

What is it?
Brainstorming is one of the oldest, fastest and most widely used creativity methods. Brainstorming does need to be undertaken by experts. It can be undertaken as a group or individually. Osborn believed that brainstorming as a group was most effective. Recent research has questioned this assumption. It should be used to address a single problem. Brainstorming is worthwhile when it is part of a larger process of design.

Who invented it?
Alex Faickney Osborn 1953 is often credited with inventing brainstorming.

Why use this method?
1. It is useful for generating new types of solutions to problems.
2. Brainstorming allows each person in a group to better understand a problem.
3. It can be used to overcome creative blocks.
4. There is group buy-in to a design direction.

Challenges
1. Groupthink
2. Not enough good ideas
3. Taking turns
4. Freeloading
5. Inhibition
6. Lack of critical thinking
7. A group that is too large competes for attention.

How to use this method
1. A facilitator explains the problem to be explored and the process.
2. The problem can be written in a place where it can be seen by everyone participating
3. Defer judgment
4. Build on ideas to make them better.
5. Do not ridicule any idea.
6. One person speaking at a time.
7. Go for quantity the more ideas the better
8. No idea is too wild.
9. Stay focused on the problem
10. Be visual
11. Record everything.
12. Do not edit during a brainstorm
13. Preferred group size is from 2 to 12
14. A good facilitator should keep the ideas flowing.
15. Give a number of ideas to be generated for example 10 and time limit such as 30 minutes.
16. Analyze the results.

Resources
1. Pens
2. Post-it-notes
3. A flip chart
4. White board or wall
5. Refreshments.

References
1. Clark , Charles Hutchinson. The Dynamic New Way to Create Successful Ideas Publisher: Classic Business Bookshelf (November 23, 2010) ISBN-10: 1608425614 ISBN-13: 978-1608425617
2. Rawlinson J. Geoffrey Creative Thinking and Brainstorming. Jaico Publishing House (April 30, 2005) ISBN-10: 8172243480 ISBN-13: 978-8172243487

101 METHOD

What is it?
This is a brainstorming method focuses on creating volumes of ideas

Why use this method?
1. Leverages the diverse experiences of a team.
2. A large volume of ideas helps overcome people's inhibitions to innovating.
3. Makes group problem solving fun.
4. Helps build team cohesion.
5. Everyone can participate.

Challenges
1. Because the focus is on volume some ideas will not be useful.
2. Best used with other creativity methods

References
1. Clark , Charles Hutchinson. The Dynamic New Way to Create Successful Ideas Publisher: Classic Business Bookshelf (November 23, 2010) ISBN-10: 1608425614 ISBN-13: 978-1608425617
2. Rawlinson J. Geoffrey Creative Thinking and Brainstorming. Jaico Publishing House (April 30, 2005) ISBN-10: 8172243480 ISBN-13: 978-8172243487

When to use this method
1. Generate concepts

How to use this method
1. Define a problem
2. Select a moderator
3. Select a diverse design team of 4 to 12 people and a moderator.
4. The moderator asks the team to each generate 101 solutions to the design problem in a defined time. Allow 30 to 60 minutes.
5. Analyze results and prioritize.
6. Develop actionable ideas.

Resources
1. Pens
2. Post-it-notes
3. A flip chart
4. White board or wall
5. Refreshments

635 METHOD

What is it?
Method 635 is a structured form of brain-storming. "

Here six participant gain a thorough understanding of the task at hand and them separately writes three rough ideas for solution. These three ideas are then passed on the one of the other participants who read and add three additional ideas or modifications. This process continues until all participants have expanded or revised all original ideas. Six participants, three ideas, five rounds of supplements" (Löwgren and Stolterman 2004).

Who invented it?
Professor Bernd Rohrbach 1968

Why use this method?
1. Can generate a lot of ideas quickly
2. Participants can build on each others ideas
3. Ideas are recorded by the participants
4. Democratic method.
5. Ideas are contributed privately.

When to use this method
1. Frame insights
2. Explore Concepts

How to use this method
1. Your team should sit around a table.
2. Each team member is given a sheet of paper with the design objective written at the top.
3. Each team member is given three minutes to generate three ideas.
4. Your participants then pass the sheet of paper to the person sitting on their left.
5. Each participant must come up with three new ideas.
6. The process can stop when sheets come around the table.
7. Repeat until ideas are exhausted. No discussion at any stage.
8. No discussion.
9. Analyze ideas as a group,

Resources
1. Paper
2. Pens
3. White board
4. Large table

References
1. Rohrbach, Bernd: Creativity by rules – Method 635, a new technique for solving problems first published in the German sales magazine "Absatzwirtschaft", Volume 12, 1969. p73-75 and Volume 19, 1 October 1969.

AOKI METHOD

What is it?

The Aoki or MBS method is a structured brainstorming method that stresses input by all team members.

Who invented it?

Sadami Aoki. Used by Mitsubishi

Why use this method?

1. There is a hierarchy of ideas
2. This method requires that a quantity of ideas is generated.
3. shifts you from reacting to a static snapshot of the problem and broadens your perspective toward the problem and the relationships and connections between its components

Challenges

1. Groupthink
2. Not enough good ideas
3. Taking turns
4. Freeloading
5. Inhibition
6. Lack of critical thinking
7. A group that is too large competes for attention.

When to use this method

1. Explore Concepts

Resources

1. Paper
2. Pens
3. White board
4. Dry-erase markers
5. Post-it-notes.

How to use this method

6. Warm Up: Participants generate ideas for 15 minutes.
7. Participants present their ideas verbally to the larger group.
8. The larger group continues to generate ideas during the individual presentations.
9. For one hour the individual team members further explain their ideas to the group
10. Idea maps are created by the moderator.

References

1. Clark , Charles Hutchinson. The Dynamic New Way to Create Successful Ideas Publisher: Classic Business Bookshelf (November 23, 2010) ISBN-10: 1608425614 ISBN-13: 978-1608425617
2. Rawlinson J. Geoffrey Creative Thinking and Brainstorming. Jaico Publishing House (April 30, 2005) ISBN-10: 8172243480 ISBN-13: 978-8172243487

BODYSTORMING

What is it?

Bodystorming is method of prototyping experiences. It requires setting up an experience – complete with necessary artifacts and people – and physically "testing" it. A design team play out scenarios based on design concepts that they are developing. The method provides clues about the impact of the context on the user experience.

Who invented it?

Buchenau, Fulton 2000

Why use this method?

1. You are likely to find new possibilities and problems.
2. Generates empathy for users.
3. This method is an experiential design tool. Bodystorming helps design ideation by exploring context.
4. It is fast and inexpensive.
5. It is a form of physical prototyping
6. It is difficult to imagine misuse scenarios

Challenges

1. Some team members may find acting a difficult task.

Resources

1. Empathy tools
2. A large room
3. White board
4. Video camera

When to use this method

1. Know Context
2. Know User
3. Frame insights
4. Explore Concepts

How to use this method

1. Select team.
2. Define the locations where a design will be used.
3. Go to those locations and observe how people interact. the artifacts in their environment.
4. Develop the prototypes and props that you need to explore an idea. Identify the people, personas and scenarios that may help you with insight into the design directions.,
5. Bodystorm the scenarios.
6. Record the scenarios with video and analyze them for insights.

References

Understanding contexts by being there: case studies in bodystorming. Personal and Ubiquitous Computing, Vol. 7, No. 2. (July 2003), pp. 125–134, doi:10.1007/s00779-003-0238-7 by Antti Oulasvirta, Esko Kurvinen, Tomi Kankainen

BOUNDARY SHIFTING

What is it?

Boundary shifting involves identifying features or ideas outside the boundary of the system related to the defined problem and applying to them to the problem being addressed.

Why use this method?

1. It is fast and inexpensive.

Resources

1. Pen
2. Paper
3. White board
4. Dry-erase markers

When to use this method

1. Know Context
2. Know User
3. Frame insights

How to use this method

1. Define the problem.
2. Research outside systems that may have related ideas or problems to the defined problem.
3. Identify ideas or solutions outside the problem system.
4. Apply the outside idea or solution to the problem being addressed.

References

1. Walker, D. J., Dagger, B. K. J. and Roy, R. Creative Techniques in Product and Engineering Design. Woodhead Publishing Ltd 1991. ISBN 1 85573 025 1

BENJAMIN FRANKLIN METHOD

What is it?
A method developed by Benjamin Franklin for making decisions.

Who invented it?
Benjamin Franklin 1772

Why use this method?
1. It is simple
2. It was developed and used by Benjamin Franklin who was a successful decision maker.

When to use this method
1. Explore Concepts

Resources
1. Pen
2. Paper
3. White board
4. Dry erase markers
5. Post-it-notes

How to use this method
Quote from a letter from Benjamin Franklin to Joseph Priestley London, September 19, 1772

"To get over this, my Way is, to divide half a Sheet of Paper by a Line into two Columns, writing over the one Pro, and over the other Con. Then during three or four Days Consideration I put down under the different Heads short Hints of the different Motives that at different Times occur to me for or against the Measure. When I have thus got them all together in one View, I endeavour to estimate their respective Weights; and where I find two, one on each side, that seem equal, I strike them both out: If I find a Reason pro equal to some two Reasons con, I strike out the three. If I judge some two Reasons con equal to some three Reasons pro, I strike out the five; and thus proceeding I find at length where the Ballance lies; and if after a Day or two of farther Consideration nothing new that is of Importance occurs on either side, I come to a Determination accordingly.

And tho' the Weight of Reasons cannot be taken with the Precision of Algebraic Quantities, yet when each is thus considered separately and comparatively, and the whole lies before me, I think I can judge better, and am less likely to take a rash Step; and in fact I have found great Advantage from this kind of Equation, in what may be called Moral or Prudential Algebra"

320

BRAINWRITING

What is it?
Brainwriting is an alternative to brainstorming generating ideas by asking people to write down their ideas rather than presenting them verbally.

Who invented it?
Brahm & Kleiner, 1996

Why use this method?
1. Moderation of Brainwriting is easier than brainstorming.
2. Brainwriting tends to produce more ideas than brainstorming
3. Can be conducted in 15 to 30 minutes
4. Brainwriting is better if participants are shy or from cultures where group interaction is more guarded.
5. Brainwriting reduces the problems of groupthink.

Challenges
1. Not enough good ideas
2. Freeloading
3. Inhibition
4. Lack of critical thinking

When to use this method
1. Explore Concepts

How to use this method
1. Define the problem
2. Each participant should brainstorm three solutions in two minutes in written form.
3. Then have them pass the sheet of paper to their left.
4. Have the participants add to or build upon the existing suggestions by writing their own ideas underneath the original solutions. Allow 3 minutes.
5. The process should be repeated as many times as there are people around the table allowing an additional minute each time.
6. When you've finished post the ideas on a wall.
7. Get the group to vote on the most promising ideas.

Resources
1. Pens
2. Post-it-notes
3. A flip chart
4. White board or wall
5. Refreshments.

References
1. Clark , Charles Hutchinson. The Dynamic New Way to Create Successful Ideas Publisher: Classic Business Bookshelf (November 23, 2010) ISBN-10: 1608425614 ISBN-13: 978-1608425617
2. Rawlinson J. Geoffrey Creative Thinking and Brainstorming. Jaico Publishing House (April 30, 2005) ISBN-10: 8172243480 ISBN-13: 978-8172243487

DISNEY METHOD

What is it?

The Disney method is a parallel thinking technique. It allows a team to discuss an issue from four perspectives. It involves parallel thinking to analyze a problem, generate ideas, evaluate ideas, and to create a strategy. It is a method used in workshops. The four thinking perspectives are – Spectators, Dreamers, Realist's and Critics.

Who invented it?

Dilts, 1991

Why use this method?

1. Allows the group top discuss a problem from four different perspectives

Challenges

1. An alternative to De Bono Six hat Method.
2. Will deliver a workable solution quickly.

When to use this method

1. Explore Concepts

How to use this method

1. At the end of each of the four sessions the participants leave the room and then at a later time reenter the room then assuming the personas and perspectives of the next group. Time taken is often 60 to 90 minutes in total.
2. The spectator's view. Puts the problem in an external context. How would a consultant, a customer or an outside observer view the problem?
3. The Dreamers view. Looking for an ideal solution. What would our dream solution for this be? What if? Unconstrained brainstorm. Defer judgement. Divergent thinking. What do we desire? If we could have unlimited resources what would we do? They list their ideas on the white board.
4. Realists view. The realists are convergent thinkers. How can we turn the dreamer's views into reality? Looking for ideas that are feasible, profitable, customer focused and can be implemented within 18 months. They look through the dreamer's ideas on the white board and narrow them down to a short list, discuss them and choose the single best idea and create an implementation plan. What steps are necessary to implement this idea? Who can approve it, how much funding is needed? They draw the plan on the whiteboard and then leave the room.
5. The Critics view. What are the risks and obstacles? Who would oppose this plan? What could go wrong? Refine, improve or reject. Be constructive. This group defines the risks and obstacles, make some suggestions and write down these ideas on the white board.

Resources

1. White board
2. Dry erase markers.
3. Pens
4. Post-it-notes.
5. A private room

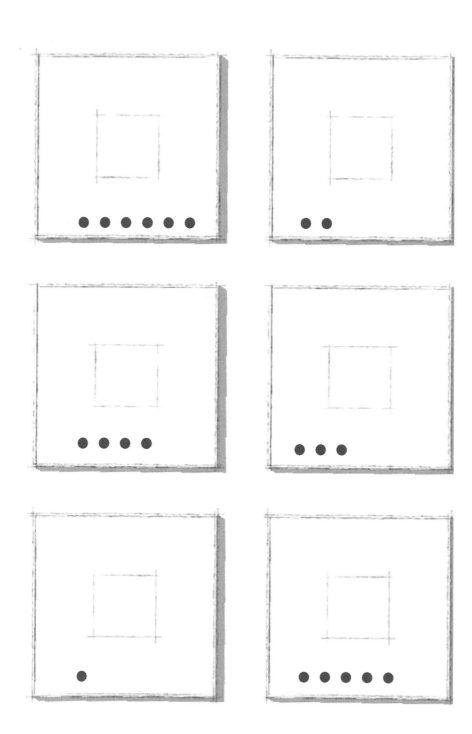

DOT VOTING

What is it?

This method is a collective way of prioritizing and converging on a design solution that uses group wisdom. Concepts can be individually scored against selection criteria such as the business proposition, ease of manufacturing, cost and usability. Each participant scores each concept against a list of assessment criteria and the scores are totaled to determine the favored ideas.

Why use this method?

It is a method of selecting a favored idea by collective rather than individual judgment. It is a fast method that allows a design to progress. It leverages the strengths of diverse team member viewpoints and experiences.

Challenges

1. The assessment is subjective.
2. Groupthink
3. Not enough good ideas
4. Inhibition
5. Lack of critical thinking

Resources

1. Large wall
2. Adhesive dots

References

1. Dotmocracy handbook Jason Diceman Version 2.2 March 2010 ISBN 45152708X EAN-13 9781451527087

When to use this method

1. Define intent
2. Know Context
3. Know User
4. Frame insights
5. Explore Concepts
6. Make Plans
7. Deliver Offering

How to use this method

1. Select a team of between 4 and 20 cross disciplinary participants.
2. Brainstorm ideas for example ask each team member to generate six ideas as sketches.
3. Each idea should be presented on one post it note or page.
4. Each designer should quickly explain each idea to the group before the group votes.
5. Spread the ideas over a wall or table.
6. Ask the team to group the ideas by similarity or affinity.
7. Ask the team to vote on their two or three favorite ideas and total the votes. You can use sticky dots or colored pins to indicate a vote or a moderator can tally the scores.
8. Rearrange the ideas so that the ideas with the dots are grouped together, ranked from most dots to least.
9. Talk about the ideas that received the most votes and see if there is a general level of comfort with taking one or more of those ideas to the next step.

OBJECTS

remote control
button
computer
phone
car
sailboat
camera
television
internet
gps
mp3 player
book

ACTIONS

smell
hear
touch
see
walk
sing
talk
dance
vision
laugh
magic
swim
play
tell a story

HEURISTIC IDEATION

What is it?
Heuristic ideation method is used to create new concepts, ideas, products or solutions.

Why use this method?
1. To create new connections and insights for products, services and experiences

Who invented it?
Couger 1995, McFadzean 1998, McFadzean, Somersall, and Coker 1998, VanGundy 1988

Resources
1. Pens
2. Markers
3. White board or flip chart
4. Dry erase markers

When to use this method
1. Explore Concepts

How to use this method
1. The group will first make two lists of words
2. Each team member selects three words from the first list and connects each word to a different word in the second list.
3. Each team members develops these ideas into concepts and illustrates or describes each concept on an index card.
4. The index cards are places on a pin board and each concept is briefly described by the team member who generated the idea.
5. The team votes to prioritize the ideas

References
1. McFadzean, E. Creativity in MS / OR: Choosing the Appropriate Technique Interfaces 29: 5 September October 1999 (pp 110 122)

IDEA ADVOCATE

What is it?
This method involves appointing advocates for ideas that were previously created during a brainstorming session.

Who invented it?
Battelle Institute in Frankfurt, Germany

Why use this method?
1. Idea advocate is a simplified form of the dialectical approach
2. To ensure fair examination of all ideas.
3. To give every presented idea equal chance of being selected.
4. To uncover the positive aspects of ideas

Challenges
1. Consideration should be given to also assigning a devil's advocate for a more balanced assessment of certain proposed ideas.
2. There should be little difference in status amongst the idea advocates.

When to use this method
1. Explore Concepts

How to use this method
1. The team reviews a list of previously generated ideas.
2. Assign idea advocate roles to:
3. A team member who proposed an idea, will implement an idea, or argues for the selection of a design direction.
4. The idea advocates present arguments to the design team on why the idea is the best direction.
5. After the advocates have presented the team votes on their preferred idea.

Resources
1. Pens
2. Markers
3. White board or flip chart
4. Dry erase markers

KJ METHOD

What is it?
The KJ method is a form of brainstorming. The KJ method places emphasis on the most important ideas. It is one of the seven tools of Japanese quality management and incorporates the Buddhist value of structured meditation.

Who invented it?
Kawakita Jiro

Why use this method?
1. There is a hierarchy of ideas
2. This method generates many ideas.
3. This method highlights the connections between ideas which is the starting point for a design solution.

Challenges
1. Groupthink
2. Not enough good ideas
3. Taking turns
4. Freeloading
5. Inhibition
6. Lack of critical thinking
7. A group that is too large competes for attention.

Resources
1. Paper
2. Pens
3. White board
4. Dry-erase markers
5. Post-it-notes.

When to use this method
1. Explore Concepts

How to use this method
1. The moderator frames the design challenge.
2. Team members generate ideas in up to 25 words on post-it notes.
3. Cards are shuffled and then handed out again to the participants.
4. Each participant should not gat any of their own cards back.
5. Each post-it note is read out by the participants, and all participants review the post-it notes that they hold to find any that seem to go with the one read out, so building a 'group'.
6. Organise post-it notes into groups.
7. Group the groups until you have no more than ten groups.
8. Sort categories into subcategories of 20-30 cards.
9. Refine groups into 10 post-it notes or less.
10. Use a white board or smooth wall.
11. Write the individual post-it notes arranged in groups on the white board or arrange the post-it notes on a wall.
12. The moderator will read out the groups and record the participant's ideas about the relationships and meaning of the information gathered.

328

LOTUS BLOSSOM

A1	A2	A3	B1	B2	B3	C1	C2	C3
A4	**A**	A5	B4	**B**	B5	C4	**C**	C5
A6	A7	A8	B6	B7	B8	C6	C7	C8
D1	D2	D3	**A**	**B**	**C**	E1	E2	E3
D4	**D**	D5	**D**		**E**	E4	**E**	E5
D6	D7	D8	**F**	**G**	**H**	E6	E7	E8
F1	F2	F3	G1	G2	G3	H1	H2	H3
F4	**F**	F5	G4	**G**	G5	H4	**H**	H5
F6	F7	F8	G6	G7	G8	H6	H7	H8

LOTUS BLOSSOM

What is it?

The lotus blossom is a creativity technique that consists a framework for idea generation that starts by generating eight concept themes based on a central theme. Each concept then serves as the basis for eight further theme explorations or variations.

Who invented it?

Yasuo Matsumura, Director of the Clover Management Research

Why use this method?

1. There is a hierarchy of ideas
2. This method requires that a quantity of ideas is generated.
3. shifts you from reacting to a static snapshot of the problem and broadens your perspective toward the problem and the relationships and connections between its components

Challenges

1. It is a somewhat rigid model. Not every problem will require the same number of concepts to be developed.

When to use this method

1. Explore Concepts

How to use this method

1. Draw up a lotus blossom diagram made up of a square in the center of the diagram and eight circles surrounding the square;
2. Write the problem in the center box of the diagram.
3. Write eight related ideas around the center.
4. Each idea then becomes the central idea of a new theme or blossom.
5. Follow step 3 with all central ideas.

Resources

1. Paper
2. Pens
3. White board
4. Dry-erase markers
5. Post-it-notes.

References

1. Michalko M., Thinkpak, Berkeley, California, Ten Speed Press, 1994.
2. Michalko, Michael, Thinkertoys: A handbook of creative-thinking techniques, Second Edition, Ten Speed Press, 2006, Toronto;
3. Sloane, Paul. The Leader's Guide to Lateral Thinking Skills: Unlocking the Creativity and Innovation in You and Your Team (Paperback - 3 Sep 2006);

MASLOW'S HIERARCHY OF NEEDS .

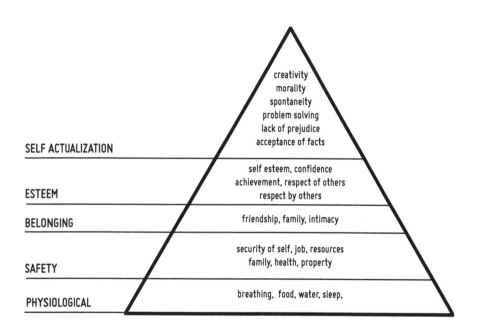

SELF ACTUALIZATION

creativity
morality
spontaneity
problem solving
lack of prejudice
acceptance of facts

ESTEEM

self esteem, confidence
achievement, respect of others
respect by others

BELONGING

friendship, family, intimacy

SAFETY

security of self, job, resources
family, health, property

PHYSIOLOGICAL

breathing, food, water, sleep,

MASLOW'S HIERARCHY OF NEEDS

What is it?
This is a psychological theory proposed by Abraham. The theory has been influential in design and marketing for half a century.

Who invented it?
Abraham Maslow 1943

Why use this method?
1. Maslow believed that these needs play a role in motivating behavior
2. Maslow believed that once these lower-level needs have been met, people move up to the next level of need

Challenges
1. The hierarchy proposed by Maslow is not today universally accepted.
2. Today it is believed that needs are not a linear hierarchy as proposed by Maslow but are more complex, systematic and interconnected.

When to use this method
1. Frame insights
2. Explore Concepts

How to use this method
The hierarchy as proposed by Maslow is:
1. Self actualization, The highest level,. personal growth and fulfilment
2. Esteem needs. Achievement, status, responsibility, reputation .
3. Social needs. friendships, romantic attachments, and families, social, community, or religious relationships.
4. Security needs. Protection, security, order, law, limits, stability
5. Physiological needs. Air, food, drink, shelter, warmth, sleep.

References
1. Maslow, Abraham (1954). Motivation and Personality. New York: Harper. pp. 236. ISBN 0-06-041987-3.
2. Kenrick, D. T., Griskevicius, V., Neuberg, S. L., & Schaller, M. (2010). Renovating the pyramid of needs: Contemporary extensions built upon ancient foundations. Perspectives on Psychological Science, 5, 292. doi: 10.1177/1745691610369469

MISUSE SCENARIOS

What is it?
This is a method that focuses on possible misuse, both unintentional and malicious, of a product or service. The method involves use of scenarios and personas to envision possible misuse cases. These may be:
1. Typical scenarios
2. Atypical scenarios
3. Extreme scenarios

Why use this method?
1. Considering misuse reduces the possibility that a product will fail in use.
2. Consider on projects where there is potential for misuse.
3. High volume manufactured products have high potential for misuse.

Challenges
1. Use customer service feedback to construct misuse scenarios.
2. It is sometimes hard to envision misuse scenarios for new products.

When to use this method
1. Know Context
2. Know User
3. Frame insights
4. Explore Concepts

How to use this method
1. Think of various types of scenarios and when they may become misuse scenarios.
2. Talk to experts and ask them to provide scenarios of misuse.
3. Consider the context of use and how that may influence misuse.
4. Brainstorm with team to create scenarios of misuse.
5. Create a list of misuse scenarios.
6. Brainstorm remedies for misuse and modify design to remedy misuse.

Resources
1. Pen
2. Paper
3. White board
4. Dry-erase markers
5. Camera

References
1. Alexander, Ian, Use/Misuse Case Analysis Elicits Non-Functional Requirements, Computing & Control Engineering Journal, Vol 14, 1, pp 40–45, February 2003
2. Sindre, Guttorm and Andreas L. Opdahl, Templates for Misuse Case Description, Proc. 7th Intl Workshop on Requirements Engineering, Foundation for Software Quality (REFSQ'2001), Interlaken, Switzerland, 4–5 June 2001

OUT OF THE BOX

What is it?
This is a method to perform out-of-the box brainstorming to generate outrageous and wild ideas.

Why use this method?
1. To generate wild ideas
2. To promote creative thinking among participants.

Resources
1. Pen
2. Paper
3. White board
4. Dry erase markers
5. Post-it-notes

Challenges
1. Avoid persona representations that may be harmful.
2. Groupthink
3. Not enough good ideas
4. Taking turns
5. Freeloading
6. Inhibition
7. Lack of critical thinking
8. A group that is too large competes for attention.

When to use this method
1. Explore Concepts

How to use this method
1. The moderator introduces this method.
2. The moderator shows the team several wild or out of the box ideas.
3. Participants generate concepts stressing that they must be wild and out of the box.
4. The moderator records the ideas on a white board.
5. The team reviews the ideas and selects some for further development and bringing back to reality.

Resources
1. Pen
2. Paper
3. White board
4. Dry erase markers
5. Post-it-notes

References
1. Clark , Charles Hutchinson. The Dynamic New Way to Create Successful Ideas Publisher: Classic Business Bookshelf (November 23, 2010) ISBN-10: 1608425614 ISBN-13: 978-1608425617
2. Rawlinson J. Geoffrey Creative Thinking and Brainstorming. Jaico Publishing House (April 30, 2005) ISBN-10: 8172243480 ISBN-13: 978-8172243487

NHK METHOD

What is it?
The NHK method is a rigorous iterative process of brainstorming of ideas following a predetermined structure.

Who invented it?
Hiroshi Takahashi

Why use this method?
1. This method requires that a quantity of ideas is generated.

Challenges
1. Groupthink
2. Not enough good ideas
3. Taking turns
4. Freeloading
5. Inhibition
6. Lack of critical thinking
7. A group that is too large competes for attention.

When to use this method
1. Explore Concepts

Resources
1. Paper
2. Pens
3. White board
4. Dry-erase markers
5. Post-it-notes.

How to use this method
1. Define problem statement.
1. Each participant writes down five ideas on five separate cards.
2. Create groups of five participants
3. While each person explains their ideas, the others continue to record new ideas.
4. Collect, and create groups of related concepts.
5. Form new groups of two or three people Brainstorm for half an hour.
6. Groups organize ideas and present them to the larger group.
7. Record all ideas on the white board.
8. Form larger groups of ten people and work further brainstorm each of the ideas on the white board.

References
1. Clark , Charles Hutchinson. The Dynamic New Way to Create Successful Ideas Publisher: Classic Business Bookshelf (November 23, 2010) ISBN-10: 1608425614 ISBN-13: 978-1608425617
2. Rawlinson J. Geoffrey Creative Thinking and Brainstorming. Jaico Publishing House (April 30, 2005) ISBN-10: 8172243480 ISBN-13: 978-8172243487

NOMINAL GROUP METHOD

What is it?
The nominal group method is a brainstorming method that is designed to encourage participation of all members of the team and minimizes the possibility of more vocal members from dominating the discussion.

Who invented it?
William Fox

Why use this method?
1. To define and prioritize problems or opportunities
2. To understand the best solution to a problem
3. To create a plan to implement an opportunity

Resources
1. White board
2. Dry erase markers
3. Blank postcards

When to use this method
1. Frame insights
2. Explore Concepts

How to use this method
1. Distribute information about the process to participants before the meeting.
2. Participants drop anonymous suggestions into an unmonitored suggestion box written on blank postcards.
3. The suggestions are distributed to participants before the meeting so that they can think about them.
4. In the meeting the moderator writes the suggestions on to a white board
5. Each participant has the opportunity to speak in support or against any of the suggestions.
6. The moderator leads the team in to clarify each idea,
7. The moderator instructs each person to work silently and independently for five minutes, recording as many ideas, thoughts, or answers as possible on paper.
8. The moderator asks the group to list 5 to 10 ideas that the like the most, in order of importance, and to pass them to the moderator.
9. The moderator counts up the number of votes for each idea.
10. Each participant is given a number of votes that they record on blank postcards which are collected face down and tallied.

References
1. The Memory Jogger II: A Pocket Guide of Tools for Continuous Improvement and Effective Planning Michael Brassard (Author), Diane Ritter (Author), Francine Oddo (Editor) 1st edition (January 15, 1994) ISBN-10: 1879364441 ISBN-13: 978-1879364448

NYAKA

What is it?

The Nyaka method is a form of brainstorming. The Nyaka method places emphasis on exploring problems and solutions to problems.

Why use this method?

1. There is a hierarchy of ideas
2. This method generates many ideas.

Challenges

1. Groupthink
2. Not enough good ideas
3. Taking turns
4. Freeloading
5. Inhibition
6. Lack of critical thinking
7. A group that is too large competes for attention.

Resources

1. Paper
2. Pens
3. White board
4. Dry-erase markers
5. Post-it-notes.

When to use this method

1. Explore Concepts

How to use this method

1. Define a moderator
2. The moderator draws a vertical line on a whiteboard.
3. Time limit of 30 minutes
4. The moderator asks the team to define as many things that are wrong with a design or service or experience as possible.
5. The moderator asks the team to define solutions for as many of the problems defined as possible.
6. Create a hierarchy of problems and a hierarchy of solutions for each problem.
7. A group size of 4 to 20 people is optimum.
8. For larger groups the moderator can break the group into groups of 4 or 5 people.

References

1. Clark , Charles Hutchinson. The Dynamic New Way to Create Successful Ideas Publisher: Classic Business Bookshelf (November 23, 2010) ISBN-10: 1608425614 ISBN-13: 978-1608425617
2. Rawlinson J. Geoffrey Creative Thinking and Brainstorming. Jaico Publishing House (April 30, 2005) ISBN-10: 8172243480 ISBN-13: 978-8172243487

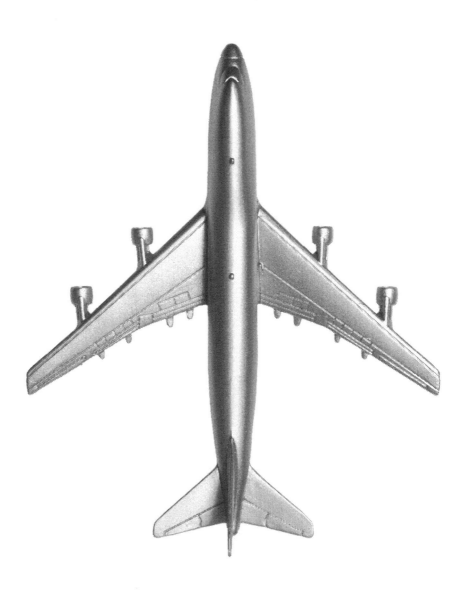

OBJECTSTORMING

What is it?
A brainstorming technique that uses found objects for inspiration.

Who invented it?
Alex Faickney Osborn 1953 is often credited with inventing brainstorming.

Why use this method?
1. Leverages the diverse experiences of a team.
2. Makes group problem solving fun.
3. Helps build team cohesion.
4. Everyone can participate.

Challenges
1. Groupthink
2. Not enough good ideas
3. Taking turns
4. Freeloading
5. Inhibition
6. Lack of critical thinking
7. A group that is too large competes for attention.

When to use this method
1. Generate concepts

How to use this method
1. The moderator introduces the method to the group.
2. The problem is defined by the moderator.
3. The larger group is broken down into groups of 4 or 5 participants. The moderator collects a diverse collection of objects before the brainstorming session.
4. Each participant is given two objects and asked to use them as inspiration to generate 10 ideas
5. Allow 20 minutes
6. The participants are asked to vote for their three preferred solutions.
7. Select the top ideas for further development.

Resources
1. Pens
2. Post-it-notes
3. A flip chart
4. White board or wall
5. Refreshments

PERSONAL

What is it?
Recent research has suggested that some individuals are more creative working alone for brainstorming sessions rather than in groups. In this case the divergent idea generation is done by an individual and the convergent phase is done by the team.

Who invented it?
Alex Faickney Osborn 1953 is often credited with inventing brainstorming.

Why use this method?
1. Leverages the diverse experiences of a team.
2. Uses the creativity of the individual free from distractions.
3. Helps build empathy.

Challenges
1. Some ideas that you generate using the tool may be impractical.
2. Best used with other creativity methods

When to use this method
1. Generate concepts

How to use this method
1. Define a problem
2. Find a quiet place
3. Generate as many ideas as possible in 30 minutes.
4. Get the team together and present the ideas to them.
5. Get the team to vote on which ideas they like the most. Two votes per person.
6. Analyze results and prioritize.
7. Develop actionable ideas.

Resources
1. Pens
2. Post-it-notes
3. A flip chart
4. White board or wall
5. Refreshments

References
1. Clark , Charles Hutchinson. The Dynamic New Way to Create Successful Ideas Publisher: Classic Business Bookshelf (November 23, 2010) ISBN-10: 1608425614 ISBN-13: 978-1608425617
2. Rawlinson J. Geoffrey Creative Thinking and Brainstorming. Jaico Publishing House (April 30, 2005) ISBN-10: 8172243480 ISBN-13: 978-8172243487

PERSONA BRAINSTORMING

What is it?
This is a brainstorming method that uses the imagined perspectives of an identified persona or group identified as one of your client's customer groups such as students look at a design problem.

Who invented it?
Alex Faickney Osborn 1953 is often credited with inventing brainstorming.

Why use this method?
1. Leverages the diverse experiences of a team.
2. Helps build empathy.
3. Makes group problem solving fun.
4. Helps build team cohesion.
5. Everyone can participate.

Challenges
1. Some ideas that you generate using the tool may be impractical.
2. Best used with other creativity methods

When to use this method
1. Generate concepts

How to use this method
1. Define a problem
2. Select a diverse design team of 4 to 12 people and a moderator.
3. Identify a persona to focus on. See personas.
4. Ask the team how they would deal with the problem if they were the persona
5. Analyze results and prioritize.
6. Develop actionable ideas.

Resources
1. Pens
2. Post-it-notes
3. A flip chart
4. White board or wall
5. Refreshments

References
1. Clark , Charles Hutchinson. The Dynamic New Way to Create Successful Ideas Publisher: Classic Business Bookshelf (November 23, 2010) ISBN-10: 1608425614 ISBN-13: 978-1608425617
2. Rawlinson J. Geoffrey Creative Thinking and Brainstorming. Jaico Publishing House (April 30, 2005) ISBN-10: 8172243480 ISBN-13: 978-8172243487

PIN CARDS

What is it?
The pin cards technique is a brainwriting process to generate ideas on colored cards that are sorted into groups and discussed. This method allows participants to think of more ideas during the writing process. This method can generate more ideas than some other brainstorming methods.

Who invented it?
Wolfgang Schnelle

Why use this method?
1. To generate ideas to solve a problem
2. To produce many ideas quickly and without filtering from other participants.

Challenges
1. Cards need to be passed on quickly
2. Participants may feel time stressed.
3. Some participants may want to make their ideas confidential.

Resources
1. Colored blank index cards
2. Pins
3. Pin Board
4. Pens
5. Markers

When to use this method
1. Explore Concepts

How to use this method
1. The moderator writes the problem statement on a white board.
2. The participants should be seated around a large table.
3. The moderator distributes 10 cards of the same color to each participant.
4. Each participant receives different-colored cards.
5. Participants record one idea per card.
6. Ideas can be a cartoon sketch or a sentence
7. Completed cards are passed to the person on the participant's right hand side.
8. Participants can review cards from a person on their left hand side.
9. After 30 to 45 minutes all the participants pin the cards that they have to a wall.
10. Each participant should aim to produce at least 40 ideas.
11. The team sorts the cards into a number of groups by association. The type of association are determined by the group.
12. The participants prioritize the groups and combine the ideas in the favored group for further development.

References
1. Nancy R. Tague .The Quality Toolbox, Second Edition. SQ Quality Press; 2 edition (March 30, 2005) ISBN-10: 0873896394 ISBN-13: 978-0873896399

RELATED CONTEXT

What is it?

A method that involves discovering and projecting the thinking of another sector, brand, organization or context onto a design problem.

Why use this method?

A method of discovering affinities that can facilitate innovative thinking and solutions.

1. Scenarios become a focus for discussion which helps evaluate and refine concepts.
2. Usability issues can be explored.
3. Scenarios help us create an end to end experience.
4. Personas give us a framework to evaluate possible solutions.

Challenges

1. Strong personalities can influence the group in negative ways.
2. Include problem situations
3. Hard to envision misuse scenarios.

When to use this method

1. Know Context
2. Know User
3. Frame insights
4. Generate Concepts

How to use this method

1. Identify a design problem
2. Put together a design team of 4 to 12 members with a moderator.
3. Brainstorm a list of sectors, organizations, or contexts that may imply a different approach or thinking to your design problem.
4. Imagine your design problem with the associated list.
5. Generate concepts for each relationship
6. Vote for favored directions using dot voting method.
7. Analyze and summarize insights.

Resources

1. Post-it notes
2. White board
3. Paper
4. Pens
5. Dry-erase markers

References

1. "Scenarios," IDEO Method Cards. ISBN 0-9544132-1-0
2. Carroll, John M. Making Use: Scenario-based design of human-computer interactions. MIT Press, 2000.
3. Carroll J. M. Five Reasons for Scenario Based Design. Elsevier Science B. V. 2000.

RESOURCES

What is it?
This is a brainstorming method that uses the availability of resources to look at a design problem.

Who invented it?
Alex Faickney Osborn 1953 is often credited with inventing brainstorming.

Why use this method?
1. Leverages the diverse experiences of a team.
2. Helps build empathy.
3. Makes group problem solving fun.
4. Helps build team cohesion.
5. Everyone can participate.

Challenges
1. Some ideas that you generate using the tool may be impractical.
2. Best used with other creativity methods

References
1. Clark , Charles Hutchinson. The Dynamic New Way to Create Successful Ideas Publisher: Classic Business Bookshelf (November 23, 2010) ISBN-10: 1608425614 ISBN-13: 978-1608425617
2. Rawlinson J. Geoffrey Creative Thinking and Brainstorming. Jaico Publishing House (April 30, 2005) ISBN-10: 8172243480 ISBN-13: 978-8172243487

When to use this method
1. Generate concepts

How to use this method
1. Define a problem
2. Select a diverse design team of 4 to 12 people and a moderator.
3. Identify a resource to limit or make more available such as finance, time, people, materials or process.
4. Ask the team how they would deal with the problem if the resource was changed as proposed
5. Analyze results and prioritize.
6. Develop actionable ideas.

Resources
1. Pens
2. Post-it-notes
3. A flip chart
4. White board or wall
5. Refreshments

ROLESTORMING

What is it?
Rolestorming is a brainstorming method where participants adopt other people's identity while brainstorming.

Who invented it?
Rick Griggs1980s

Why use this method?
1. Helps reduce inhibitions which some team members may have in suggesting innovative solutions.

Challenges
1. Avoid persona representations that may be harmful.
2. Groupthink
3. Not enough good ideas
4. Taking turns
5. Freeloading
6. Inhibition
7. Lack of critical thinking
8. A group that is too large competes for attention.

When to use this method
1. Explore Concepts

How to use this method
1. Select moderator
2. Conduct a traditional brainstorming session
3. At the conclusion of the first brainstorming session the moderator identifies a number of identities to be used for the second session
4. The identities can be any person not in the brainstorming group such as a competitor, a famous person, a boss. They should be known to the team members.
5. The Moderator asks some questions
How would this identity solve the problem?
What would this persona see as the problem?
Where would this persona see the problem?
Why would the persona see a problem?
6. Brainstorm in character.
7. Use words such as "My persona"
8. Share ideas.

References
1. Clark , Charles Hutchinson. The Dynamic New Way to Create Successful Ideas Publisher: Classic Business Bookshelf (November 23, 2010) ISBN-10: 1608425614 ISBN-13: 978-1608425617
2. Rawlinson J. Geoffrey Creative Thinking and Brainstorming. Jaico Publishing House (April 30, 2005) ISBN-10: 8172243480 ISBN-13: 978-8172243487

SENSORIAL METHOD

What is it?

Design in northern Europe and the United States focuses on the visual sense which is only a component of the design experience. A design such as an Italian sports car gives greater consideration to other senses such as hearing, smell touch to give a consistent experience of through all senses to a product user.

Who invented it?

Rob Curedale 1995

Why use this method?

1. It gives a design a greater experience of quality than a design that focuses on the visual sense.
2. It gives a consistent experience.
3. It provides a more stimulating experience than a design that focuses on the visual experience.

Challenges

1. Groupthink
2. Not enough good ideas
3. Taking turns
4. Freeloading
5. Inhibition
6. Lack of critical thinking
7. A group that is too large competes for attention.

When to use this method

1. Explore Concepts

How to use this method

1. The moderator frames the design challenge.
2. Team members generate ideas on post-it notes.
3. The team works through 20 minute brainstorming sessions in each sense, Vision, smell, touch hearing, taste.
4. Ask team members to generate 6 to 10 ideas each under each category.
5. Use up to 25 words for non visual senses and simple sketches for the visual ideas.
6. Organise post-it notes into groups through discussion with five concepts in each group, one idea from each sense group or five different senses in each group.
7. Ask team to vote on which groups have the most potential for further development.

Resources

1. Paper
2. Pens
3. White board
4. Dry-erase markers
5. Post-it-notes.

SCENARIOS

What is it?

A scenario is a narrative or story about how people may experience a design in a particular future context of use. They can be used to predict or explore future interactions with concept products or services. Scenarios can be presented by media such as storyboards or video or be written. They can feature single or multiple actors participating in product or service interactions.

Who invented it?

Herman Kahn, Rand Corporation 1950, USA

Why use this method?

1. Scenarios become a focus for discussion which helps evaluate and refine concepts.
2. Usability issues can be explored at a very early stage in the design process.
3. The are useful tool to align a team vision.
4. Scenarios help us create an end to end experience.
5. Interactive experiences involve the dimension of time.
6. Personas give us a framework to evaluate possible solutions.

Challenges

1. Generate scenarios for a range of situations.
2. Include problem situations
3. Hard to envision misuse scenarios.

When to use this method

1. Frame insights
2. Generate Concepts
3. Create Solutions

How to use this method

1. Identify the question to investigate.
2. Decide time and scope for the scenario process.
3. Identify stake holders and uncertainties.
4. Define the scenarios.
5. Create storyboards of users goals, activities, motivations and tasks.
6. Act out the scenarios.
7. The session can be videotaped.
8. Analyze the scenarios through discussion.
9. Summarize insights

Resources

1. Storyboard templates
2. Pens
3. Video cameras
4. Props
5. White board
6. Dry-erase markers

References

1. "Scenarios," IDEO Method Cards. ISBN 0-9544132-1-0
2. Carroll, John M. Making Use: Scenario-based design of human-computer interactions. MIT Press, 2000.
3. Carroll J. M. Five Reasons for Scenario Based Design. Elsevier Science B. V. 2000.
4. Carroll, John M. Scenario-Based Design: Envisioning Work and Technology in System Development.

WORD LISTS

VERB LIST	ADJECTIVE LIST	ADVERB LIST	PRODUCT LIST
walk	adaptable	accidentally	GPS
stand	adventurous	anxiously	marine
reach	affable	beautifully	printer
sit	affectionate	blindly	copy
jump	agreeable	boldly	chair
fly	ambitious	bravely	sofa
accept	amiable	brightly	video
allow	amicable	calmly	game
advise	amusing	carefully	camera
answer	brave	carelessly	desk
arrive	bright	cautiously	tv
ask	broad-minded	clearly	music
avoid	calm	correctly	floor
stop	careful	courageously	bookcase
agree	charming	cruelly	tools
deliver	communicative	daringly	fence
depend	compassionate	deliberately	cart
describe	conscientious	doubtfully	car
deserve	considerate	eagerly	house
destroy	convivial	easily	bean bag
disappear	courageous	elegantly	audio

SEMANTIC INTUITION

What is it?
Semantic intuition is a method of generating ideas based on word associations.

Who invented it?
Warfield, Geschka, & Hamilton, 1975. Battelle Institute

Why use this method?
1.   To find new solutions to a problem.

When to use this method
1.   Explore Concepts

Resources
1.   Pens
2.   Paper
3.   Post-it -notes
4.   White board
5.   Dry erase markers.

How to use this method
1.   Define the problem to be explored.
2.   The team brainstorms two to four word lists that are related to the problem. They could be for example a list of nouns, a list of verbs and a list of adjectives.
3.   The team makes a forth lists of associations of two or three words from the lists that can form the basis of new ideas.
4.   Combine one word from one set with another word from the other set.
5.   The team visualizes new products services or experiences based on the word associations.
6.   Each team member produces five to ten ideas based on the word associations over a 30 minute period.
7.   The ideas are prioritized by the group by voting.

References
1.   Warfield, J. N., H. Geschka, and R. Hamilton, Methods of Idea Management, Approaches to Problem Solving No. 4, Columbus: Academy for Contemporary Problems, August, 1975.

SCAMPER

What is it?
SCAMPER is a brainstorming technique and creativity method that uses seven words as prompts.
1. Substitute.
2. Combine.
3. Adapt.
4. Modify.
5. Put to another use.
6. Eliminate.
7. Reverse.

Who invented it?
Bob Eberle based on work by Alex Osborne

Why use this method?
1. Scamper is a method that can help generate innovative solutions to a problem.
2. Leverages the diverse experiences of a team.
3. Makes group problem solving fun.
4. Helps get buy in from all team members for solution chosen.
5. Helps build team cohesion.
6. Everyone can participate.

Challenges
1. Some ideas that you generate using the tool may be impractical.
2. Best used with other creativity methods

When to use this method
1. Generate concepts

How to use this method
1. Select a product or service to apply the method.
2. Select a diverse design team of 4 to 12 people and a moderator.
3. Ask questions about the product you identified, using the SCAMPER mnemonic to guide you.
4. Create as many ideas as you can.
5. Analyze
6. Prioritize.
7. Select the best single or several ideas to further brainstorm.

Resources
1. Pens
2. Post-it-notes
3. A flip chart
4. White board or wall
5. Refreshments

References
1. Scamper: Creative Games and Activities for Imagination Development. Bob Eberle April 1, 1997 ISBN-10: 1882664248 ISBN-13: 978-1882664245

SCAMPER QUESTIONS

Substitute

1. What materials or resources can you substitute or swap to improve the product?
2. What other product or process could you substitute?
3. What rules could you use?
4. Can you use this product in another situation?

Combine

1. Could you combine this product with another product?
2. Could you combine several goals?
3. Could you combine the use of the product with another use?
4. Could you join resources with someone else?

Adapt

1. How could you adapt or readjust this product to serve another purpose or use?
2. What else is the product like?
3. What could you imitate to adapt this product?
4. What exists that is like the product?
5. Could the product adapt to another context?

Modify

1. How could you change the appearance of the product?
2. What could you change ?
3. What could you focus on to create more return on investment?
4. Could you change part of the product?

Put To Another Use

1. Can you use this product in another situation?
2. Who would find this product useful?
3. How would this product function in a new context?
4. Could you recycle parts of this product to create a new product?

Eliminate

1. How could you make the product simpler?
2. What features, parts, could you eliminate?
3. What could you understate or tone down?
4. Could you make the product smaller or more efficient?
5. Would the product function differently if you removed part of the product?

Reverse

1. What would happen if you changed the operation sequence?
2. What if you do the reverse of what you are trying to do?
3. What components could you substitute to change the order of this product?
4. What roles could you change?

STP METHOD

What is it?

STP is a brainstorming method designed to help define ways of reaching a goal.

Who invented it?

Ava S Butler 1996

Why use this method?

1. To generate new ideas

Challenges

1. Groupthink
2. Not enough good ideas
3. Taking turns
4. Freeloading
5. Inhibition
6. Lack of critical thinking
7. A group that is too large competes for attention.

Resources

1. Pens
2. Post-it-notes
3. A flip chart
4. White board or wall
5. Refreshments.

References

1. Butler, Ava S. (1996) Teamthink Publisher: Mcgraw Hill ISBN 0070094330
2. Rawlinson J. Geoffrey Creative Thinking and Brainstorming. Jaico Publishing House (April 30, 2005) ISBN-10: 8172243480

When to use this method

1. Explore Concepts

How to use this method

1. The moderator writes three headings on a white board. Situation, target and proposal.
2. The moderator reviews the rules of brainstorming. Go for quantity.
3. The moderator asks the question "What do you see as the current situation?"
4. When all ideas have been recorded the moderator asks "Which comments need clarification?"
5. After team members provide clarification the moderator asks " What is our ideal goal?"
6. After all ideas have been recorded and clarifies the moderator asks" What is our preferred target?"
7. After the team votes and a preferred target is selected the moderator asks "How can we get from our current situation to our preferred target?"
8. After all ideas have been recorded and clarified the team selects a preferred way to get to the target by voting.

SIX THINKING HATS

What is it?

Six thinking hats is a tool for thinking described in a book by the same name by Edward de Bono. It can help a design team understand the effects of decisions from different viewpoints.

1. White Hat thinking is information, numbers, data needs and gaps.
2. Red Hat thinking is intuition, desires and emotion.
3. Black Hat thinking is the hat of judgment and care.
4. Yellow Hat thinking is the logical positive.
5. Green Hat thinking is the hat of creativity, alternatives, proposals, provocations and change.
6. Blue Hat thinking is the overview or process control.

Who invented it?

Edward de Bono 1985

Challenges

1. When describing your concept, be specific about your goal.
2. Utilize your thinking for practical solutions.
3. Always think in the style of the hat you're wearing.
4. Stick to the rules.

Why use this method?

The key theoretical reasons to use the Six Thinking Hats are to:

1. Encourage Parallel Thinking
2. Encourage full-spectrum thinking
3. Separate ego from performance
4. Encourage critical thinking.

When to use this method

1. Know Context
2. Know User
3. Frame insights
4. Generate Concepts
5. Create Solutions

How to use this method

1. Optimum number of participants is 4 to 8.
2. Present the facts White Hat.
3. Generate ideas on how the issue should be handled Green Hat.
4. Evaluate the ideas. Yellow Hat.
5. List the drawbacks Black Hat.
6. Get the feelings about alternatives Red Hat.
7. Summarize and finish the meeting. Blue Hat.
8. Time required 90 minutes.

Resources

1. Paper and
2. Pens,
3. Descriptions of different hats
4. Symbols of hats
5. Space to sit in the circle

References

1. de Bono, Edward (1985). Six Thinking Hats: An Essential Approach to Business Management. Little, Brown, & Company. ISBN 0-316-17791-1 (hardback) and 0316178314 (paperback).

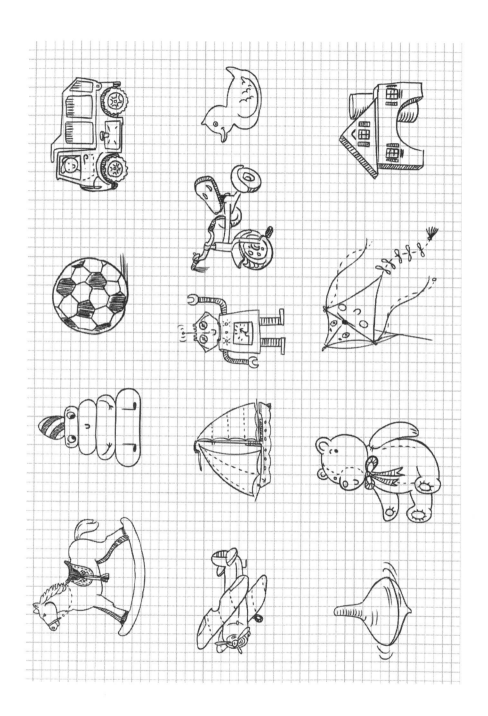

10 X 10 SKETCH METHOD

What is it?

This method is an approach to making early concept generation sketching more efficient in use of time than the method that stresses finished sketches early in the design process. It allows more time to explore ideas and so stresses the quality of thinking and the final solution. The 10 x 10 method involves creating ten rows with ten thumbnail sketches per row on each page.

Why use this method?

1. It allows more exploration of alternative ideas in a shorter time
2. May lead to a final concept which is a better design than traditional approaches.
3. Prevents sketches from becoming jewelry in the mind of the designer and more important than the quality of the final design solution.

Challenges

1. This method takes discipline

When to use this method

1. Explore Concepts

How to use this method

1. Traditional design concept exploration involves a designer producing six to 12 alternative design concepts presented as attractive renderings
2. This method involves a designer making ten rows of ten simple fast cartoon like sketches per page.
3. Each sketch should be no larger than one inch by one inch.
4. The designer produces 5 to 20 pages of very fast sketches during first phase of concept exploration
5. Designs are reviewed and ranked by the design team following a discussion and presentation by the designer and a relatively small number are selected for iteration, recombination and further development.
6. At the next stage more finished and larger concept sketches are produced

Resources

1. Paper
2. Fine line pens
3. Sharpie markers

SYNECTICS

What is it?

Synectics is a structured creativity method that is based on analogy. Synectics is based on observations collected during thousands of hours of group process and group problem solving and decision making activities (Nolan 1989)The word synectics combines derives from Greek "the bringing together of diverse elements."

Who invented it?

George Prince and William Gordon 1976

Why use this method?

1. Use to stimulate creative thinking and generate new problem solving approaches.
2. Synectics provides an environment in which risk taking is validated.
3. Synectics can be fun and productive.

Challenges

1. Synectics is more demanding than brainstorming,
2. If the analogy is too obvious, then it may not promote innovative thinking.
3. Synectics works best as a group process.

When to use this method

1. Frame insights
2. Generate Concepts

How to use this method

1. Problem definition.
2. Create an analogy. Use ideas from the natural or man-made world, connections with historical events, your location, etc.
3. Use this Sentence Stem: An is a lot like a y because...
4. Use a syntectic trigger Mechanism like a picture, poem, song, drawing etc. to start your analogical reasoning.
5. The group generates as many solution approaches, called springboards, as possible.
6. Idea selection.
7. Excursions – Structured side trips.
8. Develop the selected ideas into concepts.
9. Analyze the connections in the analogy you have created.

Resources

1. Paper
2. Pens
3. White board
4. Dry-erase markers

References

1. Gordon, William J.J. Synectics: The Development of Creative Capacity. (New York: Harper and row, Publishers, 1961
2. Nolan, Vincent. "Whatever Happened to Synectics?" Creativity and Innovation Management, v. 21 n.1 (2003): 25.

DESIGN CHARETTE

What is it?

A design charette is a collaborative design workshop usually held over one day or several days. Charettes are a fast way of generating ideas while involving diverse stakeholders in your decision process. Charettes have many different structures and often involve multiple sessions. The group divides into smaller groups. The smaller groups present to the larger group.

Who invented it?

The French word, "charrette" spelt with two r's means "cart" This use of the term is said to originate from the École des Beaux Arts in Paris during the 19th century, where a cart, collected final drawings while students finished their work.

Why use this method?

1. Fast and inexpensive.
2. Increased probability of implementation.
3. Stakeholders can share information.
4. Promotes trust.

Challenges

1. Managing workflow can be challenging.
2. Stakeholders may have conflicting visions.

When to use this method

1. Define intent
2. Know context and user
3. Frame insights
4. Explore concepts
5. Make Plans

Resources

1. Large space
2. Tables
3. Chairs
4. White boards
5. Dry-erase markers
6. Camera
7. Post-it-notes

References

1. Day, C. (2003). Consensus Design: Socially Inclusive Process. Oxford, UK, and Burlington, MA: Elsevier Science, Architectural Press.

PICTIVE

What is it?

PICTIVE (Plastic Interface for Collaborative Technology Initiative through Video Exploration) is a low fidelity participatory design method used to develop graphical user interfaces. It allows users to participate in the development process. A PICTIVE prototype gives a user a sense of what a system or a piece of software will look like and how it will behave when completed.

Who invented it?

Developed by Michael J. Muller and others at Bell Communications Research around 1990

Why use this method?

1. Less development time.
2. Less development costs.
3. Involves users.
4. Gives quantifiable user feedback.
5. Facilitates system implementation since users know what to expect.
6. Results user oriented solutions.
7. Gets users with diverse experience involved.

Challenges

1. Designers can become too attached to their prototypes and allow them to become jewelry that stands in the way of further refinement.
2. Do not worry about it being pretty.

When to use this method

1. Explore Concepts

How to use this method

1. A PICTIVE is usually made from simple available tools and materials like pens, paper, Post-It stickers, paper clips and icons on cards.
2. Allow thirty minutes for initial design.
3. Allow ten minutes for user testing.
4. Ten minutes for modification.
5. Five minutes for user testing.
6. Create task scenario.
7. Anything that moves or changes should be a separate element.
8. The designer uses these materials to represent elements such as drop-down boxes, menu bars, and special icons. During a design session, users modify the mock up based on their own experience.
9. Take notes for later review.
10. Record the session with a video camera
11. The team then reviews the ideas and develops a strategy to apply them.
12. A PICTIVE enables non technical people to participate in the design process.

References

1. Michael J. Muller PICTIVE an exploration in participatory design. Published in: ·
Proceeding CHI '91 Proceedings of the SIGCHI Conference on Human Factors in Computing Systems Pages 225-231 ACM New York, NY, USA ©1991 table of contents ISBN:0-89791-383-3 doi 10.1145/108844.108896

APPEARANCE PROTOTYPE

What is it?

Appearance prototypes look like but do not work like the final product. The are often fabricated using a variety of rapid prototyping techniques from digital 3d models or by hand in materials such as hard foam, wood or plastics. Usually, appearance prototypes are "for show" and short term use and are not designed to be handled.

Challenges

1.   Designers can become too attached to their prototypes and allow them to become jewelry that stands in the way of further refinement.
2.   Clients may believe that the design is finalized when more refinement is required.
3.   They are expensive to produce,

Why use this method?

May be used to get approval for a final design from a client or to create images for literature or a web site prior to the availability of manufactured products.

When to use this method

1.   Explore Concepts

How to use this method

1.   They give non-designers a good idea of what the production object will look like and feel like.

References

1.   Constantine, L. L., Windl, H., Noble, J., and Lockwood, L. A. D. "From Abstraction to Realization in User Interface Design: Abstract Prototypes Based on Canonical Components." Working Paper, The Convergence Colloquy, July 2000.

DARK HORSE PROTOTYPE

What is it?

A dark horse prototype is your most creative idea built as a fast prototype. The innovative approach serves as a focus for finding the optimum real solution to the design problem.

"Dark horse prototypes are three dimensional physical prototypes that are built to explore a previously rejected idea. In the world of horse racing, a dark horse is a bet that has the least likely odds to win, but which ultimately may have the greatest chance of reward. Likewise, designers may have rejected certain ideas because they were perceived as being too risky, radical, impossible, unacceptable, and so on. The dark horse prototype gives designers the permission to think bigger and more creatively. In practice, a dark horse prototype is an iteration of an existing prototype. What CFI has found is that designers often dismiss their earlier intuition and gut sense, and the early ideas often become more predictive of the final success of the project deliverable than subsequent iterations. Prof. Cutkosky realized that students often became enamored of the prototypes they built, to the point that they narrowed their solutions too early in the design process.
"The 'dark horse' was added ... to help preserve ambiguity (keep the design solution space from shrinking too fast). It asks teams specifically to invest some time on a prototype that uses a concept or technology that they did not seriously consider" *Source: ICED'09/493 International Conference Stanford University,*

Who invented it?

The concept of the dark horse prototype was brought to our attention by Professor Mark Cutkosky of Stanford University's Mechanical Engineering Department in January 2000.

Why use this method?

1. This method is a way of breaking free of average solutions and exploring unknown territory
2. A way of challenging assumptions.

Challenges

1. Fear of unexplored directions
2. Fear of change
1. Designers can become too attached to their prototypes and allow them to become jewelry that stands in the way of further refinement.
2. Client may believe that system is real.

How to use this method

1. After initial brainstorming sessions select with your team the most challenging, interestingly or thought provoking idea.
2. Create a low resolution prototype of the selected idea.
3. With your team analyze and discuss the prototype.
4. Brainstorm ways of bringing back the dark horse concept into a realizable solution.

LOW FIDELITY PROTOTYPING

What is it?

Cardboard prototyping is a quick and cheap way of gaining insight and informing decision making without the need for costly investment. Simulates function but not aesthetics of proposed design. Prototypes help compare alternatives and help answer questions about interactions or experiences.

Why use this method?

1. May provide the proof of concept
2. It is physical and visible
3. Inexpensive and fast.
4. Useful for refining functional and perceptual interactions.
5. Assists to identify any problems with the design.
6. Helps to reduce the risks
7. Helps members of team to be in alignment nn an idea.
8. Helps make abstract ideas concrete.
9. Feedback can be gained from the user

Challenges

1. Producer might get too attached to prototype and it becomes jewelry because it is beautiful rather than a design tool.

When to use this method

1. Know Context
2. Know User
3. Frame insights
4. Explore Concepts

How to use this method

1. Construct models, not illustrations
2. Select the important tasks, interactions or experiences to be prototyped.
3. Build to understand problems.
4. If it is beautiful you have invested too much.
5. Make it simple
6. Assemble a kit of inexpensive materials
7. Preparing for a test
8. Select users
9. Conduct test
10. Record notes on the 8x5 cards.
11. Evaluate the results
12. Iterate

Resources

1. Paper
2. Cardboard
3. Wire
4. Foam board,
5. Post-it-notes
6. Hot melt glue

References

1. Sefelin, R., Tscheligi, M., & Gukker, V. (2003). Paper Prototyping — What is it good for? A Comparison of paper — and Computer — based Low fidelity Prototyping, CHI 2003, 778-779
2. Snyder, Carolyn (2003). Paper Prototyping: the fast and easy way to design and refine user interfaces. San Francisco, CA: Morgan Kaufmann

GENERATIVE PROTOTYPING

What is it?
A method also called "Thinkering" where participants build simple prototypes from supplied materials to explore ideas.

Who invented it?
Pioneered by Liz Sanders 2002 and Lego Johan Roos and Bart Victor 1990s.

Why use this method?
1. Creative way to generate ideas involving users
2. Discovering user needs
3. Developing concepts with users
4. Designing prototypes with users

Challenges
1. Demanding of participants:
2. Good moderation needed
1. Designers can become too attached to their prototypes and allow them to become jewelry that stands in the way of further refinement.

When to use this method
1. Know Context
2. Know User
3. Frame insights
4. Explore Concepts

How to use this method
1. "In generative prototyping users are asked to together with designers built low-tech prototypes or products using a large set of materials during a workshop. For example, in creating ideas for a new playground, children were asked to built their favorite playground element using ice lolly sticks, foam balls, etc
2. The basic idea is that by building, you start thinking and new ideas are generated."

source: Geke Luken

Resources
1. Toy construction kits such as lego
2. Pop sticks
3. String
4. Tape
5. Post-it-notes
6. Cardboard
7. Paper
8. Markers

References
1. Statler, M., Roos, J., and B. Victor, 2009, 'Ain't Misbehavin': Taking Play Seriously in Organizations,' Journal of Change Management, 9(1): 87-107.

CREATIVE TOOLKITS

What is it?
Collections of modular objects that can be used for participatory modeling and prototyping to inform and inspire design teams. Often used in creative codesign workshops. It is a generative design method which facilitates creative play. The elements can be reused in a number of research sessions in different geographic locations.

Who invented it?
Pioneered by Liz Sanders and Lego Johan Roos and Bart Victor 1990s.

Why use this method?
Helps develop:
1. Problem solving
2. Change management
3. Strategic thinking
4. Decision making
5. Services, product and experience redesign
6. Can be fun
7. Identify opportunities
8. Re frame challenges
9. Leverages creative thinking of the team

When to use this method
1. Know Context
2. Know User
3. Frame insights
4. Explore Concepts

How to use this method
1. Form cross-disciplinary team 5 to 20 members. It's best to have teams of not more than 8
2. Identify design problem. Create agenda.
3. Start with a warming up exercise.
4. Write design problem in visible location such as white board.
5. Workshop participants first build individual prototypes exploring the problem.
6. Divide larger group into smaller work groups of 3 to 5 participants.
7. Ask each participant to develop between 1 and design solutions. Can use post-it notes or cards.
8. Through internal discussion each group should select their preferred group design solution.
9. The group builds a collective model incorporating the individual contributions.
10. Each group build a physical model of preferred solution and presents it to larger group.
11. Larger group selects their preferred design solutions by discussion and voting.
12. Capture process and ideas with video or photographs.
13. Debriefing and harvest of ideas.

References
1. Statler, M., Roos, J., and B. Victor, 2009, 'Ain't Misbehavin': Taking Play Seriously in Organizations,' Journal of Change Management, 9(1): 87–107.

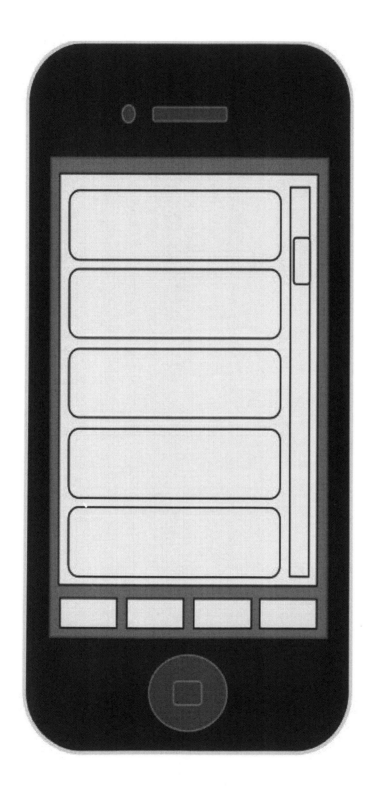

WIREFRAME

What is it?

Website wireframes are a simplified outline of the elements of a web page. They are useful for communicating the functionality of a website in order to get feedback on the design. The wireframe depicts the page layout, interface and navigation, and how these elements interact in use.

WHO INVENTED IT?

Matthew Van Horn claims to have invented the term around 1994 in New York.

Why use this method?

1. Wireframes are useful for getting feedback on a design.
2. Wireframes can speed up the iteration process of a website design.
3. Enable online collaboration
4. Helps Identify needed changes early on in the development.
5. Wireframes are low cost

Challenges

1. Notes to explain behavior are usefull
2. Wireframes do not explain interactive details involving movement.

When to use this method

1. Define intent
2. Know Context
3. Know User
4. Frame insights
5. Explore Concepts

How to use this method

1. There are a several ways to create wireframes. These include drawing by hand. Using Adobe Photoshop or Illustrator and using wireframe software.
2. Start by listing all of the elements that you want on your website.
3. Use simple boxes or outlines of the shape of elements, and name them. These elements can include: navigation: buttons, Company logo: can just be represented by a box, content areas and search box.
4. Review your design and adjust as necessary.
5. Make wireframe for each page in your site.

Resources

1. Paper
2. Pens
3. Wireframe software
4. Computer

REFERENCES

1. Brown, Dan M. (2011). Communicating Design: Developing Web Site Documentation for Design and Planning, Second Edition. New Riders. ISBN 978-0-13-138539-9.
2. Wodtke, Christina; Govella, Austin (2009). Information Architecture: Blueprints for the Web, Second Edition. New Riders. ISBN 978-0-321-59199-9.

366

APPENDIX A
CRITICAL THINKING SCORING RUBRIC

LEVEL	EXCEEDS EXPECTATIONS	STRONG	EFFECTIVE	DEVELOPING	EMERGING	NEEDS IMPROVEMENT
SCORE	6	5	4	3	2	1
SUMMARIZES THE PROBLEM	Clearly identifies the challenge and relationships of the design problem	Clearly identifies the challenge and relationships of the design problem	Summarizes the issue. Some aspects are incorrect or confused	Summarizes the issue. Some aspects are incorrect or confused	Summarizes the issue. Some aspects are incorrect or confused	Fails to identify the challenges and relationships of the design problem
CONSIDERS CONTEXT	Analyzes the design problem with sense of scope. Identifies the influence of context.	Analyzes the design problem with sense of scope. Identifies the influence of context.	Explores context in a limited way. Relies on authorities.	Explores context in a limited way. Relies on authorities.	Explores context in a limited way. Relies on authorities.	Analyzes the problem with bias of own context. Fails to justify opinion
COMMUNICATES ORIGINAL PERSPECTIVE	Demonstrates own perspective supported by experience and unassigned sources. Integrates contrary interpretations	Demonstrates own perspective supported by experience and unassigned sources. Integrates contrary interpretations	Presents own perspective . Addresses other views inconsistently	Presents own perspective without addressing other views	Single view simplistic position adopted with little consideration. Fails to justify opinion	Single view simplistic position adopted with little consideration. Fails to justify opinion
ANALYZES SUPPORTING EVIDENCE	Examines evidence and questions bias accuracy and relevance	Examines evidence and questions bias accuracy and relevance	Selective use of evidence. Discerns fact from opinion. May not recognize bias.	Selective use of evidence. Discerns fact from opinion. May not recognize bias.	Repeats information without question. Does not distinguish between fact and opinion	Repeats information without question. Does not distinguish between fact and opinion
ASSESS CONCLUSIONS CONSEQUENCES	Considers context, assumptions and evidence. Ideas are qualifies. Considers ambiguities	Considers context, assumptions and evidence. Ideas are qualifies. Considers ambiguities	Conclusions consider evidence. Present implications that may impact other people.	Conclusions consider evidence. Present implications that may impact other people.	Fails to identify conclusions. Conclusions are absolute and from an external source.	Fails to identify conclusions. Conclusions are absolute and from an external source.
USES OTHER PERSPECTIVES	Addresses divers perspectives to inform analysis. Justifies own view while respecting views of others	Addresses divers perspectives to inform analysis. Justifies own view while respecting views of others	Integrates multiple viewpoints in a limited way. Some evidence of self assessment	Integrates multiple viewpoints in a limited way. Some evidence of self assessment	Presents single perspective. Fails to recognize other perspectives	Presents single perspective. Fails to recognize other perspectives

APPENDIX B
DESIGN THINKING SCORING RUBRIC

LEVEL	EXCEEDS EXPECTATIONS	STRONG	EFFECTIVE	DEVELOPING	EMERGING	NEEDS IMPROVEMENT
SCORE	6	5	4	3	2	1
AMBIGUITY	Comfortable when things are unclear	Comfortable when things are unclear	Limited comfort when things are unclear	Limited comfort when things are unclear	Uncomfortable when things are unclear	Uncomfortable when things are unclear
EMPATHY AND HUMAN VALUES	Sees and understands others point of view. Focuses on user needs	Sees and understands others point of view. Focuses on user needs	Has limited understanding of other points of view	Has limited understanding of other points of view	Sees only own point of view	Sees only own point of view
COLLABORATIVE	Collaborates effectively with people from other disciplines with different backgrounds and viewpoints	Collaborates effectively with people from other disciplines with different backgrounds and viewpoints	Collaborates with people from other disciplines with different backgrounds and viewpoints in a limited way	Collaborates with people from other disciplines with different backgrounds and viewpoints in a limited way	Cannot collaborate with other. Sees only own point of view.	Cannot collaborate with other. Sees only own point of view.
CURIOUS	Is interested in things that are not understood and seeing things with fresh eyes.	Is interested in things that are not understood and seeing things with fresh eyes.	Shows limited interest in things that are not understood and seeing things with fresh eyes.	Shows limited interest in things that are not understood and seeing things with fresh eyes.	Is not interested in things that are not understood and seeing things with fresh eyes.	Is not interested in things that are not understood and seeing things with fresh eyes.
HOLISTIC	Balances perspectives of business, human values, the environment and technology	Balances perspectives of business, human values, the environment and technology	Considers the perspectives of business, human values, the environment and technology in a limited way	Considers the perspectives of business, human values, the environment and technology in a limited way	Does not consider the bigger context focusses on only one aspect such as business profitability	Does not consider the bigger context focusses on only one aspect such as business profitability
NON JUDGMENTAL	Crafts ideas with no judgement of the idea or idea creator	Crafts ideas with no judgement of the idea or idea creator	Some judgement of ideas and other idea creators	Some judgement of ideas and other idea creators	Extensive judgement of ideas and other idea creators	Extensive judgement of ideas and other idea creators
OPEN MINDSET	Is able to tackle problems regardless of industry or scope. Out of the box thinker	Is able to tackle problems regardless of industry or scope. Out of the box thinker	Can address problems over a number of industries and a limited range of scope	Can address problems over a number of industries and a limited range of scope	Can only address problems in a single industry of limited scope	Can only address problems in a single industry of limited scope
BIAS TOWARD ACTION	Creates prototypes and physical embodiments of ideas and actions that effectively move project forward	Creates prototypes and physical embodiments of ideas and actions that effectively move project forward	Creates some prototypes and progress but in a limited way	Creates some prototypes and progress but in a limited way	Talks about ideas but does not create physical prototypes or move project forward through actions	Talks about ideas but does not create physical prototypes or move project forward through actions
EXPERIMENTAL	Embraces experiment as an integral part of work	Embraces experiment as an integral part of work	Experiments in a limited way	Experiments in a limited way	Does not experiment	Does not experiment
COMPLEXITY	Creates clarity from complexity	Creates clarity from complexity	Limited ability to address complex problems	Limited ability to address complex problems	Cannot address complex problems	Cannot address complex problems
PROCESS	Is mindful of process	Is mindful of process	Follows process in a limited way	Follows process in a limited way	Has no process	Has no process
SHOSHIN	An attitude of openness, eagerness, and lack of preconceptions even when at an advanced level,	An attitude of openness, eagerness, and lack of preconceptions even when at an advanced level,	Some openness, and eagerness. Some preconceptions	Some openness, and eagerness. Some preconceptions	Lack of openness, and eagerness. Many preconceptions	Lack of openness, and eagerness. Many preconceptions
ITERATIVE	Makes improvements with prototyping feedback loops and cycles regardless of design phase	Makes improvements with prototyping feedback loops and cycles regardless of design phase	Limited ability to refine or improve ideas through iterative user feedback and prototyping	Limited ability to refine or improve ideas through iterative user feedback and prototyping	No ability to refine or improve ideas through iterative user feedback and prototyping	No ability to refine or improve ideas through iterative user feedback and prototyping

index

index

index

index

index

T

index

structured workshops

The author presents workshops online and
in person in global locations for executives,
engineers, designers, technology professionals
and anyone interested in learning and
applying these proven innovation methods.
For information contact: info@curedale.com
The author presents workshops online and
in person in global locations for executives,
engineers, designers, technology professionals
The author presents workshops online and
in person in global locations for executives,
engineers, designers, technology professionals
and anyone interested in learning and applying
these proven innovation methods. For more
information contact: info@curedale.com

Other titles from this author

Design Methods 1
200 ways to apply design thinking
Author: Curedale, Robert A
Publisher: Design Community College.
Edition 1 November 2013
ISBN-10:0988236206
ISBN-13:978-0-9882362-0-2

Design Methods 2
200 more ways to apply design thinking
Author: Curedale, Robert A Publisher: Design
Community College.
Edition 1 January 2013
ISBN-13: 978-0988236240
ISBN-10: 0988236249

Design Research Methods
150 ways to inform design
Author: Curedale, Robert A
Publisher: Design Community College.
Edition 1 January 2013
ISBN-10: 0988236257
ISBN-13: 978-0-988-2362-5-7

50 Brainstorming Methods
for team and individual ideation
Author: Curedale, Robert A
Publisher: Design Community College.
Edition 1 January 2013
ISBN-10: 0988236230
ISBN-13: 978-0-9882362-3-3

50 Selected Design Methods
to inform your design
Author: Curedale, Robert A
Publisher: Design Community College.
Edition 1 January 2013
ISBN-10:0988236265
ISBN-13:978-0-9882362-6-4

Mapping Methods
for design and strategy
Curedale, Robert A
Publisher: Design Community College.
Edition 1 April 2013
ISBN-10: 0989246817
ISBN-13: 978-0-9892468-1-1

about the author

Rob Curedale was born in Australia and worked as a designer, director and educator in leading design offices in London, Sydney, Switzerland, Portugal, Los Angeles, Silicon Valley, Detroit, and China. He designed and managed over 1,000 products and experiences as a consultant and in-house design leader for the world's most respected brands. Rob has three decades experience in every aspect of product development, leading design teams to achieve transformational improvements in operating and financial results. He has extensive experience in forging strategic growth, competitive advantage, and a background in expanding business into emerging markets through user advocacy and extensive cross cultural expertise. Rob's designs can be found in millions of homes and workplaces around the world.

Rob works currently as a Adjunct Professor at Art Center College of Design in Pasadena and consults to organizations in the United States and internationally and presents workshops related to design. He has taught as a member of staff and presented lectures and workshops at many respected design schools and universities throughout the world including Yale, Pepperdine University, Art Center Pasadena, Loyola University, Cranbrook, Pratt, Art Center Europe; a faculty member at SCA and UTS Sydney; as Chair of Product Design and Furniture Design at the College for Creative Studies in Detroit, then the largest product design school in North America, Art Institute Hollywood, Cal State San Jose, Escola De Artes e Design in Oporto Portugal, Instituto De Artes Visuals, Design e Marketing, Lisbon, Southern Yangtze University, Jiao Tong University in Shanghai and Nanjing Arts Institute in China.

Rob's design practice experience includes projects for HP, Philips, GEC, Nokia, Sun, Apple, Canon, Motorola, Nissan, Audi VW, Disney, RTKL, Governments of the UAE,UK, Australia, Steelcase, Hon, Castelli, Hamilton Medical, Zyliss, Belkin, Gensler, Haworth, Honeywell, NEC, Hoover, Packard Bell, Dell, Black & Decker, Coleman and Harmon Kardon. Categories including furniture, healthcare, consumer electronics, sporting, homewares, military, exhibits, packaging. His products and experiences can be found in millions of homes and businesses throughout the world.

Rob established and manages the largest network of designers and architects in the world with more than 300,000 professional members working in every field of design.

Made in the USA
Lexington, KY
26 January 2014